R. Barnett

Speaking Is
A Practical Matter

Bernard P. McCabe, Jr.
SOUTHERN CONNECTICUT STATE COLLEGE

Coleman C. Bender
EMERSON COLLEGE

Speaking Is a Practical Matter

Boston
Holbrook Press, Inc.

TO NORMA
AND
EVELYN

Preface

I S SPEAKING a practical matter? Is it just as important to the house-wife as it is to the politician? Just as vital to the apprentice as to the tycoon? To the four-year-old as to the man of sixty? Of course! Speaking is one of our most practical means of everyday communication. Indeed, it is with this practicality in mind that we have developed and arranged *Speaking Is a Practical Matter.* The aim is not to produce orators, or even "public" speakers, but rather to increase effectiveness in the speaking process.

In general, a "speech" refers to an unprepared or prepared, informal or formal talk. An "address" is a prepared, formal talk usually dealing with an important subject or delivered during a special occasion. The "oration" is a formal address on a special occasion and has the further obligation of artistic eloquence and style. We shall concentrate upon the "speech" because it is more directly applicable to daily communication.

Effective speech is not limited to certain occupations or special events. The ability to speak well is necessary to anyone who talks. Every day we have feelings or ideas we want to express and to do this satisfactorily means to speak well. Therefore, why not improve our speaking through study and practice? This is the way we usually better our writing, reading, dancing, driving, and any number of other activities. Considering the constant and continual use of speech and its social and occupational importance, it seems only reasonable we should also study speaking.

We have, therefore, eliminated from our book the purposes or types of speaking which are uncommon or infrequently used. We shall concentrate upon the development of two essential foundations of proficient everyday communication—speeches of explanation and speeches of opinion. In a speech of *explanation*, we aim at *clarification* of ideas, procedures, concepts, and opinions. In a speech of *opinion*, we are asking the listeners for *consideration of, agreement with, or action on* our ideas. Preparation, of course, is included as basic and preliminary to all oral communication.

To help achieve this functional speaking, a step-by-step procedure providing orderly direction is used as a practical method of building effective speaking. This constructive guide will allow recognition of strengths and weaknesses. A particular step can then be easily enlarged by incorporating additional material.

Contents

Contents

Contents

Contents

Speaking Is
A Practical Matter

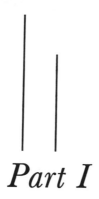

Part I

Speech: the oral communication process

What is speech?

DICTIONARY DEFINITIONS of speech will include meanings as diverse as "vocalization," "talk," and "dialect." Some dictionaries solve this problem by defining speech as "the act of speaking."

The following diagrams will aid in explaining our concept of "speech."

COMMUNICATION PROCESS

Medium or Channel

One Person
group
organization

print
pictures
sound

One Person
group
organization

ideas

thoughts

feelings

attitudes

concepts

etc.

Transmitter

Receiver

Feedback

In this simple sketch of the complicated communication process, speech is included as one of the forms of communication. Therefore, our definition of speech is:

Speech is that form of communication in which "humans" are the initiators, transmitters, and the receivers. In other words, if you (as a human) wish to send a message to me (as a human) you can print it, send it by flag signal system, or tell me. If you use yourself as the transmitter (vocal or visual) rather than write or draw a picture, then you are using speech.

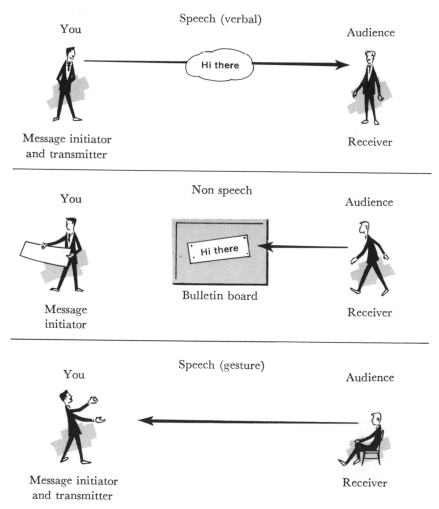

Even if another medium (radio, television, telephone, or film) is used, the original transmitter system is a human one now carried by another medium or transmitter.

You   Secondary   Receiver   Audience
            Transmitter

Message initiator
and transmitter

In summary, speech is the system of communication which uses humans as initiators and transmitters (visual and/or auditory) and humans as auditors or receivers.

Why the emphasis on speech?

... it is absurd to hold that a man ought to be ashamed of being unable to defend himself with limbs, but not of being able to defend himself with speech and reason, when the use of rational speech is more distinctive of a human being than the use of his limbs. (*Rhetoric,* Bk. I, Ch. 1)

In this statement made by Aristotle more than 2000 years ago, we find the answer to our question. Upon careful analysis of Aristotle's reasoning, the essence of all communication becomes apparent.

First, the ancient rhetorician noted the rather obvious fact that speech is a distinguishing characteristic of man. Man takes justifiable pride in his position as a highly developed being. He can reason. He can communicate. By combining the two, man has virtually conquered land, sea, and now space. Communication has helped to establish and to maintain all of man's social institutions. Undeniable? So it would seem. Try remaining mute for a day. How much could you accomplish?

Looking more closely at the Aristotelian comment, we find that he

5

considered speech a means of defense. Historically there are instances in which the sword proved mightier than the word. Yet, even there, one wonders whether the need for the sword might not have existed if the word had been more skillfully used.

When does today's man have the opportunity to "defend" himself with speech? Constantly! Every time man speaks he defends his capacity for rational, intelligent thought. In doing so, he must express himself clearly, concisely, and logically.

Take, for example, the business man at a departmental conference about to make an oral presentation on a new advertising approach. Immediately, he must consider his "defense." He must present his report in a manner which, through an intelligent defense of his proposals, gains the respect of his colleagues. Nearly everyone in our modern society faces similar circumstances. Simply alter the scene a little and the person in defense could be you. Think for a moment, how many times you defend yourself every day. The number can be amazingly high. While we do not consciously label the varied communication situations a defense, the term fits. Each of us attempts to defend our image before others. This image is often changing. It is usually self-determined and varies with the situation.

Consider the student. In the classroom, he defends his position as a scholar, a thinker, or a humorist. In the cafeteria, he becomes a charmer, a philosopher, or a brilliant conversationalist. In the fraternity, he is the leader, the promoter, or the entertainer. Whatever the circumstances, this student defends his role with speech and action. Although his many roles may change after he leaves school, he still finds the need to defend himself through the spoken word. In all probability however, the defense has grown in importance and the competition from others has increased.

Even after he has obtained a job by defending his qualifications for the position, speech continues to be important. This occupational defense is often called "selling oneself." Whatever the name, it unquestionably exists. In fact, the use of speech consumes so much of all our professional time it is surprising that we do not collapse from oral exhaustion. From the moment we enter the office in the morning, our defense begins—greeting colleagues, giving and receiving orders, and carrying out the business of the day. Throughout the working day we continually defend our position—taking directions, giving directions, explaining procedures to subordinates, and justifying actions to superiors. The salesman is not the only one who must sell. All of us must do it.

This defense does not end by simply closing the office door. Besides meeting the expectations of your own family, you must satisfy the home community. You are still on trial before the neighbors, the church group, the P.T.A., the bowling league, the fraternal club, the country club, and on and on. Each one challenges you in a different way and is met with some degree of oral "defense."

It is evident the oral aspect of life begins with the first wail at birth and continues throughout the life of every man. We do have the gift of speech and we should expect the quality of communication to be of the highest possible degree.

What are the basic types of speech?

WHEN CONSIDERED in its broadest sense, speech is simply talk. Every conversation is a speech. This is a very important point to remember. Too often the student of speech imagines he is only being prepared to deliver orations or formal speeches before the public. This is not necessarily true. Even though the different forms of speaking are given specific academic titles, the ultimate objective of each remains the same—to transfer ideas, thoughts, attitudes, feelings, or emotions.

We know that all speaking situations aim for effective communication of ideas. Remembering this, let us preview the various circumstances. We must now use certain academic labels to avoid confusion. Note the similarities between each type.

Conversation

First, there is the most familiar and least feared type—conversation. Conversation is simply talk with certain distinguishing characteristics. In fact, conversation is *basic* to *all* other speech types. Conversation is characterized in three ways:

1. It is delivered *within* a small informal group of listeners.
2. The expression of thoughts may be continual or intermittent with possible interruption by listeners.
3. The speaker does not prepare his talk beforehand.

Conversation is the most frequently used form of oral communication. The study of speech will certainly improve one's conversational skills.

Public speaking

Second, there is the more formal communicative type—public speaking. Actually, public speaking is a form of modified conversation:

1. It is delivered *before* a group of listeners.
2. The expression of thoughts is continued until completed without interruption from the listeners.
3. The speaker plans his comments before the time of speaking.

A comparison of conversation with public speaking reveals that public speaking is more organized and generally more formal. No matter how this planned conversation is used—for a committee report, a formal statement of opinion, a sales presentation, or a banquet address—the element of *time* is the factor causing the change. Time is valuable and both the speaker and the listener want conservative use of it. Thus, a speaker is generally required to "speak his piece" as concisely and clearly as possible. This type of formal conversation is called public speaking.

Discussion

A third type of communication is discussion. Although its settings vary, discussion always involves a number of contributing speakers. In discussion, people gather together to talk about a specific subject. The usual purposes of discussion are: to exchange information, to identify problems, and to evaluate possible solutions. Each individual is expected to contribute. Thus, its characteristics take on those of both conversation and public speaking:

1. Speaking is done within a small group, meeting informally, yet in a relaxed atmosphere.
2. Each member of the group has an opportunity to speak briefly on the various aspects of the subject and there may be interruptions.
3. Each speaker usually has given thought to the discussion subject prior to the meeting and may even have prepared notes.

So we see that discussion has the characteristics of conversation as well as of public speaking. We will explore the variations of this form of speaking in a later section.

Debate

Another formal situation is debate. Debate is a speech situation where definite opposing views are usually presented under formal rules. While discussion is a casual cross between conversation and public speaking, debate is more rigid in format. In the great presidential debates of 1960, for example, each candidate attempted to win the listener and his opponent to a particular view. With such an aim, the debater must be specifically prepared, and yet remain flexible to listener reaction. Here, a set procedure is established before the speaking event:

1. The speaking is done *before* a group of listeners.
2. The speaker is given a specific period of time to present his views uninterrupted.
3. The speaker plans his initial argument prior to the speaking situation and is ready to answer any questions or opposing arguments.

Debate is the most formal and carefully structured pattern of speaking we have discussed. In this type, points of view have already been predetermined and the speakers are trying to win support for their position.

Now that we have previewed the basic forms of oral communication, a brief summary statement is in order. As we have noted, conversation is the basis of all other forms of speaking. The format of speaking may be changed from informal to formal, from less structured to more carefully structured, from unprepared to carefully prepared, and single to multiple speakers. However, in each case the aim is always the same—the effective transfer of ideas, thoughts, attitudes, feelings, or emotions.

What are the methods of presentation?

Impromptu

The most common method of presentation is impromptu. Conversation is impromptu speaking. It is a talk given without previous preparation and is spontaneous speech.

Everyone gives impromptu talks throughout the day. Regardless of occupational or recreational activities, anyone who comes in verbal contact with other people engages in impromptu speaking.

The impromptu speaking situation can arise under more formal circumstances than casual conversation. A person could, for instance, be present at an organizational meeting where the head of the group requests an explanation or an opinion from him. Since there had been no previous warning of this request, there had been no formal preparation. Therefore, he speaks "off-the-cuff," or ad-lib—the impromptu method. Similar situations could occur whenever people gather together for any reason—political rallies, business meetings, professional conventions, banquets, or reunions. The possibility of impromptu speaking is ever present.

How can one prepare for impromptu speaking? Perhaps the greatest danger is the initial shock of being asked to speak unexpectedly. Probably you should always be aware of the possibility of being called upon to say a few words. However, if you did not expect it to happen, and it *does*—do not let the surprise turn to panic. Instead, allow yourself time to become calm before saying anything of importance. Often you can shed the initial shock by assuming your position slowly, or if this is not possible, use the standard introduction: "Mr. Chairman, members of the. . . ." By the time your introduction is finished, you have probably collected your thoughts and can proceed.

Although there is really no one format for impromptu speaking which is universally accepted, the following steps may serve as a guide:

1. Obtain listener attention while gaining self-composure by polite recognition of the audience present and by stating the purpose of speaking. (Avoid trite clichés or admitting any fear.)
2. State the main points on which you will speak.
3. Elaborate on each of these points by explaining their meaning to the listeners.
4. Give an example for each main point.
5. Conclude by summarizing.

Naturally, the impromptu speaker is the only one capable of determining what to say, and how to say it at the time. He is the one experiencing the surprise situation. He alone must decide how and what to say.

One final word of advice: always be a good listener! If you are listening attentively, the impromptu situation is much easier. You will have already been thinking on the subject and, if called upon, will be able to translate your thoughts into spoken words. Stay alert. Remain composed.

Extemporaneous

The first type of prepared speech we will consider is the extemporaneous speech. Since the speaker is not bound by a pre-determined expression of ideas, extemporaneous speech is the most flexible method of presentation. While the content of such speeches is considered beforehand, the exact wording is reserved for the moment of speaking. Hence the extemporaneous speech has a quality of spontaneity.

In preparing an extemporaneous speech, a speaker studies the subject, selects his specific ideas on the topic, develops these ideas, and then constructs an outline organizing the materials. The extemporaneous speech is *not* written out like a composition. Only key items are recorded and then used as a guide while speaking. The presentation, freed from the restrictions of a rigid text, can be more informal and more like ordinary conversation.

Unlike the impromptu speaker, the extemporaneous speaker practices his speech. Some rehearse before a mirror or members of the family while others simply review in their mind.

To relieve you from the burden of memorizing the complete speech, it is completely acceptable to record an outline of the speech on *cards* to be used while speaking. You may even on occasion read some items from these cards. This is quite permissible. In fact, it is not only recommended that all extemporaneous speeches be outlined but that the cards be used openly at the time of speaking. Most professionals do, so why not you? Here are a few pointers for preparing an extemporaneous speech:

1. On cards write an outline that is immediately and clearly understood by you.
2. Number each card to prevent a mix-up in sequence.
3. Write on cards which are easy to manipulate.
4. Use the cards openly and do not attempt to hide them from the listener.

Use the extemporaneous speech whenever possible. Aside from having greater appeal to the listener, it is valuable training for devloping a person into a skilled speaker.

11

Manuscript

The manuscript speech has every word to be spoken in written form. All you need to do is read it. Immediately the novice sighs in relief and thinks: "Here is the answer to all my worries." The manuscript form does partially solve some problems of speaking. When a speech is completely written, there is no danger of forgetting content or fumbling for words. However, as you might expect, there are also definite disadvantages.

The greatest and perhaps most common problem with the manuscript speech is its boring effect upon the listener if it is poorly read. How often have you listened to someone read a speech? Did you find your interest was maintained during the entire reading? Or did it waver? In fact, did you begin thinking of everything but the speech? Perhaps you struggled to shake off a creeping drowsiness? If you have ever experienced this then you have had firsthand knowledge of the ineffective reading of a manuscript speech.

When you are writing a speech it is essential to remember that the manuscript speech is not an essay designed for silent reading. There is a major difference between reading and listening. The reader of the printed page can re-read at will. The listener cannot. The style for oral presentation must be composed for *instant* comprehension. Furthermore, the silent reader can set his own pace. He may pause to rest, to contemplate, or to consult another source. Obviously, the listener to a speech is unable to do any of these. Therefore, the manuscript speech writer must *make allowances* for the oral situation.

How should a speech manuscript be written? The answer is actually quite simple. *Write exactly as you speak!* A conscious effort must be made to write orally. We are so conditioned to write in one style and speak in another that our pen habitually writes for the silent reader. The words you are now reading are not specifically designed for oral reading. The following is a sample speech manuscript designed for oral reading:

> At this very moment/ and I mean this *very* moment/ there is an *abundance* of *fine* men and women in our nation/// Men and women of *high intelligence* and *education*/// *Gifted* men and women/// *Concerned* men and women/// What are they doing??? Working for private business and the federal government/// So what??? Yet throughout America there are children who *need* these

men and women/// Children who are *ripe* for *learning*/// Children who *thrive* on *learning*/// Children who *demand* these *talented* persons as *teachers*/// Yet *too many* are *unavailable*/// Why??? Because of *you* the *parent*!!! Yes/ that's what I said/// You're the *main* reason for the *shortage* of *outstanding* teachers///

Absurd!!!! Ridiculous!!!! You haven't chased *any* teachers away/// Ah/ but *maybe* you *did*/ *inadvertently*///

Think along with me for a moment///

Do you tell a physician how to do his work???? A dentist???? A lawyer???? A veterinarian???? Of course you *don't*///

What about a plumber??? An auto mechanic??? A carpenter??? A TV repairman??? Again you *don't interfere*////

You let the *specialist* do his job/// All *you* do is present the problem to him/// It's the *specialist* who finds the *solution*/// After all/ *he's* the one with *specialized training*///

Now/ what about the *school teacher*??? The situation *should* be the *same*/// But it *isn't*!!!

How is the speech manuscript different from other writing? Essentially, it is the writing of words, sentences, and paragraphs in an oral style.

Some of the variations found in the speech manuscript differentiating it from an essay are:

1. Vertical "pause" lines replace punctuation as being more quickly recognized by the eye when the speaker is reading.
2. The number of "pause" lines indicates the length of the pause.
3. Expressions are informal and often grammatically incomplete.
4. Contractions are used.
5. Some colloquialisms are acceptable.

The result of the "extemporaneous" technique of writing the manuscript is a speech which can be more easily and more effectively read by a speaker. You not only give a better performance but the listener is more attentive. The strain on both of you is minimized. Just remember how you have reacted to a pedantic reading of an essay and avoid making the same mistake. The *conversational norm* is the guide to all styles of presentation.

Memorized

Another method of presentation is the completely memorized speech. In this, the speech is written in manuscript form and then committed to memory. A high degree of talent is needed for effectiveness. Added to the difficulty of reading a manuscript, you must have an unfailing memory to be able to recite all the words. This presentational style is fraught with dangers and you are advised to avoid it. Fully memorized speeches are not particularly common today although there may be times to use this method for portions of a speech.

What are the requirements of speaking?

THE PRINCIPAL REQUIREMENT of speech is the transfer of subject matter between speaker and listener. For most of us, this speaking process is performed unconsciously. But are our thoughts understood by others? We live in a world of talk and efficient speech is a necessity. Since we are continually confronted with situations requiring oral response, each of us has certain responsibilities as a communicator:

1. He must be effective in speech *preparation.*
2. He must be capable of *explanation.*
3. He must be proficient in the expression of *opinion.*

Since each of these elements—preparation, explanation, and opinion—is basic to communication, it is essential to master their ingredients to be effective in all forms of oral communication.

Preparation

We recognize that man transmits thoughts to others through speech. At least part of the time the situation goes beyond conversation. Therefore, the effective speaker must be aware of the steps of preparation necessary to communicate under somewhat more formal circumstances. This is the first responsibility of any speaker.

You may have thought concern over preparation was limited to the professional. But we are all professionals in a sense. We build our entire lives around oral communication. Thus, in a general way, we can all qualify as "professional" speakers.

Speech preparation involves more than just the practice of oral sounds. It is a combination of fundamentals which should be familiar to all of you before you move on to the actual construction of a speech for a specific situation. To facilitate the practical study of these fundamentals, steps arranging the elements of preparation in a sequence of importance to you as a potential speaker follow:

1. How do you choose a topic?
2. How do you gather materials?
3. How do you outline the topic?
4. How can you use visual aids?
5. How can you use language?
6. How should you look?
7. How should you sound?
8. How are you to manage stage fright?

Once you are familiar with each step of preparation you will be ready to meet the demands of actual speaking situations.

Explanation

When you are chatting with friends, there are only two possible reasons for doing so. The first is to *explain*. Explanation may be given different labels of identification or it may take different forms. However, the process remains the same and is basic to all forms of communication. Moreover, it is vital to effective speaking and therefore becomes the second responsibility of a speaker.

Let us consider three representative forms of explanation commonly given other labels:

1. *Description* explains what took place, what happened, or what something looks like. .
2. *Demonstration* explains the functioning of equipment, instrument, or product.
3. *Informing* explains the what, how, when, and where of a subject.

In each of these cases, the process remains explanation although the form varies.

Man converses everytime he explains. Explanation, therefore, is basic to all speaking. An entire section will be given to the speech of explanation because of its importance. A speaker constructing a speech of explanation will find the following progression of steps in preparation helpful:

1. Analyzing the speaking situation.
2. Gathering the materials.
3. Selecting content materials.
4. Recognizing the means of developing content.
5. Organizing the content.
6. Evaluating the completed speech.

These steps lead naturally toward the finished product.

Opinion

How many people have the opportunity to give an opinion? Everyone! Opinions on a multitude of matters are an everyday affair. Expressing opinion is another major purpose of speaking.

Essentially, the speech of opinion is a process of explanation. However, the speaker of opinion has certain *additional* requirements carrying this use of speech beyond that of simple explanation. He must substantiate an opinion to make it logically, reasonably, and intellectually acceptable. Therefore, a separate section is devoted to this important process of oral communication.

The speech of opinion has three goals. First, to make the listener *consider* the opinion as intelligent, whether he agrees with it or not; second, to foster *agreement* between the speaker and the listener; third, to direct the listener to a specific course of *action*. Although a speaker might not aim for all three goals, it is necessary to accomplish acceptance or consideration of his opinion before moving to the others.

Consider for a moment the following people who use speech. Each has an opinion to offer the listener for consideration:

1. The *politician* seeks acceptance of his opinion on his qualifications for an office or on legislation. *Purpose*: action through voting.
2. The *salesman* seeks acceptance of his opinion about the superiority of his product or about customer need for the product. *Purpose*: action through buying.

3. The *clergyman* seeks acceptance of a religious opinion. *Purpose*: agreement and action in behavior.
4. The *administrator* seeks acceptance of his opinion on the organization or operation of matters within his charge. *Purpose*: agreement and action on his directions.
5. The *philosopher* seeks acceptance of his theoretical opinion. *Purpose*: agreement through belief.

You can probably think of other instances where opinions are presented for consideration.

It will be noted that in all of the above instances, there is a need for soundness of substance and reasoning before the opinion is accepted. No intelligent speaker or intelligent listener would consider an opinion unless there were substantiation of all expressed ideas. An opinion that is merely a personal view founded upon superficiality is unacceptable. To accept this kind of opinion is to be moved by prejudice and bias.

Once there is an opinion based on sound, constructive thinking, its expression finds *persuasive* purpose through the intent of the speaker. Therefore, it is important to remember that *before there can be persuasion, there must first be an opinion.*

Because of its very nature, the speech of opinion goes beyond simple explanation. Here, the topic is initially controversial or at least questionable. There is a positive need for applying sound reasoning to the process of explanation. And, due to the persuasive purpose of the speech, there is need for special listener adaptation. The steps in the speech of opinion are arranged to satisfy both these aspects of the speech:

1. Analyzing listener attitudes.
2. Recognizing human motivations.
3. Applying psychological patterns.
4. Organizing content into reasoning patterns.
5. Evaluating the completed speech.

These steps of the speech of opinion will guide you in the construction of a speech designed to gain acceptance of your opinion.

In this general preview of oral communication we have simply noted those ideas known to everyone. First, we recalled that ours is a world of talk. We are all public speakers, and the quality of our expression of thoughts plays an important role in our work and play. Secondly, we observed that all speaking is a form of conversation. Whether it is called public speaking, discussion, or debate, it is still a manner of conversing. It does not matter whether the talk is impromptu, extemporaneous, read, or delivered from memory. These are only styles of presentation or variations of conversation. Finally, we outlined the major units of study—speech preparation, speech of explanation, and speech of opinion. By condensing the various elements of oral communication into these three basic categories and subdividing each into a step-by-step procedure, we have presented speaking as a practical process useful in our daily activities.

It must always be remembered throughout any study of oral communication that there is a need for the practical application of theory. As Plato observed in his *Phaedrus* and Aristotle echoed in the *Rhetoric*, pages of printed rules and observations cannot be substituted for practical experience. Intelligent speaking can be achieved only by adapting the theory to personal needs. The following procedural sections are, therefore, aimed at meeting the requirements of a man of speech in a modern society.

Part I | Exercises ∽ Assignments

1. Select a vocation that is of interest to you and make a list of the speaking situations necessary for successful performance of duties in that vocation.

2. Reflect back over the speaking situations in which you engaged during the past 24 hours. Which situations were explanation and which opinion?

3. Make a list of your present assets and liabilities as a speaker. Ask one of your friends to make a similar list. Compare these two lists.

4. Describe the speaking characteristics of the most competent speaker that you have heard.

5. Make a list of the characteristics that you, as a listener, personally prefer in a speaker. Arrange this list in order of importance. Do the same for those characteristics that you dislike.

6. Keep a diary of your speaking activities for one week. Include the following:
    Type of speech activity
    Type of listener

Explanation or opinion
Success level of experience

7. List in order of importance those primary forces which have shaped your current speaking pattern.

8. Prepare two lists of vocations that differ in speech requirements (i.e. lawyer vs. typesetter). Justify your selections.

9. Prepare a talk on either side of one of these subjects:
   Speakers are born not made.
   Good speakers always have good personalities.
   You can be a success in many vocations without good speech.
   Speech has more social value than economic value.
   Practice is more important than theory in speech improvement.

10. Define "natural" and "habitual" as terms applied to speech behavior.

Part II

Preparing

for speaking

YOU may have a variety of reactions to the speech situation. These reactions may range from fear and panic to calm consideration of the task. We heartily recommend the latter.

Certainly you should show concern! You and your ideas will be exposed to listeners for their approval or disapproval. However, you should turn this concern into action aimed at preparation for the speech situation.

You will find the steps in this section of value in preparing the content of your talk. These steps are suggested as a prerequisite to preparation of a specific talk. Follow the guidelines and you will systematically approach the speaking task.

Step 1

How do you choose and adapt a topic?

THE choice of a good topic is essential for effective communication. Whether the speaker be a student, salesman, lawyer, nurse, or housewife, the selection of a specific subject for a speech gives direction to the entire speaking event. This is true of all speaking situations in which the communicant is being judged on what he says.

The businessman goes to the board meeting prepared to discuss specific items. Before doing so, he has given positive thought to the various topics and to the comments which may be made. The lawyer plans his case. The educator prepares the lecture. The salesman lays out his sales approach. The politician develops his argument. Each, after careful selection of the specific topic, enters the speaking situation from which the speech will be developed.

You should approach the speaking situation with the confidence that comes from knowing that your topic has been carefully selected for this specific group of listeners.

There are three fundamental factors in the selection of a topic for a speech:

1. It must interest the speaker.
2. It must be specific.
3. It must be adapted to the listener.

It must interest the speaker

IT WOULD SEEM only natural that the subject of a speech should be of interest to the speaker. A speaker must have a *reason* for talking or he should remain silent. Although a speech is fluently delivered, listeners appear to have a sixth sense which exposes the uninterested or insincere speaker.

We all know that the individual who is enthusiastic and interested in his work produces results significantly different from those of an efficient but uninterested worker. Though on the surface the end product may appear the same, there is a difference. Two secretaries assigned to an office may be equally efficient. But here the similarity ends. One does her duty while the other does more. The second enthusiastically takes charge of the endless details that could clog a businessman's day. She opens, sorts, and prepares correspondence for inspection. She reviews the daily program for her employer. She duplicates and files dictations. She thoughtfully schedules appointments. She screens calls. She traces information. She checks supplies. In short, this secretary has become an assistant. Interest and enthusiasm have carried her from the acceptable to the superior. Whose work is considerably better? That of the interested person, of course,

A similar situation exists in speaking. As listeners we recognize the work of the uninterested speaker and he will not need to wait to be pensioned off. We discharge him immediately by not listening. On the other hand, the sincere, interested speaker is promoted by receiving our earnest attention. Every listener appreciates an interested speaker. An interested speaker means an interesting speaker!

Where do you go for subjects and subject-matter that arouse your interest? You are not only aware that the first step for gaining listener interest is your *own* interest but you know the occasion requiring the speech. The answer is actually quite simple. Look to your *own experience* and look to your *own knowledge*. What better sources? Both are part of you. So both should interest you. Adjust your experience and knowledge to the specific speaking occasion and you will bring your interest to the listener. Remember that the intersection where the lines of interest of the speaker and the lines of interest of the listener cross is the location of a potential subject for a stimulating talk. However, if you have a subject that holds a strong interest for you alone, this enthusiasm can be communicated to the listener and can arouse interest that did not exist before.

Subject from your own experience

Is there anything in your experience that interests and involves you? Anything in your daily routine? Matters that you experience every day and perhaps as a result tend to ignore? Sometimes repetition can cause you to block regular occurrences from your conscious thoughts. Yet they are there. Some please you. Others annoy you. Some concern you directly, others only indirectly. Yet they are there. Take a fresh look at your surroundings. What do you really see? What really happens? Here is where a possible speech subject begins. And here is where you may find the substance of speaking. Think of the politician, the social worker, the clergyman, the businessman, the salesman, or the housewife. Where do they find subjects for speaking? From their experience.

The politician lives in the world of his constituents. He experiences their experiences. He sees the needs of his voters, for he has the same political needs. When he goes before the public, this politician recalls his experiences and relates them to the people. If he has had unsatisfactory public schooling, he discusses this before proposing corrective measures. If experience has taught the politician that better highways are needed, this becomes part of his speech. If he has observed through experience matters of law, social welfare, health, or safety, these become an integral of his speech.

The social worker finds his interests are also those of experience. The needs of the aged, the poor, the immigrant, and the young are experienced in part by the social worker. Observing the many needs of our society becomes the interest of this person. The young children who have a need for recreational facilities or for guidance are a part of the life of the social worker. There are the aged who are ignored, families in need of help, and immigrants lost in a new environment. These among others become the experiences of the social worker. Not only are there numerous topics for speaking in the daily routine of the social worker, but there is an abundance of materials for the development of any of them.

The clergyman lives within the spiritual and social lives of his parishioners. Their lives become his as his becomes part of theirs. This uniting of experiences becomes a storehouse of subjects and materials for speeches. When speaking to the members of his parish, he talks from the experiences of both himself and the people. Experience becomes a part of the substance from which he speaks. Therefore,

25

the clergyman brings his own interest to his subject and to the interest of the listener.

The businessman searches his experience for the policy to use in the operation of his business activity. His experiences as an employee become the key to his discussions on personnel matters. His experiences as a consumer are found in his proposals for the development of consumer goods and consumer marketing. His experiences in management enter his talks to assistants on company policy. As the businessman's experiences with the various aspects of his position increase daily, he recognizes the greater complexities of the business operation. This understanding can then be found in talks on business subjects. Here lies his interest and he brings it to the listener.

The salesman faces the public daily in speaking situations. He has to convince the customers of their need for his product as well as of the superiority of his goods over those of his competitors. His success depends solely on his ability to communicate successfully. It is not enough simply to know a sales presentation to achieve this goal. The successful salesman dips into his own experiences and observations to find the key to effective communication. Undoubtedly, you have encountered such a man. He does not list a catalogue description of his commodity. If he did, you would not buy. Instead, he talks about the significance of the product in your life. How would you find it useful, enjoyable, or efficient? He actually adapts his product to your experiences. How is he able to do this? He simply recalls his own experience and recognizes how the product has been one that worked to his own advantage. He then merely transfers this image to include you. His interest in his own experience enables him to convey this interest when selling to you. Again the experience of the speaker has become the foundation for effective communication.

Finally, let us consider the housewife. Technically, she is not employed or charged with selling ideas or goods. Yet in her diversified role she practices a bit of each of the preceding professions. Like the specialists, the housewife calls upon her experience. Listen to this woman talk. She discusses politics as they affect her children, her husband, her neighborhood, and herself. She sees what needs to be done politically and socially and uses this interest as the starting point for her speaking. When considering business matters, the housewife likewise draws understanding from that which involves her special world. From the smallest appliance to the cost of living, she turns to her experience during times of discussion. In dealing with human nature, the housewife's experience is essential to her understanding and to her communication of ideas. How often have we heard the mother say to a child in need of an answer, "Well, when I was a girl. . . ." Even for the housewife, therefore, experience is the primary foundation for ideas and discussion.

Probably every one of us has used experience in the selection of an occupation. As adolescents approach adulthood, they notice, and possibly try, the various occupations in their environment. Periodically, a young person announces an ambition to pursue a certain occupation when he grows up. Finally, he reaches that period of life and a choice must be made. What influences this selection? Most often experience provides the general interest from which the specific goal is determined.

Since many of our decisions and interests stem from experience it should be a good place to look for a speech topic and materials for subject development. There are dozens of potential speech topics waiting to be noticed. Once you know what you are to say, it is easy to gather additional information to provide further details.

Subject from your knowledge

Your own knowledge is another source for speeches. This does not mean just what you have learned in formal education. Day to day living also increases your knowledge. Here, you may learn more about the intricacies of your occupation, national and local problems, dealing with human nature, eliminating ragweed from the front lawn, or even changing a diaper. As your knowledge grows your interest increases. Think about yourself for a moment. Did you have an interest in golf, bowling, or skiing when you knew nothing about them? Your interest changed after you learned more about the games. Would you have a strong interest in child care, baby formulas, the little league, or the P.T.A. before you became a parent? Would you care about interior decorating, landscaping, outdoor barbecues, or heating systems before you became a home owner? What about your occupation? Has your interest intensified as your knowledge of its many aspects increased?

The beginning teacher is interested primarily in maintaining order and covering a scheduled amount of subject-matter. However as her knowledge of the job increases, her interest is more fully captured.

The nursing novice concentrates on what she learned in nursing school and on trying to avoid any mistakes. As she becomes more familiar with the many aspects of her profession, she finds her interests centering more and more upon caring for the ill.

Undoubtedly all of us have found that we, too, grow more interested in our work as our knowledge of it increases. This is true of everything—work or play—in our lives. As our knowledge expands, our interest increases.

Moreover, this learned interest may be unplanned. It can be quite accidental. For instance, a subject on television might strike an interest in the viewer, a chance conversation might stir up interest in a totally unfamiliar topic, or a national event might lead to further investigation of the incident. A student is given information on various subjects and as a result, may become interested in one or more of them. In the beginning, only a small amount of information may be necessary to capture his attention, but as his knowledge grows, more details are needed to increase his interest.

Search your mind to find speech subjects. At some time an interest has been aroused. Find it and you are on your way to discovering a topic for communication and a means for developing it.

Benefits of an interesting subject

Having an interest in the subject of a speech certainly makes the event more enjoyable for everyone. Why talk about something which holds no interest for either you, the speaker, or the listener? It is much easier to *want* to speak than to force yourself to say something.

Inasmuch as it is the speaker who is being judged and has the task of communication, let us consider his personal gains from selecting a subject which interests him:

1. Since he is already interested in the subject, the speaker is motivated to seek out an abundance of detailed information and ideas on the topic.
2. With this depth of knowledge, the speaker can easily use greater selectivity for the content of the speech.
3. By not being forced to exhaust all his knowledge during the speech, the speaker has a self-assuring cushion of reserve information.

We can see that the speaker reaps many benefits by expressing his interest in a speech. He has something to say, and therefore, has a reason for speaking.

What about the listener? How does he gain from the speaker's interest?

1. The listener is confronted by a poised, confident speaker.
2. He hears the delivery of a speaker who wants to communicate.
3. The listener learns from the knowledge of the speaker, thereby supplementing his own interest.

Because both parties are interested in the speech, there is a greater rapport between the speaker and the listener. Effective communication has not only been accomplished but it has also been furthered.

The topic must be specific and concise

ONCE A SUBJECT is selected, the speaker's duty is not yet completed. Speaking is neither filibustering nor a simple matter of talking. Merely doing either one is an imposition on the listener. Therefore, a *specific topic* must be abstracted from the general subject.

Usually a specific speech topic is chosen by simply narrowing the general material until a limited aspect is reached. For example, you may be interested in community theater. Yet, if you were to talk to the local dramatic group, it would be almost impossible to cover all the elements of the subject—directing, acting, costuming, settings, lighting, managing, producing, and advertising. These are simply too much to be handled by one speaker in one speech. A series of lectures would be needed to cover the entire subject adequately. Each lecture would be limited to one specific topic within the subject.

We can learn an important lesson from this example. For the most part, the speaker should not attempt to speak on a broad subject. Instead, he should limit the speech to a specific topic from within the general area. This applies not only to the speaker making just one appearance before the listener but to the one making several speeches to the same listener as well. There are times when a broad overview of a subject is in order. However, the beginning speaker should be very cautious in making a talk of this type.

The narrowing process

You should always select limits for the speech subject. Within the limited topic, there can be expansion of detail and thus an opportunity for you to display your knowledge. You know where you are heading and the listener knows where you are leading him.

As soon as the general speech subject is chosen or assigned, you should immediately begin considering ways of limiting the topic. Even though the subject may seem to be adequately limited at first sight, further limitation is probably still needed. As the speaker, you have knowledge of the subject, and therefore your mind begins functioning, seeing details at first glance. As a result, you may think the subject is already specific. Do not be trapped into such a misconception. Think of the listener! How much does he know? Will he immediately recognize the specific elements of the general subject? Will the listener have the same interpretation as you? Will he know what specific areas you will cover? Clear the air by breaking the general down into the specific. Do this every time and avoid the pitfalls of attempting to speak on a general subject.

Look carefully at the following condensed examples of the narrowing process. Consider which would be the easiest and the most interesting for you to use in constructing a speech and which would be more meaningful to the listener—the general or the specific:

SPEECHES OF EXPLANATION:

General Subject: The Public Health Nurse.
Narrowed: The role of the Public Health Nurse is *to care for* the *sick* shut-in.
Narrowed: The Public Health Nurse is the *principal* source of *medical service* for the sick shut-in.
Specific Topic: The Public Health Nurse bridges the gap between *the hospital* and the *aged, the handicapped,* the *financially needy* who are *confined* to their homes.

∽ ∽ ∽

General Subject: The United States Coast Guard.
Narrowed: The United States Coast Guard is a *help* to the *weekend sailor.*

Specific Topic: The U. S. Coast Guard serves the weekend sailor with *instructions, weather forecasts,* and *rescue.*

〜 〜 〜

General Subject: The social worker in American cities.
Narrowed: *Activities* of the social worker in *slum neighborhoods* of American cities.
Specific Topic: The *techniques* of the American social worker *versus police enforcement* in the slums of *our* city.

〜 〜 〜

General Subject: American education today.
Narrowed: The *State University* in the United States today.
Narrowed: The *cost* of State University education today.
Specific Topic: The cost of *our* State University education to the *student,* the *taxpayer,* and the *state.*

〜 〜 〜

General Subject: American foreign aid.
Narrowed: American foreign aid to *South America.*
Specific Topic: American foreign aid in the form of *farm surplus* to South America.

Speeches of Opinion:

General Subject: Merging with our competitor is a wise course of action.
Narrowed: Merging with a competitor with *greater assets* will be a wise move.
Specific Topic: Merging with a competitor having greater *working capital, wider stock distribution,* and more *advanced sales promotion* will be a sound business move.

〜 〜 〜

General Subject: Automation is good.
Narrowed: Automation *in industry benefits the consumer.*
Specific Topic: Automation in industry benefits the consumer with *lower cost, faster service,* and *improved quality.*

〜 〜 〜

General Subject: Socio-economic reforms are needed.
Narrowed: Socio-economic reforms are needed in *American agriculture.*

Narrowed:	*Wage* reforms are needed for the *migrant farm worker* of the South.
Specific Topic:	*Minimum wage laws* should be extended to include migrant farm labor from *Mexico* working in the South.

$\backsim \;\; \backsim \;\; \backsim$

General Subject:	Pay television is impractical.
Narrowed:	Pay television would have to be *approved* by *Congress.*
Specific Topic:	Pay television is *too complicated* and *too costly* to warrant congressional approval.

$\backsim \;\; \backsim \;\; \backsim$

General Subject:	Our sports coupe is the best buy.
Narrowed:	Our sports coupe model has *more standard equipment* for the *money.*
Narrowed:	Our sports coupe model is the best buy because it comes equipped with more *safety features.*
Specific Topic:	We sell the best value in our sports coupe model because it comes equipped with the extra safety features of *disk brakes, heavy-duty suspension,* and *puncture-proof tires.*

In each of the above examples a general subject was narrowed until a more specific topic had been reached. Although the degree of narrowing varied, the end result was the same. Obviously, the more specific the topic, the easier it is to construct a speech for presentation. The speaker knows precisely what should be said and has greatly simplified the development and organization of content. Narrowing a subject is one important key in making the task of speaking easier. As a result, the listener's attention is captured earlier and quicker.

The topic must be adapted to the listener

As we noted earlier, a speech topic should interest the speaker and should be specific. We must now consider one additional matter. The main idea of the speech needs to be adapted to the particular listener.

Would it be sensible to discuss graduate college scholarships before vocational training students? Foreign aid before welfare persons? Auto racing before a swimming team? No! Such topics have no relationship to the interests of the specific listening group.

In adapting the topic to the listeners, the speaker needs some background information. The degree of specificity here is governed by the speaking purpose and the particular type of person present. There are two elementary questions which a speaker can ask himself to gather much information for use in determining the means of speech adaptation:

1. Why is there a meeting between speaker and listeners?
2. Who are the listeners?

The answers to these questions can reveal such useful information as:

1. Whether the audience is voluntary or captive.
2. The familiarity of the listeners with the speaker.
3. The familiarity of the listeners with the speaker's subject.
4. The socio-economic level of the listeners.
5. The initial rapport existing between the speaker and the listeners.
6. The educational level of the listeners.
7. The logical interests of the listeners.
8. The apparent values of the listeners.

With such information you can select the elements of speaking more efficiently and effectively. You can avoid discussing a topic which does not relate to the listeners. Similarly, you may find the use of time and talk to be more constructive by presenting the topic in a more practical state of development. The level and amount of detail is also determined by the nature of the listeners. Just about every aspect of a speech is affected by the listeners.

A politician must be prepared to discuss a subject in different ways to different listeners. When speaking on aid to agriculture, for example, he must select the specific subject topic that will satisfy the needs or interests of his immediate listeners. The city audience would hear a different speech than the rural audience. The general legislature would hear one speech and the agricultural committee another. Even though there is expression on the same general subject, the specific topic and its development varies according to the type of listeners. If this were not done, there could be a loss of communication.

When an educator teaches the American Revolution to different grade levels, the fourth grade hears a different lecture from that delivered to the eighth grade. Yet another lecture is presented to the twelfth grade. Again, the same general subject is specifically adapted to the particular listeners.

The salesman also alters his salesmanship to correspond to the consumer. If he is selling typewriters, he would use a different approach for the student, the parent, the small office manager, and the large corporation. Although the product is the same, the listener is different, thus the need for adaptation. Moreover, the salesman would not make the same presentation to interested prospects as he would to the completely uninformed prospects. He would need to adapt to the knowledge and interest level of the listeners.

Adaptation is continually taking place. Wherever there is a speaker and a listener, the effective communicant adjusts the speech to fit the situation. The speaker thinks of his presentation in terms of effectiveness. Placing himself in the position of the hearer, he asks the following *listener* questions:

1. Why tell me?
2. Who cares?
3. So what?
4. So?

A speaker has the responsibility of selecting a specific topic and refining it to satisfy the listener. It is not the duty of the hearer to *force* interest or understanding.

It is the speaker who knows the subject and has the interest in the topic. He must narrow the speech until it becomes specific. Then he must adapt it to the listener.

1. What is the purpose of speaking to the particular listener?
2. How does it concern the listener?
3. What is expected of the listener?
4. What does the listener expect of the speaker?

Unless there is *adaptation* to the *particular* listener, the speech may be meaningless. Every main point of a speech should mean something to the listener. To give a speech relevancy is to give it meaning.

Once you have chosen a topic, ideas regarding it will come to mind. Now is the time to be ready to record the items you may want to talk about.

Step 1 | Exercises ∿ Assignments

1. Make a list of ten general subjects which interest you from each of the following:
   a. your experiences
   b. your knowledge

2. From the list above take two general subjects. Now from each of these find five specific topics.

3. During the next few days, pay special attention to being a listener in informal conversation. Draw up a list of particular characteristics about conversation that are appealing to you as a listener. Next, consider and be prepared to discuss how these characteristics can be made applicable to formal speaking.

4. Listen to a lecture or speech on television. Pay special attention to the speaker's adaptation to the listeners. Did the speaker adapt? If so, how? If not, how could he have done so?

5. Members of the class take turns putting a general subject on the board. Now each member of the class is given five minutes to list as many specific topics as possible.

6. Divide the class into groups of four. Appoint one member of each group as "lead speaker." Have the lead speaker give a one-minute impromptu speech on a subject of his own choice—without revealing the subject to the other members of his group. Immediately following the lead speaker, each member of the group must give a one minute impromptu based upon the lead speech.

7. Take the general topic, "Education," and show how the topic may be narrowed by:
   Geography e.g., United States——New England——Massachusetts——Boston——Boston Latin

   | Period of time | Methods |
   | Type | Financing |

8. Narrow the following general topics into specific topics:

   | Patriotism | Public Speaking |
   | Public Welfare | Productivity |

9. List topics that may interest your class in the following areas:

   | International Problems | National Problems |
   | State Problems | Local Problems |

10. Narrow and adapt the following topics to the list of suggested audiences:
    Topics: Economics
                 Preventing War

Alcoholism
Automobile Accidents
Controls on World Population Growth

Audiences: Parent-Teacher Association
Future Farmers of America
Rotary Club
Automobile Mechanics
Fuel Oil Dealers

Step 2 | *How do you*

gather materials for

the development

of the topic

NO speaker is expected to know everything. It would be impossible to have all the materials needed for the speech stored conveniently in his mind. The speaker and the speech topic will naturally determine the amount of content materials needed. Even if the speaker knows most of the content, he should verify the information as a safeguard against incorrect statements. Moreover, he usually needs added details for expansion.

As a speaker, after you have selected a specific topic, you should make a survey of all knowledge on the subject matter. It is often wise to put the recalled information on cards which you can then easily catalogue by specific content. Next, you supplement this immediate knowledge by gathering additional materials for the complete development of the topic. If you are a cautious speaker you will have more details than you expect to use on the speech topic. Do not stop the process of gathering materials simply because you have enough to satisfy the speaking situation. It is better to gather a comprehensive collection of specific details from many sources—observation, talking and listening, public communication, and the library. You will be much more effective as a communicator if you can select the most effective materials from a broad collection.

From observation

AFTER YOU HAVE selected your speech subject, take special notice of the environment. When you know what to look for, it is amazing how quickly your vision improves. Perhaps you ride the same bus every morning. As the ride becomes routine you take less notice of fellow travelers. However, one day you are discussing white- and blue-collar workers and suddenly there is a purpose for noticing specific characteristics of the passengers around you. Fellow commuters appear in different focus. The collar color becomes obvious. You discern differences within each group and implied facts begin to appear before you. Although nothing conclusive can possibly be determined from such a personal, uncontrolled survey, you will get ideas which prompt further investigation. You are on the way to new discoveries because of a new concern with the environment.

Take a tour of a city, for instance, and through observation you can construct a premise upon which a talk can be developed. Stroll through the museum and the art-gallery section of the city. No longer are these areas quiet secluded places. The museum has waiting lines outside. Inside, the rooms are as crowded as a cafeteria at noon. Do you see matronly sponsors of the arts? Or is there a conglomeration of people—a mixture of minks, sport shirts, dungarees, dress suits, and sweat shirts? In the art galleries the scene is different. What might all this suggest? What might be the state of cultural interest? Ideas can be formulated from such an observation and the experience can be used for a speech on the subject.

Take a drive through your home community and this time *look*. What meets the focused eye of the observer? Houses of nearly identical design touched with attempts at individuality. Lawns with rhododendrons and barbecue grills. Garages with station wagons. Roofs with color-television antennae. No sidewalk, just street and driveway. Here again the observed facts can be the exemplification of concrete subject matter.

An interesting speaker is an alert observer. He is always on the alert to see the intricacies of man in society. Questions are forever running through his mind. He does not bury his head in a sound-proof, vision-proof vault. He looks and he *sees*. Many speech materials are found in the environment. The medical researcher, the philosopher, the sociologist, and the educator are only a few of those who make use of observation for the formation of ideas, theories, and procedures. The same can be true for you. Remember, observations are valuable as examples bringing more factual details and personal qualities to a speech.

From talking and listening

MAN IS A creature of talk. Much of his time is spent talking and listening. It sometimes is claimed that we learn much by conversing with others. Certainly this is true. Conversation with different persons gives us an insight into personalities, ideas, and problems. There is little doubt about this. There once was a time when a man simply chatted with others and called it teaching. Today, although education itself is more formal, there is still much to be learned from simply chatting.

Through conversation with others there can be the reward of hearing the ideas of others. This information—abstract or concrete, general or specific—may enlighten a listener or stir his intellectual curiosity.

At lunch the first day of a new job, the conversation usually centers around the company. The old timers talk about the organization, the department heads, the work itself and may pass on advice to the newcomer. The new employee gets a casual insight into the company and the other employees. He has learned casually. He gets a view which cannot be found in books.

Perhaps while relaxing at the health club, you are drawn into a conversation where one of the group, an amateur horticulturist, discusses a blight threatening the elm trees in the park and laments that nothing is being done about it. You join the talk, learn the problems, and his solution to save the town park. Although you were unaware of the situation before, you have learned now through oral exchange.

We are daily presented with the opportunity to gain knowledge or to awaken interest in innumerable subjects just through talking and listening.

When oral communication takes place under informal circumstances, you should be a good listener as well as a proficient talker. When the other party is doing the talking, hear what is being said rather than plan what to say when it is your turn. Mentally note what is being said either to increase your knowledge of a subject or to understand the workings of the human mind.

If the occasion for gathering speech materials is more formal, be prepared to record all important details in writing. When the situation is that of lecturer and listener, recognize your position as listener. Avoid the temptation to give silent thought to the matter. This can come later. While the other person has the stand, listen attentively, keeping accurate and objective notes. After the complete expression of the subject by the lecturer, you will have time for your own thinking on the subject.

Interviewing is another means of learning through oral communication. The interviewer is able to gain specific information from the interviewee. To do so, however, he needs careful preparation before the actual meeting:

1. The interview should be pre-arranged at the convenience of the person to be interviewed.
2. The interviewee should be told of the purpose of the meeting, the subject of inquiry, and the questions to be asked.
3. The interviewer should be prepared to ask specific questions.
4. Answers to questions should be accurately recorded or taped with the permission of the person interviewed.

In all instances where materials are gathered through oral exchange, there is need for high-quality listening.

From public communications

TODAY SOME MATERIALS for speaking can be found right in the home. Television and radio bring a vast assortment of subjects—news reports, news analyses, public service programs, and special coverages—into nearly every living room. Programs pass through microphones and cameras carrying information on a limitless variety of subjects. All of this is available to you by simply turning a knob. Selective tuning can not only give the individual specific information but can awaken interest and provoke fresh thinking. Television and radio can be a major source of materials for speaking. Where else can one see a history of the political, social, or economic developments of another country? Even within our own nation, television brings us to city slum areas with an intimate view of the people and conditions. We can watch the physical development of a community thousands of miles away. The agricultural industry of Iowa can be seen by the Floridian. The political conventions of California's Cow Palace are observed in Maine. Oklahoma Indian reservations, Wisconsin dairy farms, Vermont skiing, Texas cattle ranches, and any number of other matters are compressed into the television screen. What one views can be included into speeches as information or as examples.

In addition to the mass media you can get information from listening to speakers. Despite the trend of people to remain at home, lecturing is still popular in our country. Schools and colleges often have an active program of guest speakers who discuss a variety of subjects. The same is true of church groups, business organizations, educational associations, and social clubs. Experienced people are invited to address the membership and the public on topics of concern to thinking persons. As a student of speech, you should take advantage of hearing such lectures. You will be able to observe a professional speaker at work as well as hear the specialized subject matter.

Regardless of the source of public communication—electronic or live—the auditor is still responsible for accurate and objective listening. To listen, to record, and to think are the three main steps of gathering material from public communications.

From the library

THE LIBRARY IS a most important source of speech materials. Within the library are stored printed works on a multitude of subjects. It is a most efficient and complete friend to a speaker.

Libraries often give the appearance of formality. Once you are familiar with the quiet operations of these buildings of compiled learning, you will move within their walls with ease and assurance. All libraries follow similar methods of organizing their materials and the system can be learned quite easily.

Books and the card catalogue

The *card catalogue* is the key system for efficiently locating books in a library. It is the alphabetical directory of all books. If you are familiar with this easy-to-use system, a minimum of time and effort are consumed in discovering any text in the building.

Each work is listed on a separate card and filed alphabetically in cabinets. As a further aid, each book is classified and filed under more than one heading: author, title, subject. For example, the book, *Federal Union,* by John D. Hicks, could be found under three different catalogue sections:

1. *author heading*—Hicks, John D.
2. *title heading*—Federal Union
3. *subject heading*—Early American History to 1865

All you need to use the card catalogue to locate a specific text is the author, title, or the subject of the work. Simply go to the card files and search the alphabetical listing until the card bearing the name of the book and a description of its contents is located. You will notice a *number* printed on one of the upper corners. This is a code number indicating the specific location of the book on the library shelves. Record this number and the other information requested on a special library call form, give it to the librarian, and the book will be delivered to you. In some cases, you will do the work yourself. You simply look on the shelves through the books having numbers similar to yours until you find your specific number.

The card catalogue is also valuable when searching for information without a specific text in mind. In that case, the subject file is particularly useful. Simply go to the cabinet containing the cards on your subject and browse through the cards, reading the descriptions of the books listed. You can find specific texts in this way.

Magazines

Magazines are often important to a speaker. Since magazines are usually restricted to certain subject-matters and are published periodically, you can find current information on specific subjects. Libraries generally have a special room for the great number and variety of periodicals. The card catalogue has the name and location of each individual periodical kept by the library. In addition, there are special publications, listing the thousands of articles found in most magazines, to help locate a specific article.

Readers' Guide to Periodical Literature is the most available source for finding specific magazine articles. These yearly volumes contain a cumulative index of articles for over a hundred different magazines dating back to the beginning of the century. The listing is by author and subject of the article. To find an article, select the volume of the *Readers' Guide* by appropriate date, turn to the proper subject heading, and there you will find all the information needed to get the magazine from the librarian—author, title, name and volume of magazine, and date of publication.

In addition to *Readers' Guide,* there are *special* indexes available. Poole's *Index to Periodical Literature* covers periodicals published from 1802–1906. The *International Index to Periodicals* lists learned journals in arts and sciences. Others which are self explanatory for subject-matter are: *Educational Index, The Agricultural Index, Art Index, The Industrial Arts Index,* and *The Bulletin of the Public Affairs Information Service, Newsweek Index,* and *Time Index.*

Newspapers

For information on daily happenings throughout the world, the newspaper is an important source. Back issues of newspapers are also available for researching reports of past events.

While private individuals do not collect newspapers over the years, a library has the facilities to preserve actual or microfilm copies of leading papers. Some libraries keep microfilm reproductions of a local paper. Usually, *The New York Times* is available on microfilm. The *Times* publishes *The New York Times Index,* containing an alphabetical listing of articles, by subjects, for a number of years, to accommodate the researcher. In addition to its principal purpose, the *Times Index* is also a guide to articles published in other newspapers at the same time. In other words, by using the dates of the *Times* article, the researcher can correspond with the publishers of any other newspapers to obtain photostatic copies of their articles on the same subject. For instance, if an event took place in Any City the specific date of articles on this event can probably be found in the *Times Index.* Then a request for copies of the local article can be made directly to the newspaper of Any City using the information obtained from the *Index.*

For articles representing the views of Europe there are the indexes of *The London Times.* There are two other indexes—*Palmer's Index,* which catalogues articles since 1790, and the *Official Index* containing a comprehensive listing since 1906.

Government publications

The federal government publishes a considerable quantity of materials that are not classified as books. Therefore, reference must be made to special indexes and bibliographies.

The *Monthly Catalog: United States Government Publications* lists many pamphlets of the government. *Statesman's Yearbook* identifies world political leaders. *Statistical Abstract of the United States* and *United States Census Reports* index statistical facts on the nation. Boyd's *United States Government Publications: Sources of Information for Libraries* contains those bibliographies which are distributed by the federal government.

The Congressional Record is a most useful source of information on the daily happenings of the legislative branches of the government. The daily activities of each congressional session are recorded in these special volumes.

Miscellaneous materials

For biographical information, there are several sources: *Who's Who, Who's Who in America, Webster's Biographical Dictionary, American Men of Science, Directory of American Scholars.*

Summarized or specialized information can be found in encyclopedias such as *The Encyclopedia Britannica, The Encyclopedia Americana,* and *The New International Encyclopedia.*

Recording materials

A RESEARCHER SHOULD HAVE some system of recording the materials gathered. It would, of course, be impossible to remember all information found. It would be too awkward to fill a notebook with the details of the readings. A simpler system is needed.

For convenience of collecting, recording, and filing, the use of note cards seems best. Putting information on cards allows easy handling, shuffling for organization, and storing. In addition, the same cards can be used for reference during a speech.

Clarity and simplicity are essential when using note cards. Each card should be complete in itself, that is, contain only *one complete point* of information. To make certain that each card of recorded material is meaningful, it should have the following:

1. The *subject* of the recorded point.
2. The *information* quoted or paraphrased accurately.
3. The details on the complete *source*.

DISTRICT MANAGER RESPONSIBILITIES TO THE LOCAL OFFICES

"The District Manager of a national organization is forever forced into the dual role of 'Big Daddy' and 'Tyrant.' 'Big Daddy' must encourage subordinates who continually seek recognition simply for executing the normal functions of a particular position. The pat on the back, cliché compliments of, 'Well done, my boy,' are the vital trivia of leadership. And, just as in any strong father image, there are times when the subordinate must feel the strong, reassuring domination of the Tyrant."

Hoff, Gerald, *The Dual Role of Managerial Leadership* (Chicago: Emerson & Co., 1966), p. 10.

If other information were to be taken from the same work, the format would remain the same.

The use of quotation marks is important to signify an exact copy of the material. This ensures accuracy when using the information and removes the necessity of double checking.

When recording material from a periodical, a similar form is used:

NORMA GALBLAY—HUMOR IN SPEECHES

"A continual use of sparkling humor enlivened Miss Galblay's refutation. Amusing comparisons, clever satire, and biting wit abound in her political attacks. She cut to the quick in the manner of a Twain so even the opposition laughed with the rest."

Laidlaw, Leslie, "The Woman Suffrage Argument of Norma Galblay," *Journal of Political Debate*, Vol. XXI, No. 6 (April, 1960), p. 132.

It is most important to record the material correctly. Without the proper subject heading, categorizing is either impossible or disorganized. You are always subject to embarrassing correction if the information is incorrectly quoted or paraphrased. There is also the danger of the information becoming meaningless to you between the time of collection and the time of intended use. The source of the material should always be fully noted, permitting verification and referral.

You will vary the type of research from speech to speech. However, do not slight this step. Always gather much more materials than you need so that you can select the best for the actual speech situation.

Step 2 | *Exercises ∾ Assignments*

1. Take a subject out of the current news. Prepare to talk about it using materials which you collect from three of the following:
   - a. observation
   - b. talking
   - c. listening
   - d. interview
   - e. public communication
   - f. library

2. Arrange a class tour of the library. Have the librarian explain the procedure for making the most effective use of each department for research—reference room, circulation department, reserve room, periodical department, documents department and any others.

3. Divide the class into groups. Assign a library department to each group for investigation. Have a group report on department materials and what type of information can be found in the materials.

4. Select an original subject and do the research. Use all the means of gathering materials. Then report your research procedures and results to the class.

5. Conduct an interview with an authority on some subject, perhaps a faculty member. Keep accurate notes on how the interview proceeded. Report to the class the results of the interview, its difficulties, its success and how it could have been better.

6. Prepare a bibliography on one of the following subjects:
   The Language of the Bees
   Unidentified Flying Objects

Theater of the Absurd
Automobile Safety Features
Computer Language

7. Select a current "name" in the news. Hand in a work sheet showing your steps in researching background on this person.

Step 3

How is the topic outlined?

ONE of the most valuable steps in the construction of a speech is to outline the main ideas. The speaker sets down his ideas in an outline form which permits easy analysis, development, and organization.

The outline serves *you,* the speaker. You should always remember this. If outlining seems inconvenient, it is only because it forces you to sit down and give constructive thought to the content of a speech. It is not a hindrance but an asset. The clarity of topical points, content, and arrangement of a speech is tangible evidence of efficient pre-delivery outlining.

The speaker who uses an outline in the preparation of the speech finds the effort returns confidence through positive construction. The lazy or careless person avoids the outline or scribbles an inadequate one. To regard outlining as a burden or an imposition upon free thought is sheer rationalization. The speaker should look upon the outline as a valuable aid and reap the rewards of time saved, anxiety abandoned, and successful communication advanced.

Although the system of outlining is essentially the same for any speech, methods of outlining differ, ranging from very simple to very complex. More important than the difference between the outline for the speech of explanation and that for the speech of opinion is the purpose of the outline.

The system of outlining

AN OUTLINE IS the skeleton of the speech. It is the frame supporting and giving form to speaking. It is the system enabling a speaker to organize ideas into a complete whole. It is the speech.

The first characteristic noticed in a complete outline is its basic divisions. The outline contains three units, each complete in itself:

INTRODUCTION

I.————————————————————————————
II.————————————————————————————

BODY

I.————————————————————————————
   A.————————————————————————————
   B.————————————————————————————
II.————————————————————————————

CONCLUSION

I.————————————————————————————
II.————————————————————————————

Each of the three outline divisions serves a special purpose. The *introduction* reveals the speech topic. The *body* elaborates on the topic. The *conclusion* reviews and ends the speech. Knowing what to put into each unit of an outline in itself gives some organization to the construction of a speech.

Main speech points outlined

Each outline unit is composed of ideas or points to be expressed. Not all the points of a speech have equal value. Some are more basic

49

to listener comprehension than others. The most fundamental are called *main points* and comprise the principal structure around which the complete speech is constructed.

There is need for a noticeable symbol to distinguish main points in an outline. Since outline markings are limited to numbers and letters, the only choice for the main point is the distinctive *Roman numeral*.

Using the body of the outline, the main points of a speech are added as follows:

SUBJECT: A TYPICAL NEW ENGLAND HOME TOWN

(BODY)

    I. Location
   II. History
  III. Residency
  IV. Future

We can quickly see that just listing the main points is not a completely satisfactory aid to speaking. More insight into the topic is needed.

Secondary speech points outlined

Because of the need for elaboration, *secondary points,* amplifying each main point, are added to the outline. Because these points are second in importance, identification is made with a less significant symbol than that for the main point. A *capital letter* is used to heighten the distinction between these two points. Also, this letter is *indented*.

The same sample outline is now expanded to include both main and secondary points. Greater clarity of content can immediately be seen:

I. Location
   A. Within the nation
   B. Within the state

50

II. History
   A. From settlement to Revolutionary War
   B. Independence to Civil War
   C. Civil War to World War II
   D. World War II to present

III. Residency
   A. Economic opportunity
   B. Social activities

IV. Future Prospects
   A. Present activities for growth
   B. Potential for progress

Thus the addition of the secondary points greatly improves the outline. The method of development has become clearer. What is to be said is more specific. The outline has become a more positive aid to the speaker.

Specific speech details outlined

Can the outline be made more useful? It can by bringing in *specific details* for each secondary point. Specific detail has a symbol indicating its subordination to both main and secondary points. Still following the traditional outlining system, a symbol, lower in class, is used. Therefore, the *Arabic number* is the proper symbol of specific detail.

In the sample outline, the speech is now expanded by the addition of specific detail:

I. Location
   A. Within the nation
      1. New England coast
      2. State of New Hampshire
   B. Within the state
      1. Southeastern border
      2. Third largest city

II. History
   A. From settlement to Revolutionary War
      1. Originally in Massachusetts Bay Colony
      2. A major seaport for foreign trade

51

    B. Independence to Civil War
      1. One of 13 states ratifying Constitution
      2. Grew as an economic and cultural center
    C. Civil War to World War II
      1. Industry reached a peak
      2. Decline as a cultural center at turn of 19th century
    D. World War II to present
      1. Industrial recession in the post-war period
      2. Results of the lack of economic progress

III. Residency
    A. Economic opportunity
      1. Skilled labor in limited demand
      2. Professional persons always welcomed and needed
    B. Social activities
      1. Both a summer and winter sporting area
      2. Nightclubs limited to private organizations
      3. No theater, concert, dance

IV. Future Prospects
    A. Present action to implement growth
      1. Political leaders offer concession to industry
      2. Chamber of Commerce conducts advertising program
    B. Potential for progress
      1. Limited attraction for new industry because of the lack of technically trained labor
      2. Adherence to status quo tends to retard effect of public relations program

With each expansion of the outline, the substance of the speech becomes more positive. A stranger to the topic could now read the outline and have some idea of the subject and the speaker's approach to the development and organization of the content.

Supplementary speech details outlined

Thus far, the outline has main points, secondary points, and specific detail. The addition of *supplementary detail* makes the outline about as complete as most speakers would want or need. This added detail gives special clarity to speaking.

As we see in the final, completed form of the sample outline, the indented *small letter* indicates supplementary detail:

I. Location
   A. Within nation
      1. New England coast
         a. Ten mile coastal line on Atlantic Ocean
         b. Second largest seaport in New England
      2. State of New Hampshire
   B. Within the state
      1. Southeastern border
         a. Separates Maine coast from Massachusetts coast
         b. Only state seaport
         c. Only city on Atlantic coast
      2. Third largest city
         a. Population 25,000
         b. Property value in excess of $5 million

II. History
   A. From settlement to Revolutionary War
      1. Originally in Massachusetts Bay Colony
      2. A major seaport for foreign trade
   B. Independence to Civil War
      1. One of 13 states ratifying Constitution
      2. Growth as an economic and cultural center
         a. Shipping activity drew other business
         b. With business activity and financial wealth came the opera and the theater
   C. Civil War to World War II
      1. Industry reached a peak
         a. Shipping by sailing vessels was at its climax
         b. Federal government opened a naval shipyard
      2. Decline as a cultural center at turn of 19th century
         a. Greater growth of Boston attracted cultural activities
         b. Interest of a seaport worker turned to other forms of entertainment
   D. World War II to present
      1. Industrial recession in the post-war period
         a. Shipping decreased because of lack of facilities
         b. Labor costs forced industry south
      2. Results of the lack of economic progress

III. Residency
   A. Economic opportunity
      1. Skilled labor in limited demand
         a. Lack of industry requiring skilled labor causes little interest in such training

             b. Yet, industry does not come because of the lack of such skilled workers

             c. The paradox of all New England

          2. Professional persons always welcomed and needed

             a. Physicians, dentists, and teachers in short supply

             b. Increased population requires the services of the professions

      B. Social activities

          1. Both a summer and winter sporting area

             a. Fine beaches and lakes near-by

             b. Hunting and fishing areas among the best in the country

          2. Nightclubs limited to private organizations

          3. No theater, concert, dance

IV. Future Prospects

      A. Present action to implement growth

          1. Political leaders offer concessions to industry

             a. Special tax rates

             b. Low rent on public land

          2. Chamber of Commerce conducts advertising program

             a. Branch offices in all major cities in country

             b. Representatives approach individual businesses

             c. Advertisements in national business magazines

      B. Potential for progress

          1. Limited attraction for new industry because of the lack of technically trained labor

             a. Skilled workers go to Boston

             b. Vocational training programs now in operation

          2. Adherence to status quo tends to retard effectiveness of public relations programs

             a. Local business men pressure against new, competing industry

             b. Land owner refuses to sell or lease land

             c. Older citizens prefer historical status to industrial status

The outline is now ready for use by the extemporaneous speaker or for writing a manuscript speech. It is fairly complete. Further specific facts can be added at the discretion of the speaker.

The outline began with a listing of main points and grew in detail until it was completed. With this type of outline, you are fully prepared to present the speech. Effective speakers use outlines similar to the one shown here. Although there may be some minor differences, the system remains the same:

I.   (main point)
  A.   (secondary point)
    1.   (specific detail)
      a.   (supplementary detail)

This is the *system* of outlining a speech topic in preparation for presentation.

Methods of outlining

METHODS OF OUTLINING involve the technique of composing the outline. Generally there are three styles of outlining—single word, phrase, and sentence.

Single word

The single-word outline uses a key word for each section of the outline:

I. Location
  A. Nation
    1. New England
    2. New Hampshire
  B. State
    1. Southeast
    2. Coastal

This method is rather barren in detail and its use is limited. Some speakers may only want the single-word outline to guide them through an entire speech. More often your needs are greater and require more clues to content. A single word outline is best used as an initial guide to speech development. It can be a means of selecting main points and corresponding elaboration. The simplicity of this outline form allows you to see the overall framework of the talk. The major supporting materials are compressed into single word clues.

Phrase

Phrase outlines are more satisfactory for the building of a complete speech and are better guides when presenting the speech. In this method, each point of the outline is written as a phrase:

I. Location of city
   A. National location
      1. New England seacoast
      2. New Hampshire state
   B. State location
      1. Southeast section
      2. Directly on the Atlantic

The phrase gives just enough more additional detail than the single word to make the outline more understandable. Therefore, its usefulness is increased.

This expanded method is more valuable in constructing the speech. First, it allows more thoughts in the written guide. When the outline is being revised, the meaning of each step is more apparent and thus needed changes are more obvious. Second, there is no need to give time and thought to compositional technique. Third, there is a fairly substantial script to use for practice. Fourth, the outline can be used during the actual delivery of the speech since its higher degree of completeness stimulates immediate recall of detailed content.

Sentence

The sentence outline is written entirely with complete sentences and is the most thorough of outlines. The next step would be to compose a speech manuscript.

I. To discuss the home town, its location should be known.
   A. First, let us get the general area nationally.
      1. It is in New England on the Atlantic Coast.
      2. The state of its location is New Hampshire.
   B. Second, its placement within the state is noteworthy.
      1. It is in the southeast coastal corner.
      2. Its limits are bordered on the east by the Atlantic.

The sentence method is an extension of the phrase outline. Because it keeps the outline format and allows a greater degree of flexibility in presentation than does the manuscript, changes can still be made during delivery. However, the speech should be a spontaneous speech. If a manuscript is to be written, the sentence outline is plainly the best source.

Which outline method is best? No definite answer can possibly be given. The decision rests upon the speaker and the requirements of the speaking situation. Probably a combination of all three will be used most frequently. One suggestion on method applies to the speech of opinion. When you are expressing a controversial opinion in an outline, a complete sentence is advised to ensure *absolute* clarity of your idea.

Outlines of explanation and opinion speeches

THE TWO MAJOR TYPES of speeches—explanation and opinion—use different approaches to outlining. The following section will illustrate these differences.

For speech of explanation

The outline for explanation is made up of the principal items to be explained or the materials of explanation:

Main Points: The major parts, ideas, items to be covered in explanation.

Secondary: The actual explanation for the appropriate main point.

Specific: The exemplification of the explanation.

Supplementary: Additional details on the exemplification.

The complete outline found in Step 3 is an example of an outline for the speech of explanation. The speaker, knowing the requirements of the speaking situation, selects the method for outlining the speech of explanation. Probably, the main points and secondary points will be single words and phrases. The specific points will be sentences in order to include their details.

For speech of opinion

Since the speech of opinion has a purpose beyond that of explanation, the content of the outline differs. The outline contains the principal statements of opinion plus proof and elaboration:

Main Points: Basic reasons behind the opinion.
Secondary: The proof, logic, or explanation of the reason.
Specific: Materials which complement the proof, explanation, or logic by furthering clarity, identification, credibility, or interest.
Supplementary: Refined detail clarifying the specific.

If the final main point of the Home Town outline were revised to be an expression of opinion, it might look like the following:

I. The program to attract new business is inadequate.
  A. Tax concessions offered are insufficient.
    1. Offering a two year period without a business tax cannot compete with the rest of the state.
      a. Three neighboring cities are offering five year plans.
      b. Elsewhere in state there are many 10-15 year concessions.
    2. A long term real estate tax concession can be offered to new business.
      a. At least 75% of public land is idle with no income.
      b. Private land would be lower in cost.
  B. Publicity efforts are too narrow.
    1. Advertising is primarily directed toward vacationists.
      a. Last year about 92% was just for summer tourists.
      b. Only 8% for all other types.
    2. National branches of Chamber of Commerce are stagnant.
      a. They only think of our area as an historical site.
      b. Little is being done to promote the location as a potential industrial center.

In the foregoing sample outline, the use of the sentence method was necessary to have complete development of the opinion. Although some shorter techniques may occasionally be used, the full sentence is generally best for the speech of opinion.

Purposes and values of outline

WHEN READING A textbook, a student often makes markings on the pages to aid in future study. Many underline the various important points made by the author, that is, the main and secondary points. Some even put brackets around specific and supplementary details. What are they really doing? The printed material is being *outlined*.

If outlining the printed page enables the *reader* to better understand the content and idea, is it not reasonable to conclude that outlining is valuable for the *speaker*? Probably the author of the printed matter even began with an outline before composing the finished product. The use of an outline has great value whether for writing or speaking.

Aid to development

The outline, because of its form, aids speech construction. First, you erect a frame of main points. Next you add the reinforcement of secondary points. You next use specific points to add to completeness. Finally you support the whole with supplementary points.

By eliminating all superficial compositional elaboration, the outline assists the speaker immeasurably during construction:

1. It relieves the speaker of grammatical and compositional construction.
2. It gives greater freedom for concise expression.
3. Its form permits ease of checking completeness of content.
4. It reveals and aids the precise arrangement of content.
5. It promotes objective consideration of points and development.
6. It can be easily corrected or reorganized.

One real value of an outline is its presentation of the speech as a unit to the speaker. With this total picture in mind, he can then rearrange, revise, or edit the speech with much greater ease. Investing time in outlining seems to be a waste to the novice speaker. Do not be misled. This initial investment pays real dividends in clarity of organization of the finished product.

Aid to delivery

The complete outline is also an aid to delivery:

1. It lets the speaker study the speech content with ease.
2. It is a simple guide to speech practice.
3. It can easily be converted into a manuscript speech.
4. It acts as a guide during the extemporaneous speech.
5. It allows an extemporaneous speaker to think and to adapt during delivery.
6. Its use helps the speaker have a natural, spontaneous expression of content when speaking.

The outline is beneficial to delivery for all types of speeches—formal or informal, extemporaneous or manuscript, explanation or opinion—and promotes pleasant, effective communication. It is a very valuable adjunct in speech construction and speech delivery.

You have a topic and are ready to plan it on paper. Now is the time to turn your attention to the matters of presentation.

Step 3 | Exercises ∽ Assignments

1. Read a short article in a magazine or newspaper. Locate the introduction, body and conclusion. Determine the main points. Now, outline it showing these elements.

2. Using the same article, take the first main point and outline it, showing the secondary points, specific detail, and supplementary detail.

3. Exchange the detailed single main point outline of No. 2 with a fellow student. Review the unfamiliar outline for a few moments. Now, talk about the substance contained within the outline. Can you do it easily? How could the outline be improved to aid you?

4. Each class member prepares an outline for a short speech on a vacation trip. Take turns putting an outline on the blackboard. Discuss it and make suggestions for improvement.

5. Prepare a two minute speech on an experience. Deliver the speech to the class. During the speech the class outlines the main points and secondary points. After the speech, compare the outlines of the speaker and the class. Are they the same?

6. Tape record a short impromptu talk. Listen to the recording and try to outline the talk.

7. Put your outline on the board or duplicate it for the class. Have them follow the written outline as you give your talk.

8. Outline in complete sentence form a printed speech from the newspaper, *Vital Speeches* or other collections of speeches.

9. Describe situations where you would use the single word outline in preference to the complete sentence outline.

10. Prepare a simple outline. Remove each identification symbol from each item and list the items in random order. See if a member of the class can rearrange them into an outline form.

Step 4

How can visual aids help?

OFTEN the subject of a speech is complicated. Perhaps you are describing a new sales promotion plan, an organizational blueprint, or tactics for solving a problem. It would seem only natural to use a pencil and paper in your explanation to help the listener grasp the complete idea while keeping track of the individual parts.

Too often a speaker fails to use visual aids, the most practical means of ensuring clarity of content. With visual aids the audience can see what is being discussed whether the aid is a graphic design, a list of words, or a sketch. By *seeing* as well as *hearing,* the audience's understanding of the speech is increased.

The speaker, too, benefits from the use of a visual aid. It allows him to move physically and with purpose and gives him something to do. As a result, he does a better job of speaking. Moreover the aid, an integral part of the speech, reminds him what to say and also helps to relieve any tension.

This step will introduce you to the major types of visual aids available to the speaker. You will gain stature as a speaker if you strengthen your visual communicative skills. Together the visual and audio channels can combine to aid both speeches of explanation and opinion.

Types of visual aids

THERE ARE many types of visual aids—written, graphic, and model. The speaker, after considering the nature of the listener and the speech, determines the type of aid to use.

Listing points or statistics

The written visual aid consists of printed words or numbers on a blackboard, a large sheet of cardboard or heavy paper. Its style varies with the needs of the speaker. You should be familiar with the following commonly-used styles:

I. *LISTING OF MAIN POINTS OF THE SPEECH:*

EFFECTIVE SPEECH TRAINING MUST BE ADOPTED

1. Teaches poise.
2. Teaches thought organization.
3. Teaches sound reasoning.
4. Teaches listener analysis.

ADVERTISING PLAN FOR EUROPEAN MOTORS

1. Television Auto Special.
2. SCCA and NASCAR races.
3. Motor Journal road tests.
4. National Auto Show.

II. *NUMBERS OR STATISTICS OF IMPORTANCE:*

CRIME AND PREVENTION IN OUR TOWN

1. Crime rate up 38%.
2. School dropouts have increased gangs
3. Social workers number 25 units.
4. 75 police officers assigned.

63

COST PERCENTAGES FOR LAST YEAR

1. Materials up   9%
2. Labor up   3%
3. Advertising up   7%
4. Shipping down   1%

HISTORY OF TONNAGE MINED

1900	2.5 million
1920	5.0 million
1930	4.0 million
1940	3.5 million

STOCK SALES FOR FIRST QUARTER

January	105,500
February	97,000
March	83,100
TOTAL	285,600 shares

III. *NAMES OF PERSONS, PLACES, OR THINGS:*

CANDIDATES FOR VICE PRESIDENT OF SALES

1. Alex Foster—Section Chief, Chemical Analysis
2. Coleman Barnes—Head, Public Relations
3. Harriet Borbes—Asst. Coordinator, American Sales
4. Bernard McDonald—Unit Supervision, Research

COMPARATIVE CLASSES OF AMERICAN VS. FOREIGN CARS

Low priced: Ford *vs.* Volkswagen
Medium priced: Pontiac *vs.* Rover
High priced: Cadillac *vs.* Mercedes Benz

Use the written visual aid whenever you feel it will help clarify your material. If the material is complicated and a blackboard is available, prepare the material on it before the speech. However, putting the material on the board while speaking gives an appearance of spontaneity. Often when a blackboard is not available or inconvenient to use, you can write the material on large sheets of cardboard or heavy paper prior to the speech and show it at the appropriate time.

Undoubtedly, you will find this type of visual aid can be used in many speeches. The listener can see and hear simultaneously—thereby doubling the impression. You will be considered a better speaker simply because you took the time to prepare the aid for the listener.

Graphs and charts

Graphic visual aids are simply-constructed charts or geometric designs offering a compact view of specific items in relation to the whole. They help the listener to make easy comparisons, see changes, or grasp the entire picture.

I. LINE GRAPH

The line graph permits the listener to see at a glance the increases and decreases occurring over a period of time. It thereby makes obvious in a brief moment what otherwise would require many words and much time to explain. The line graph improves listener understanding and aids listener recall.

II. PROFILE GRAPH

The profile graph is similar to the line graph. The difference is in the use of shading beneath the data line. Although both types of graphs convey the same visual information, the profile is recommended as a

65

variation when showing large or significant changes in data in relation to specific intervals. It helps the listener concentrate on such special fluctuations.

GROWTH PERCENTAGES OF PROFESSIONAL MEMBERSHIP

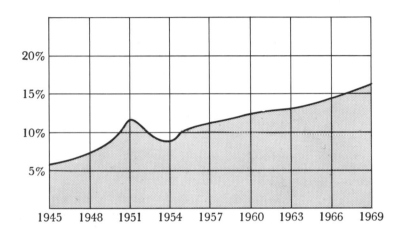

III. Bar Graph

Bar graphs have the advantage of presenting the listener with blocks of information in a form allowing visual comparison. Unlike the line graph, the bar graph condenses data not needed to be shown in exact detail thereby quickly achieving listener understanding.

AVERAGE CASE WORKER RESPONSIBILITY IN MAJOR CITIES

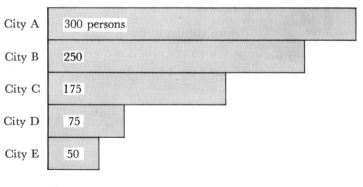

IV. ORGANIZATION CHART

Organization charts are especially important when a speaker is discussing a complex subject consisting of many divisions of influence. Whether the subject be a political group or procedure, a business complex or chain-of-command, or even the local social group, this particular visual aid is essential for the listener trying to place the pieces in the organizational jigsaw.

LOAN STRUCTURE OF PLYMOUTH STATE BANK

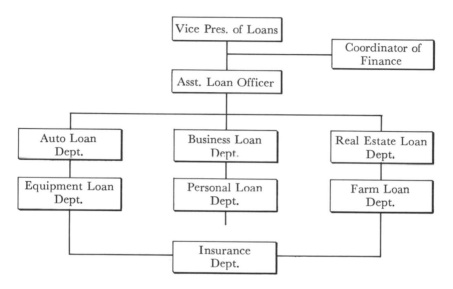

V. "PIECE OF PIE"

The visual aid called the "piece of pie," has a rather unique characteristic. It clearly illustrates the divisions or pieces in relation to one another while remaining within the visual setting of the whole. The listener is not only shown a combination of elements but can compare their relationships.

67

EXPENSES DURING THE CAMPAIGN

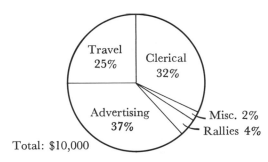

Total: $10,000

Like the written visual aid, the graphic can be sketched on a blackboard either during the speech or before it. However, if the graphic aid is especially complicated or is a test of draftsmanship, it is advisable to construct it beforehand on large sheets of cardboard or heavy paper. The advantage of the graph is that the listener can clearly and easily see the relationship of the parts to the whole and can, therefore, find greater meaning in the speaking process.

VI. Pictograph

The pictograph shows the same type of information as other graphs but uses a representative figure rather than a line or bar. This graph can be used to highlight certain features of a presentation.

NUMBER OF MEN AND WOMEN IN SELECTED PROFESSIONS

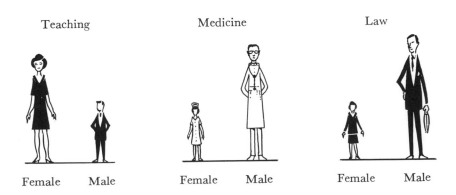

SALES OF CHRISTMAS TREES FROM CANADA

Each figure represents 1000 trees

VII. Flow Chart

The flow chart is a visual aid that shows the viewer a series of sequences or relationships.

PROCESSING RAW MATERIALS

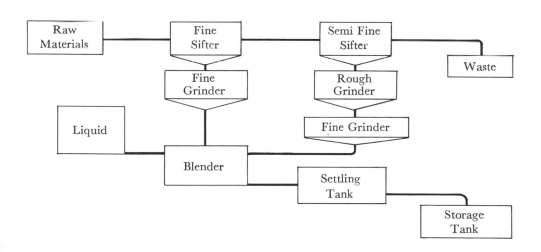

Objects, models, and specimens

At times it may be wise to consider the use of the actual object, a specimen, or model rather than a chart or diagram. Displaying and

69

talking about a special golf club can be much more meaningful than talk alone. Showing a model of the new X100 will add clarity to your talk on the new plane. An enlarged model of the human larynx or ear can be of help in explaining how these organs function. Specimens sometimes are too small for the speaker to exhibit but they can be passed to the listeners or made available for examination at the conclusion of the talk.

Diagrams and cutaways

A diagram may be a simplification of a complex concept or process. If you wish to show certain features you can prepare a diagram highlighting those features. A cutaway will allow you to show the various layers or parts of the object or process.

LINES OF FORCE IN MAGNETS

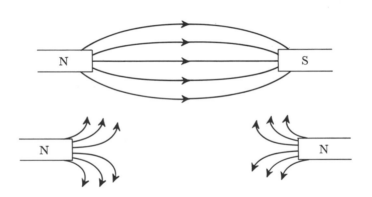

Flannel board and strip chart

These two special types of visual aids allow the speaker to reveal material at the appropriate time. The flannel board is, as the name suggests, a stiff board covered with flannel or other heavy adhesive cloth. The material to be placed on the board also has a flannel backing. The speaker takes the item that he wishes to show to the listener and places it firmly on the flannel board.

The strip chart is prepared before the talk and the items to be shown are covered. At the appropriate time the paper covering is removed and the item revealed.

STRIP CHART

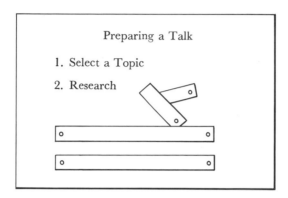

Construction and use of visual aids

THE VISUAL AID, used effectively, is a definite asset to a speaker. Often, however, a potentially good aid is wasted because it does not meet the requirements of construction or of use.

Requirements of construction

The visual aid is of major value to the listener only if it can be easily seen. Simply because you can see all parts of the visual aid does not mean the listener can also see it. The following check list is handy to have when you are planning a visual aid:

1. Make the *entire* visual aid twice as large as it may seem necessary.
2. Print or draw with heavy black letters or lines.
3. Print rather than write.
4. Use a blackboard or large sheets of cardboard or large sheets of heavy paper.
5. Keep the aid simple.
6. Use two or more simple aids rather than one complicated one.

Requirements of use

Effective use of a visual aid must be planned. It does not necessarily come naturally. Before delivering the speech, carefully plan the use of the visual aids according to the following guide:

1. Check the aid for completeness, order, and function.
2. If using more than one visual aid number them consecutively.
3. Show at the center of the listening group.
4. Keep aid at shoulder height.
5. Do not stand between listener and aid.
6. Allow enough time for all to see.
7. Only look at aid when making specific reference to it.
8. Coincide use of aid with speech content.

If a visual aid is to be distributed to the listener, use the following method:

1. Do NOT distribute the aid before the speech.
2. Distribute at that point in the speech when needed.
3. Inform the listeners of the intended distribution.
4. Emphasize that reference will be made to the aid.
5. THEN make the distribution as quickly as possible.
6. Allow ample time for listener to receive aid and return attention to you.
7. IMMEDIATELY discuss the aid.

Visual aids can serve an important purpose for both you, the speaker, and the listener. However, you must plan its construction and manner of use wisely. The effective speaker knows his visual aid and handles it smoothly. As a result, he becomes a more efficient speaker and the audience more efficient listeners.

Step 4 | Exercises ∾ Assignments

1. Collect a sample of visual aids for each of the following and discuss their usefulness in speaking:

a. written
b. line graph
c. profile graph
d. bar graph
e. organizational chart
f. piece of pie

2. Take two of the sample visual aids and transfer them to a blackboard or to cardboard sheets. Present them to a group of listeners. Have the listeners evaluate them as visual aids.

3. Watch two weather reports on television. Describe the visual aids used, then compare them for effectiveness.

4. Give an impromptu talk on the route you follow in getting to a specific place, such as class, work, home. Draw a diagram on the blackboard to aid your explanation.

5. Show the class how to do something. Use a visual aid during the explanation.

6. Explain the arrangement of furniture in a room in your house or office. Include placement of windows and doors. Use the blackboard and fill in the drawing as you describe the room.

7. Bring to class an actual object and explain how it is used (golf club, tool, etc.) .

8. Prepare a chart that will show the organizational structure of a business, club, or campus group. Prepare a talk using this chart.

9. Locate a chart in one of the professional journals in the library. Enlarge this chart and present a short talk using the information in the chart.

10. Prepare a handout that can be used to advantage by listeners. Prepare a short speech incorporating the handout.

How can language be used more effectively?

THE language of a speaker is the means of communicating thought to others and, therefore, must be *clear* and *stimulating*. The better the language is, the better the process of communication will be.

Clarity—the first requirement

ORAL COMMUNICATION has a specific goal in the use of words. There must be *instant understanding*. The listener must *immediately* comprehend the meaning of the language used by a speaker. Since speech is invisible and momentary, there is no time for the listener to contemplate. Therefore, the speaker must be positive all the words he uses will be instantaneously understood by the hearer.

An auditor who must ask himself the question, "I wonder what the speaker meant by that?" is an auditor who has stopped listening. Aim for instant understanding in oral communication.

Consider the background of the listeners. What words might have meanings out of the range of their experiences? What words might have meanings that are special for the speaker or listeners?

The following list illustrates words that may need explanation or substitution for special listeners:

WORD	AUDIENCE
Support	Military *vs.* Scientist
Protest	Student *vs.* Faculty
Spontaneous	Teacher *vs.* Fireman
Channel	Television Repairman *vs.* Geologist

Concrete language

Words are symbols with more or less specific meaning. Be specific in language by using words that are concrete. Ambiguity in language is a barrier to the effective transmission of content.

An effective speaker always considers the possibility that his listeners may apply different interpretations to his words. Therefore, to prevent misinterpretation, he avoids abstractions. For instance, the businessman may refer to the need for well-qualified personnel working in his department. Fine, but what does "well-qualified" mean? To the listener, the term may mean personable, industrious persons, holding college degrees in business, who like the security of a major corporation. Yet to the businessman speaker, it may mean employees who are thirty-five to forty years old with a law degree, have ten years experience in marketing and stand aloof from the traditions of organizational team work. What can this difference in interpretation do to the executive's speech? It minimizes effective communication. Generalization has broken down the process of understanding. Concrete specific language would have saved the situation. To avoid being too general, a speaker should attempt to state specifically and exactly what he means in each significant statement throughout the whole speech. Notice the following pairs of sentences. They may have the same meaning but one minimizes the differences in interpretation by being more specific and exact.

GENERAL VS. CONCRETE SENTENCES

1. Many parents attended the P.T.A. meeting.
   Ninety-five parents attended Tuesday's P.T.A. meeting.
2. Our sales have recently increased considerably.
   Our sales have increased by 37% this month.

3. It takes many years to become a physician.
   It takes eight to ten years to become a specialist or general practicing physician.
4. Experts agree that my plan will work.
   The American Testing Foundation agrees that my plan will work.
5. Our candidate is supported by local businesses.
   Our candidate has been endorsed by the local Chamber of Commerce.

It is obvious which sentences are more exact. Not only do the more concrete statements eliminate vagueness but they create a greater impact through specific meaning. Moreover, the use of more precise language makes a more interesting talk. Examine the following two passages to see if they illustrate this principle.

A nurse's work never ends. She is on her feet for hours covering her assigned hospital section. She serves the patients, gets their food and medicine and generally cares for their personal needs. In addition, today's nurse has great quantities of paper work to do. When she finishes her duty for the day, she is completely exhausted.

〜 〜 〜

What does a nurse do each day? She walks approximately twenty-five miles of hospital corridors in her daily eight-hour shift of duty. What does she do in these endless miles? The vital signs—blood pressure, pulse, respiration, and temperature—are periodically checked and recorded. She not only makes sure the supportive measures—intravenous apparatus, oxygen tents, electrocardiogram monitoring—in use are performing correctly, but has an apparently never-ending source of equipment and supplies prepared for any emergency. Prescribed medication is carefully measured, delivered, and administered on a precise schedule. She follows the doctors' orders for every patient—getting x-rays, laboratory tests, and other studies; turning, moving and ambulating those who cannot do it themselves; calling in the requested consultants; measuring input and output liquids; and ordering specific diets—in addition to answering the patients' own requests. Is this all she does? No! She routinely bathes the patients, changes bedding, adjusts the beds, supervises the serving of meals, talks with the patients, families, and visitors, and makes rounds with the doctors. Does she rest now?

If she can do it while writing her reports—recording medications given, her observations on the patient's condition and other related information, ordering supplies—supervising the student nurse, nurses' aides, and non-nursing personnel, and answering patients' calls. Is it any wonder that the nurse, going off duty, is physically, emotionally, and mentally exhausted?

Is there any question which sample passage is more specific? Concrete, exact language does make a difference. Where one description lets the listener supply the details, the other gives them to him in the expected concrete language.

Simple language

A second characteristic of clear language is *simplicity*. An effective speaker does not try to express ideas with complex wording. The main concern of a speaker is the positive communication of precise ideas and specific content. Anything standing in the way of this aim should be eliminated from the speech.

Listeners often compliment a speaker for directness and speaking to the point. All speakers should seek such listener gratitude. However, many still cannot resist the temptation to make sounds which they believe resemble those of classical orators of the "grand school of eloquence." Such a speaker might wish to impress his listeners with his "verbal erudition," his "rhetorical sensitivity," and his "euphonious and phonetic elegance," by speaking "trippingly on the tongue." Instead, we hear the "euphemistic affectations of sesquipedalians" from a speaker who uses a lot of words but communicates little.

The wise speaker concentrates on conveying the message of his speech in language the listener can understand. This is your task as a communicator. You have something to say and the audience is there to listen. Why waste everyone's time and energy? Although it may be entertaining or even impressive to hear an utterance of high-flown words, the substance of such a speech will remain in the notes of the speaker rather than in the minds of the listener.

Look at the following pairs of sentences. Which is more readily understood? If you had to listen for thirty minutes or longer, which style would you prefer?

1. My pleasure finds reward in pecuniary pursuits.
   I like to make money.

2. Shall we partake of our repast?
   Shall we eat?

3. Better not to repine on going to business.
   Don't complain about going to work.

4. Her culinary efforts are exquisite.
   She cooks well.

5. The remunerations for his endeavors are moderate.
   He makes an average wage.

Although the more flowery expressions may be more entertaining in a single instance, imagine what it would be like listening to a complete speech presented in this manner. Compare the next two passages on the same subject.

> The organization with which we find ourselves most amiably affiliated strikes a rather unique note in an age of discordant rapport between those of the managerial strata and those on the performing strata. The true worth of today's *dramatis personae* is most justly found in the homophonic copartnership between our two groups. And this, gentlemen, is the very goal which we have most zealously pursued and, in fact, have obtained.
>
> ∽ ∽ ∽
>
> There is a significant difference in the personnel policy of our company and that followed by other businesses. In most instances, organizational segregation exists; management is the boss; the rest are the workers. This where we differ. Every employee is integrated into our company as a family of cooperation.

Have you decided which would produce more effective communication? If there is still any doubt in the merits of simplicity over verbosity, here is another example. Again, both are on the same subject and both say essentially the same thing. Only the use of language differs.

> Pedagogically, one might consider the modern man-of-letters to have cloistered himself in that venerable white tower, adorning his

being in scholasticism. Indubitably, such learned retreat may be sought after. Yet the exigencies of academia inexorably beckon our monastic valedictorians down to the campus plains, *in extenso.* Arrived, our man of learning extradites the minds of his charges while implanting knowledge. Both are thereby imparadised.

~ ~ ~

We might sometimes think today's professors spend all their time in private study. Although the educator may contemplate a life of research, the needs of our students are so urgent today that the teacher gives nearly all of his time to the more practical business of teaching. There are rewards, though. The students learn from professional teachers, while the professor realizes the satisfaction of contributing to this learning process.

Imagine how you as a listener would react to the high-sounding speech of the verbose speaker. Perhaps you would marvel at the beautiful language. But would you *understand* it?

After you listen to the verbose speaker for awhile, your initial enjoyment in hearing such glibness begins to fade. The words become meaningless and the content is lost in the maze of flowery words. There is no meaningful content for the listener to hear.

Just as verbosity should be avoided so should hackneyed expressions, clichés, and platitudes. Where abstract and verbose language confuses, trite expressions bore. They are so common that they are drained of all meaning. Look over this list of well-used expressions. None are especially exciting.

OVER-USED EXPRESSIONS

hot-shot salesman	busy as a bee
tough as nails	happy as can be
dark as night	sweet as honey
smooth as glass	white-collar worker
blue-collar worker	as the old saying goes
Rome wasn't built in a day	goes without saying
lay down the law	heartfelt appreciation
give it that old college try	

Stimulating? Then why do speakers still use such phrases? Well, "as they say—you can lead a horse to water . . . ."

79

Give your ideas original expression but let the listener understand what you are saying.

Adapted language

Adapting language to the listener is another means of increasing clarity. Words or expressions which have special meaning to the listener are effective. During a political campaign, for example, candidates are continually re-phrasing and re-wording the same speech in an effort to appeal to the various listeners. They adapt not only to the section of the country they are in but also to the economic conditions, ethnic background, occupations, and other factors concerning the listener. The language of a speech delivered to midwest farmers differs from that used in addressing a group of eastern businessmen or southern clergymen. Notice how each set of phrases in the following columns contain essentially the same idea yet the wording differs in an attempt to identify more closely to the particular listener.

THE FARMER	THE BUSINESSMAN	THE CLERGYMAN
true as a furrow	correct as a computer	right as the scriptures
drought of ideas	deficit of ideas	void of ideas
sure as the Spring	positive as tax time	certain as judgment
persistent as a gnat	retaining as a lien	unshakable as truth
peaceful as sunset	quiet as a bank holiday	restful as a hymn
sprouted like wild flowers	spiraled unchecked	ascended without pause

The situation of the politician is not unique. It applies to all speakers.

In adapting language you should avoid the inappropriate use of *specialized* or *technical* words. Your profession may carry with it a certain unique working vocabulary familiar only to your colleagues. Therefore, when speaking to those unfamiliar with your professional jargon, you should translate it into language they will understand. Otherwise, how will they follow your thoughts? Here are a few examples of specialized wording adapted through translation.

Specialized Language Interpreted

Technical:	When one is examining the invention of the deliberative speech, particular attention should be given to disposition. (Rhetoric)
Interpreted:	When one is studying the content of political speeches, special attention should be given to the organization of points.

∽ ∽ ∽

Technical:	It is not uncommon for the subject of paranoid schizophrenia to experience anhedonia. (Psychology)
Interpreted:	It is not unusual for the split personality to be incapable of feeling pleasure.

∽ ∽ ∽

Technical:	A bilateral contract between vendor and vendee was confirmed with parole evidence. (Law)
Interpreted:	An agreement between seller and buyer was confirmed orally.

∽ ∽ ∽

Technical:	When output is not in proportion to a fixed input diminishing returns exist. (Business)
Interpreted:	When the amount of goods produced is less than the amount of labor involved in production, then there is a waste of labor.

∽ ∽ ∽

Technical:	A criminal is a social deviant who conforms to the norms of a delinquent sub-culture rather than the norms of the inclusive society. (Sociology)
Interpreted:	A criminal is an outcast who follows the behavior of a corrupt group within society rather than maintain the standards of society in general.

∽ ∽ ∽

When reading, you may understand the samples of the more specialized language with a little contemplation. This is fine for *reading* but what about *hearing* these same specialized statements? How much time is there for interpretative thinking? For defining? Remember, spoken language lasts for only an instant. Words are piled upon words. There is no time for translation—only understanding. If the speaker

81

has already interpreted for the listener, then the hearer needs only to concentrate on the understanding.

Language adaptation is important to the success of all oral communication. While the wording of a speech is naturally governed by the style of the speaker, you must always remember that the listener is also a participant. Adapt your language to the hearer and you will bring him closer to the subject.

Stimulation—the second requirement

WHILE CLARITY in language enables the listener to understand, stimulating language provides color, interest, and excitement. Therefore, you need to consider the addition of *forceful language* and *vivid language*.

Forceful language

Let us consider forceful language first since it is the more closely related to clarity. Simply, forceful language means stating a specific point in precise hard-hitting words. Cut away the trimmings and leave no doubts with the listener as to exactly what you mean or feel. Look at the following contrasting expressions as examples of forceful versus common wording.

CONTRASTING COMMON AND FORCEFUL LANGUAGE

Common: My opponent speaks at length while saying little.
Forceful: My opponent spews forth words—and says nothing.

〜 〜 〜

Common: Lack of education results in a state of poverty.
Forceful: Ignorance. Ignorance is poverty.

〜 〜 〜

Common: Rather than continue discussion, let us have some facts.
Forceful: Enough useless talk. What are the facts?

〜 〜 〜

Common: While discussion continues starvation takes place.
Forceful: They talk. And we starve!

∽ ∽ ∽

Common: Results must be achieved or there is no point continuing.
Forceful: Either produce or quit!

∽ ∽ ∽

Common: Advantage has been taken of us.
Forceful: Fools! That's us. Fools!

∽ ∽ ∽

Common: Our service policy is superior.
Forceful: We service. They don't. It's that basic.

∽ ∽ ∽

Common: The solution to our higher costs is an increase in prices.
Forceful: The answer? Pay more—charge more.

∽ ∽ ∽

Common: Achieve our demands by striking.
Forceful: Break them with a strike!

∽ ∽ ∽

Common: The condition of corruption concerns me.
Forceful: The stench of corruption stifles me.

∽ ∽ ∽

What is your immediate reaction to forceful language? Shock! A shock that gives impact to a specific point. The message is clear. Listener emotions are jarred and attention is heightened. The speaker is in control.

Forceful language is succinct. It is pointed. It is catchy. It is refreshing. It captures attention. It stands out in a maze of spoken words. The listener understands immediately and he remembers. He remembers long after the speaking event.

When the speaker is stimulated by his own use of forceful language, he is relieved from steady monotonous speaking in the manner. He feels a sense of self-assurance and self-assertion that arouses his own emotions. An excitement comes to speaking. Instead of a duty, it takes on a new stimulation. A speaker can draw enthusiastically from his own emotions the means of charging those of the listener. In the end, the heightened speaker-listener stimulation results in effective communication. Speaking becomes a rewarding and productive experience for both.

83

Vivid language

While forceful language stimulates the listener through dynamic expression, *vivid* language stirs the *imagination*. Vivid wording is descriptive and activates the senses of the hearer. He can *see* what you say. He may *feel* the descriptive phrasing. He might *hear* the point of your description. His sense of *smell* may even be vicariously stimulated. Each of these senses can be stimulated in the imagination of the listener with words—vivid, descriptive words. Such stimulation can be achieved by anyone with just a little thought and practice.

Too often, our descriptions appear inadequate. It seems to be difficult to convey our image to someone else. "It's hard to describe." "You'd have to be there to appreciate it." "I wish I could really tell you how I felt." These are typical excuses offered by a speaker when at a loss for descriptive words. It is a weak excuse. There is no need for inadequacy in communicating the full image of the subject-matter. The problem is habit—the habit of continually using commonplace words as substitutes for more vivid language. We all have the vocabulary but we don't use it. As a simple example, look at these two lists of phrases.

COMMONPLACE WORDING	VS.	VIVID WORDING
very good salesman		crackerjack persuader
dishonest and evil		cesspool of corruption
trouble spot		seething hell
concerned person		dedicated humanist
community-minded		neighborhood sparkplug

In both lists, we see familiar language. No unique vocabulary was needed. However, one set of phrases carries stronger meaning and activates the imagination of the listener toward a specific end. You, as the speaker, reap the benefits of this stimulating force. Knowing your meaning precisely promotes greater recognition of the speaking point.

In the following sample of vivid statements, notice again that no special vocabulary has been used. The wording is simply part of everyone's working vocabulary.

VIVID SENTENCES

1. Infants bloated from starvation demand our contributions.
2. Fierce determination for absolute justice binds us together.
3. An unquenchable curiosity for discovering knowledge is the latchkey to creative research.
4. The exhilaration of reckless speed on the highways will continue to pack hospitals with mangled bodies, homes with sobbing orphans, and cemeteries with quiet remnants of life.
5. Lagging sales now demand that each man dedicate his imagination and sacrifice his energy to drive this recession from our organization.
6. Executives are not just computing machines catalogued with data waiting to eject information.
7. Blazing defiance flashed across the five-year-old's face when his masculinity was challenged.
8. Pounding waves battered the shore spraying angry froth over the hurricane-torn land.

To use vivid language successfully, the speaker needs to release his imagination. He pictures specifically what is to be described and then fits the words to the picture. The closer the language meets the need, the more vivid will be the wording.

Five guidelines of language have been reviewed—concrete, simple, adapted, forceful, and vivid. At first, it may seem an insurmountable chore to follow all five guides. It may be in the beginning. However, remember that old habits need concentration to be changed. Remember also the language guides are constructed upon all our learned abilities, instincts, and experience. Put yourself in the place of the listener. What type of language is meaningful to you? Use this as a clue and the rest becomes easier. Soon a blend of concrete, simply adapted, forceful, and vivid language will become a new habit.

Step 5 | *Exercises* ∽ *Assignments*

1. Write a double list of ten statements both saying the same thing. Make one list clear and simple. Have the other general and vague. Let each contrasting sentence have approximately the same number of words. Can the same things be said specifically in the same number of words as a vague statement?

2. Put a list of general statements on the board. Have each student speaker privately write a specific sentence for each of the general. Compare specific sentences. Are they nearly the same? Are the interpretations similar?

3. Write a paragraph using flowery or involved words. Read it to the listeners and then have them translate. Did they get the right meaning?

4. Here is some practice for instant adaptation to listeners. Put a neutral statement on the blackboard, such as "There's no doubt about it, the weather is changeable." Let one member of the class then stand before the group and adapt the sentence to the type of listener named by the class.

5. Between class meetings carry a small notebook. Play the role of the critical listener. Record all the trite expressions you hear. How many of these do you use? Compare with other members of the class.

6. Collect a series of advertisements that illustrate vivid language.

7. Describe an incident of a person using general language. Re-do the talk, using specific language.

8. Locate a technical paragraph in one of your textbooks or in a professional journal. Translate or interpret this for the class.

9. Prepare a list of terms used by a special group such as musicians or teenagers. Translate the terms into a more meaningful series of words for non-members of that group.

10. Select a speaker for study. Report on his use of language. Several suggestions are: Lincoln, Churchill, Roosevelt, Webster.

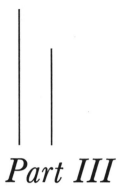

Part III

Preparing

yourself

IN addition to preparing the content of your talk you need to prepare the transmitter. In the case of oral communication, the primary
transmitter is you.

Ideas in your mind or on an outline must be translated into sound
and visual signs and symbols for the listener. In this section we will
focus on three major topics: your appearance, your voice, and stage
fright.

Preparing your voice and body as responsive instruments to the content of your talk is important. These instruments can either aid or
hinder your effectiveness in oral communication. Tune them to maximum efficiency.

Step 1

How should you look?

W HEN the planned schedule calls for your speech or you signal
your wish to speak, the critical moment has arrived. This point
is important for all communicants. The listeners see you first and,
before you have had an opportunity to utter a single sound, are judging your appearance. The effective speaker must, at all times, give
careful attention to his appearance prior to the speaking occasion.
Be prepared even if you have no intention of speaking, because the
possibility does exist.

Dress

FIRST, THERE IS the matter of dress. Naturally, it is expected that
both male and female speakers will be properly attired for the occasion. However, each individual must *objectively* evaluate his taste in
styles and combinations of clothing. It is not necessary to be a style
setter, but it is important that your image is not marred by socially
unacceptable clothing or slovenly indifference to dress.

The thought of giving suggestions on proper clothing to a speaker
may provide a few chuckles. However, have you noticed the awkward

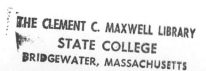

combinations worn by some men? The maroon-striped charcoal-gray sport jacket was fine. Even the faint black stripe of the dress shirt was not too noticeable. But why the glen plaid necktie? What about the chaps wearing a conservative dress suit with a vest who distort the image with bright red and black argyle socks? Or, the men who are color blind and are unable to distinguish between black and navy blue? Olive green and brown? Gray and brown? The descriptions could fill pages.

What attire should be advised for male speakers? Simply remember that you are being observed for complete appearance. Try to look at yourself as others will see you. Always be well groomed. If advice is needed, get it.

The ladies are not to be forgotten since they, too, are immediately evaluated by appearance. With the greater variety of styles and colors in women's clothing, they probably need to exercise more care. The female speaker should select a conservative dress or suit and cautiously add the right amount of appropriate jewelry. It is equally important that moderation governs the use of cosmetics. Avoid anything that might turn the listeners' attention from what you, the speaker, are saying.

A speaker whose appearance gains the immediate attention and approval from the listener also receives his initial attention for the speech. A speaker's appearance often provides the listener with reason to have confidence in the speaker and his ideas.

Posture

NOW THAT YOU are before the listener and have established a visual rapport, you must maintain the image of a person in command of both the situation and yourself. You must carry yourself with poise.

Everyone is aware of the need to stand straight and tall. Undoubtedly, over the years you have received instructions for good posture from various sources—parents, teachers, or coaches. The advice is worthy of summation here because of its importance to the speaking event.

Naturally, when before an audience, you should stand as erect as possible. We all accept this but there are temptations to break this rule. A speaker often stands behind some object. If it is a lectern, use it to hold your notes, not your body. If it is a desk or table, avoid the urge to lean. The listener does not appreciate the sight of a speaker sprawled all over a lectern or bent at a distorted forty-five degree angle. Never be so discourteous as to sit on a table or desk when a standing position should be maintained.

Similarly, a visual aid is to assist you, not to hold you up. The blackboard seems to give speakers the greatest difficulty. They lean on it. They scratch backs on it. They seem to forget that a coating of chalk dust is not particularly attractive.

The conscientious speaker looks the part. He does not lean, sit, or lie on anything. Thus, he does not indicate a casual or careless attitude toward the speech subject. How could the listener be vitally concerned with the speaking of a lackadaisical person?

What about the person who remains seated while speaking? There is still a necessity for dignified posture. Avoid sprawling across a table, slouching in a chair, or allowing your clothing to become disheveled. The listener still evaluates a speaker, even though seated, by appearance.

Be poised and the listener will think well of you.

Bodily movement

A SPEAKER IS NOT a mannequin. Although posture must be dignified, there still can be freedom of movement.

Except for occasions when microphones, cameras, or limited space force the individual to be stationary, taking a few steps is entirely permissible. Often movement is useful as an aid in relieving tension. While bodily movement is usually within the discretion of a speaker, there are certain facts to be taken into consideration.

(1) Have a reason for moving. Do not simply pace back and forth. Moving a few steps to the right or left of a lectern while introducing a new idea within the speech can be quite effective as a physical transition coincidental to the oral. At the same time, you are relieved of keeping one single position.

(2) Always remain within the range of vision of all listeners. The view of the hearer is blocked when you stand behind objects. Similarly, a position to the extreme side of the speaking area may place a visual strain on the more distant viewer. Let the listener see you with ease.

(*3*)   Unless you are using a visual aid or reading a passage, always face the listener. Eye contact with the listener causes him to return the contact. Why should the listener give attention to the speaker, if he is not interested in looking at the listener?

The key to physical movement is within the purpose of speaking. It is the aim of the speaker to communicate subject-matter. Any physical movement distracting the listener interrupts the communicative process. This is also true of no movement, for this, too, is unnatural. Although the speaker should consider how his movements look to the listener, bodily action should be natural and done with ease.

Gestures

A SPEAKER GENERALLY uses gestures during his delivery. You would think the hands would move naturally in harmony with a speaker's words. Often they do just that! And yet the speech student always says: "I don't know what to do with my hands." The answer is really quite simple. First, let the hands do what comes *naturally*. Second, learn some incidental techniques of *special* gesturing.

We all use hand motions during conversation. Look at a person while he is talking. It is almost possible to understand the intensity of the speaker without hearing a word. The more serious the convictions of the speaker, the more firm the hand movements. The lighter the subject of talk, the more casual the gestures. Gestures add to the process of communication and make speaking more vital and alive.

Some ideas on the use of gestures are presented here. Adapt them to your own speaking style and needs:

1. When saying numbers, use corresponding finger symbols.
2. When describing an object, outline it with the hands.
3. When commenting on breadth or panorama, use a sweeping movement.
4. Pointing at the listener or yourself is permissible if done for emphasis.
5. The clenched fist conveys strength, determination, anger.
6. Cupped hands symbolize unity, completeness, or wholeness.
7. Intertwined fingers can indicate integration or unity.
8. When you are speaking of opposing views or points, the right hand may represent one side, the left hand the other.

Any number of hand gestures exist and may be used at the speaker's discretion. However, they should not be artificial such as the assignment of certain movements to represent set meanings.

The preceding techniques of gesturing correspond to specific speech content. However, what to do with hands when not gesturing seems to be the greatest problem.

The hands should be free to move naturally. Stiff arms, clenched hands held in front or behind, or hands in pockets, or grasping an object, do not allow the necessary freedom for gesturing. Nothing should hinder the hands from performing just as they do in conversation. Let them work for you. It makes speaking more interesting and helps you to be more relaxed.

However, if some particular gesture appears to annoy the listeners or interfere with the communication process, eliminate or refine it. The only two gauges of gesturing are the personality of the speaker and the content of the speech.

Eye contact

EYE CONTACT is actually self-explanatory. It is a natural physical function. The listeners look at a speaker while he speaks. The speaker should return the courtesy by looking at all the audience.

Eye contact means *seeing* the hearer. Scanning the faces before you is inadequate. Moving the head like a pendulum can hypnotize the listener and can be most annoying. Furthermore, you are unable to observe the reaction of the speech upon the listener if you do actually see him. Keep in direct touch with him. The listener, sensing this directness, will return the eye contact.

One final point on eye contact. Listeners habitually look where the speaker looks. Look out the window and the listener looks out the window. Look at the clock at the rear of the room and the listener looks at the clock. Look at the floor, the door, the walls, and the listener will do the same. Therefore, you should control the listeners' eye contact and use it to your advantage. Similarly, when you are employing a visual aid, the listener will look when you look. Always be in complete command of listener eye contact by controlling your own. All eyes in the audience should be on the speaker and the speaker's should be on the listeners.

Step 1 | Exercises ∽ Assignments

1. Stand before a group of listeners. Give a short autobiography. While doing so deliberately do the following:
   a. Look at the floor.
   b. Look out the window.
   c. Snap a ball point pen.
   d. Men—put hand in pocket and jingle change.
   e. Women—arrange hair, play with jewelry.
   f. Lean on lectern, desk, table, wall.
   g. Shift weight from foot to foot.

   Listeners appraise the speaker. Did he succeed in accomplishing all the listed characteristics of poor delivery? Award a prize to the most proficient poor speaker!

2. Talk for one minute. In that time describe the appearance of some "thing" without identifying it. Use gestures as your major aid. How many different, meaningful gestures can you use? Have the listeners keep a record. Can it be identified?

3. Give a talk in which you tie a knot or a bow. Do not use the actual object. Use only gestures. Can you do it?

4. Next, have a member of the class give the same instruction. This time do not use gestures! Can this be done? Which is easier?

5. Show in pantomime five reactions or emotions. In addition to the following list use some of your own:

love	shock	anger
fear	laughter	sorrow
horror	surprise	despair

   Can the class identify your pantomime?

6. Watch five different newscasters on television. Report on their use of gestures and eye contact.

7. List those patterns or extremes of dress that are distracting to you as a listener.

8. Practice the following statements with and without gestures:
   Come *here* immediately!
   This problem is *growing* and *growing*!
   Our plan will open up *endless* possibilities for expansion.
   It is important that *we* find a solution!
   You must act now!

9. Practice improving your direct eye contact by picking out three specific listeners and directing most of your speech to them.

10. Practice this series of rhetorical questions in which you stress directness of eye contact:

> Can you do any less than this?
> Will you answer the call to duty?
> How many of us consistently do our best?
> Do you think "success" or "failure" when you face a new task?

Step 2

How should you sound?

ASSUMING there is substance in what you wish to say, you need to be aware your vocal behavior may influence the effectiveness of your total communication. We do not intend to detail all aspects of vocal behavior but only to highlight the essentials of proficient performance.

Vocal production

BASICALLY THE VOICE is a product of a series of complex anatomical adjustments. Reducing this extremely complex process to a simpler form, we have the following steps:

1. Inhalation of air.
2. Compression of air.
3. Exhalation of air.
4. Vibration of vocal folds (for voiced sounds).
5. Adjustments of the resonators.
6. Adjustments of the articulators.

The following diagram illustrates this process:

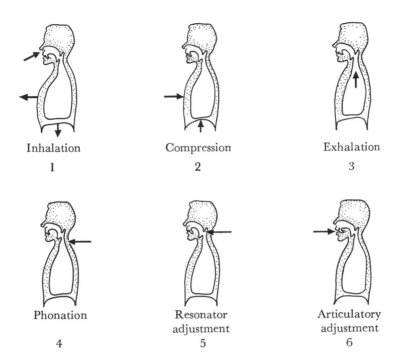

Inhalation	Compression	Exhalation
1	2	3
Phonation	Resonator adjustment	Articulatory adjustment
4	5	6

Breathing for speech

As noted in the summary of voice production the vocal apparatus uses compressed air as the power source. For adequate speech production you need both an adequate amount of air and controlled air. In other words, you need to make sure that (1) you are taking in enough air for speech and (2) you are using it properly. See how far you can count with a single breath. Be careful you are not straining to produce speech. Notice that voice quality will begin to change as you strain to produce speech with inadequate breath support. Work for both adequate breath support and breath control.

Phonation

As the compressed air stream moves from the lungs into the trachea (windpipe), it passes through the larynx (voice box). Here two vocal folds are vibrated to produce phonation. You can feel this

99

vibration on the "Z" sound if you place your finger tips on either side of the larynx.

The phonation process should be free of excessive strain. Improper use of the phonators may produce breathy, harsh, or husky voice patterns. Practice relaxation of the neck muscles if you are producing a "strained," "tight" voice.

Resonance

What is resonance? When you play tunes by blowing across the top of an empty or half empty bottle, the resulting tone is produced by resonance. In the human system the major resonators are the mouth, nose, and throat. The modification of the basic sound of phonation into the vowels is accomplished by tuning the resonators. The quality of the voice is chiefly the result of adjustments of the resonating system. Improper use of the resonators can produce voices that are thin, nasal, or flat. Try modification of the resonators while phonating a single vowel. Notice how the quality changes as you make adjustments in the size and shape of the resonators. It is very difficult to judge your own vocal quality. Try some of these changes on your friends and get their reactions or judge for yourself by using a high quality tape recording. Your aim should be pleasant, vibrant, and flexible qualities.

Articulation

The process of articulation is the modification of the air stream and the phonated sounds. The raw materials, compressed air and phonated sound, are converted into finished sounds by the adjustments and movements of the tongue, lips, teeth, and other articulators of the vocal system. Careless and inactive use of the articulation process can produce sloppy, mushy, or generally inarticulate speech. You will hear more of this problem in a later section.

Vocal characteristics

Now THAT WE have outlined the process of vocal production, we can turn to selected vocal characteristics. We can identify pitch, loudness, and rate factors when we listen to a voice. Closely related to rate are the factors of phrasing and pausing.

Pitch

Pitch can be understood by comparing this phase of voice with the range on a piano or organ. Voice also can be high or low just as a note on a piano can be high or low. Usually listeners prefer the lower rather than the higher pitch voice. However, a word of caution is in order. Do not attempt to force the voice into a lower pitch range. Higher pitches may be a result of tension. In such a case, the speaker should work for a more relaxed voice. Those who need work on relaxation should study the section on stage-fright and "relaxers."

The pitch of the voice is not consciously noticed unless it is unusual in its extremity. Obviously, the six-foot football player with the voice of a soprano will draw attention as will the petite woman speaking with the voice of an operatic baritone. These instances are not common, however, so they will not be given special attention here. If you have any doubts concerning the pitch of your voice, consult your speech instructor for a personal evaluation.

Loudness

What loudness level should you use? Certainly not one so loud that the listeners feel offended or one so quiet that the listeners must be under a constant strain to hear you. Many speakers find it difficult to judge adequate loudness levels.

Here are a few guidelines to help you with this problem. To be on the safe side, you can ask the listeners in the rear if they can hear you. Check with your instructor on an adequate loudness level. Try out the acoustics of a strange room or auditorium before you talk. Make adjustments to outside noise levels. Remember, many speakers tend to underestimate the loudness level needed for easy comfortable listening.

Practice using three levels of loudness. Try turning down your loudness to achieve a sense of intimacy or closeness with the listener. Switch back to your normal loudness. Next try adding additional loudness to achieve a sense of "highlighting" selected important ideas.

Rate

What is a good speaking rate? The obvious answer is that it is found somewhere between those rates that are too fast and those that are too slow. We all have experienced the frustration of listening to speakers who go "a mile a minute" as well as those who appear to ponder over each word and idea. Those fast speakers are probably averaging over two hundred words per minute while the slow speakers are crawling along under ninety words per minute.

What are some guidelines for selection of speaking rate? If the content is complex or new, you should use a slower rate. If the content is simple or familiar, you may wish to use a faster rate. Communication of excitement, joy and like emotions and attitudes call for a faster rate. On the other hand, to communicate reverence, serenity, or other emotions of this type use a slower rate.

Phrasing and pausing

Phrasing and pausing are closely related to rate. Phrasing is the combination of words into oral thought units. Pauses are those empty spots between words, phrases, or sentences.

As you listen to a recording of your speech you will note that you stop the flow of speech at intervals other than those stops dictated by punctuation. The above sentence might have oral phrasing like this:

As you listen to a recording of your speech/ you will note/ that you stop the flow of speech/ at intervals/ other than those stops/ dictated by punctuation.

If you try this entire sentence without phrasing or pausing, you may find yourself out of breath and the listener may lose some of the meaning. Or you could phrase it like this:

As you listen/ to a recording/ of your speech/ you will note/ that you stop/ the flow/ of speech/ at intervals/ other than those stops/ dictated by punctuation.

In this case, we see the speech pattern would lack smoothness and be staccato or jerky.

Pausing enables you to highlight ideas. If you stop after an important idea, you allow the listener to reflect back on your thoughts. The following paragraph demonstrates this concept:

It is necessary that we consider this idea. It is important to our future. It is the turning point. But we *must not be rushed* into a decision! (Pause) There is no immediate concern.

Pausing is effective in preparing your listener to receive an idea. In the following paragraph you can create better listener attention by pausing.

I have reviewed for you the history of the problem. You have seen how its significance has grown. You are probably thinking, "Should we modify our procedure?" (Pause) The answer is a most definite YES.

Articulation

The speech problem, improper articulation, deserves special attention. Articulation involves the accurate production of sounds. To omit, to distort, or to substitute sounds from a word is to be inarticulate.

Although many words can be spoken inarticulately and still be understood, proper articulation improves the process of communication.

As we relax while speaking, there is a tendency to be too casual. It is similar to driving an automobile. The beginner keeps both hands on the steering wheel and attentively watches the road ahead. The veteran driver leans against the car door, casually looks at the passing scenery, and steers with one hand while the other taps to the blare of the car radio. He notes the road occasionally. Neither careless driving nor careless speaking is satisfactory.

To correct or prevent weaknesses in articulation the individual must *consciously* hear himself. Meanwhile, there should be practice in the correct articulation of all word sounds when speaking. Pay special attention to the *middle* and *final* consonant sounds, as they are often the cause of most inarticulation.

In our rush to talk we often skim over the middle of words, especially those containing **t** and **d**. For example, "little" may sound like "li'le" or "better" becomes "be'r" and "middle" sounds like "mi'le." Repeat the following list of words making a special effort to articulate the middle consonants. Do you find it a strain? Do you notice a difference in your speech?

WORDS WITH MIDDLE **t**	*WORDS WITH MIDDLE* **d**
waiter	*harder*
potato	*lady*
better	*leading*
automobile	*pudding*
maintenance	*sadder*
butter	*loading*
thirty	*powder*
eating	*tidy*
matter	*meadow*
forty	*heading*
lettuce	*louder*
hitting	*tardy*
letter	*tinder*
batter	*body*
waiting	*bidding*

Be careful you do not change the **t** sound into a **d** sound. This distortion occurs too frequently in the middle sound. The word "letter" then becomes "ledder," "better" becomes "bedder," and "butter" sounds like "budder." Practice the following lists of contrasting **t** and **d** words, emphasizing the correct sound. Notice that the distinguishing sound is only in the middle of the words listed and this makes the difference in meaning.

PAIRS OF WORDS CONTRASTING MIDDLE **t** *AND* **d**	
bitter	*bidder*
matter	*madder*
waiting	*wading*
Patty	*paddy*
rating	*raiding*
patter	*padder*
righting	*riding*

wetting	*wedding*
knotting	*nodding*
rutty	*ruddy*
seating	*seeding*
hearty	*hardy*
carting	*carding*
sighting	*siding*

For final practice on the **t** and **d** sounds, the various words are placed into sentences. Concencrate on (1) articulation of the middle **t** or **d** sound, and (2) articulating the correct sound in its proper place. Undoubtedly at first you will slowly repeat the sentences with deliberation. Once you have the feel of the sounds being practiced, bring your speed of reading up to a normal conversation rate.

SENTENCES HAVING WORDS WITH t AND d

1. It is getting too cold to grow tomatoes.
2. It does matter which rider is in the race.
3. Her wedding was a spectacular affair.
4. Our city has great historical merit.
5. The writer of this novel concentrates on various social matters.
6. When bidding at an auction be sure you are not just nodding.
7. Sunset is a time of beauty, especially in the country.
8. Never be late to a date with a lady.
9. Sitting next to a person who mutters during a performance is hardly a pleasant evening.
10. The sales representative told his manager some hearty stories.
11. Thirty nurses are sometimes needed to cover the children's section.
12. See the maintenance department for repairs.
13. Twice he has been rated by the personnel testers.
14. Righting a wrong is hardy a matter of pleasure.
15. Sighting the railroad siding made the little boy excited.

Continue the practice of the middle sounds as we move on to the **t** and **d** in the final position.

What has been said of the middle consonants of **t** and **d** is also true of these same sounds at, or near, the end of a word. Again, the articulatory problem is either the omission of the final sound complete or interchanging the final **t** and **d** sounds. Read the following lists of words as you normally would, then read again, carefully articulating the final consonant.

WORDS WITH FINAL t	WORDS WITH FINAL d
smart	owed
fifty	old
pot	hundred
ninety	rubbed
bat	end
mighty	begged
hurt	headed
part	hanged
twenty	aid
beat	peeled
flirt	armed
party	earned
ate	pulled
forty	longed
port	eased

Let us now examine those words that differ only in the final sound. The final sound of t and d determines the meaning just as it did for the middle sounds.

PAIRS OF WORDS CONTRASTING FINAL t AND d	
plot	plod
rent	rend
pot	pod
felt	felled
shot	shod
beat	bead
meant	mend
ought	awed
ate	aid
tent	tend
chart	charred
bit	bid
bent	bend
bet	bed
ant	and

Another especially difficult test for the articulation of the final consonant sound occurs in making the plural of a word ending in a consonant which does not require a voice sound. It is difficult to articulate the final unvoiced consonant followed by the letter 's.' In practicing the word list, be sure to clearly emphasize the final unvoiced consonant sounds and the letter 's.'

PLURAL WORDS ENDING WITH AN UNVOICED CONSONANT

shirts	parks
hits	talks
gets	clients
puts	rips
meets	waits
flakes	artists
jumps	tips
takes	brakes
flirts	hurts
banks	smarts
quarts	pints
desks	presidents
mechanics	chests
sets	rakes
bakes	votes

Lastly, a rather tricky problem for the final sounds involves those words ending in the letter 's' which sounds like a z. If the final 's' follows a vowel sound or a voiced consonant sound, the letter 's' is usually pronounced as a z.

In the following words, the final sound is voiced and when made plural the letter 's' takes on the sound of z. How many do you usually articulate correctly?

PLURAL WORDS ENDING IN THE SOUND OF z

colleagues	worlds
words	dishes
cars	doctors
bleeds	customers
dogs	girls
beads	churches

107

floors	*hears*
engineers	*knives*
executives	*repairs*
voters	*discussions*
herds	*chairs*
nurses	*speeches*
heads	*doors*
teachers	*sells*
radios	*cures*

Notice that these words are easier to say when the final sound is articulated correctly as a **z** sound. Try it. Say the words both ways—as an **s** and as a **z**. They even sound better when said correctly.

The **z** sound also can be found as proper articulation in those words where a vowel sound precedes the letter 's.' Do not let the final letters 'se' fool you. In spoken language, the 'e' has no sound. If the final 'se' is preceded by a vowel sound, these letters sound like a **z**.

WORDS ENDING IN THE SOUND OF z

sales	*is*
rise	*dies*
because	*please*
bills	*phase*
cause	*does*
as	*eyes*
has	*cheese*
dues	*ease*
tease	*pause*
toys	*pays*
boys	*bows*
buys	*knees*
bees	*poise*
was	*lays*
lies	*rays*

For further practice, use the following lists for contrasting words ending in either the **s** sound or the **z** sound. As in previous words, the distinguishable sound makes the difference in meaning.

WORDS CONTRASTING s *WITH* z *SOUNDS*

ice	*eyes*
loose	*lose*
rice	*rise*
face	*phase*
bus	*buzz*
dose	*doze*
dice	*dies*
base	*bays*
moose	*moos*
fuss	*fuzz*
peace	*peas*
niece	*knees*
cease	*seize*
lace	*lays*
sauce	*saws*

For a final review of the s and z sounds, practice these sentences. Be sure to read the sentences at a normal rate as though in conversation.

SENTENCES ON THE s *AND* z *SOUNDS*

1. Does the sales department pay all expenses?
2. He lives as he sees his purpose in life.
3. The cost of eggs, soups, tomatoes, and carrots is lower.
4. The various phases of the moon control the tides.
5. A wise man will always kiss the Blarney Stone.
6. Rays of light cannot penetrate this glass.
7. Artists of all nations are supported by these foundations.
8. The interests of bankers center on the finances of business.
9. Votes are the means by which local constituents direct their representatives.
10. Stocks and bonds are good investments for economists.
11. Because it was a problem needing parental correction, the youngsters were sent back to their parents.
12. Civil servants are the mainstay of state and federal governments.
13. Good mechanics are scarce in today's age of white-collar workers.

14. Speeches by banquet speakers are not the best of desserts.
15. Years of business experience are needed to produce top executives.

Speaking a complex language in various social settings can lead to weaknesses in articulation. The preceding sounds are the principal victims. Yet, with practice and a conscious effort articulatory problems can be resolved. Listening is the key to self-evaluation. Practice is the key to correction. Develop your hearing, practice your corrections, and you will improve your speech.

Stress

Next let us consider the problem of correct stress on the proper syllables. The improper placing of primary stress on the wrong syllable is very obvious to the average listener. Stress on the first syllable of the words "police," "device," rather than the second is sometimes used on stage to indicate an uncultured, uneducated person.

Certain words will shift stress if the word is a noun or a verb. For example, note the shift in the following:

Noun	Verb
con' duct	con duct'
in' sult	in sult'

Check your dictionary when you are in doubt concerning correct stress in pronunciation.

Regionalisms

In our travels to or meeting students from other sections of the country, we immediately notice speech differences. Generally speaking, there are three major dialect groups: (1) Eastern (roughly New England and New York City); (2) Southern (those states below the Mason-Dixon line); and (3) General American (the remainder of the United States).

What group do we use as standard for each of these regions? Most guides to pronunciation suggest that the educated, careful speakers in a particular geographical area be used as the standard. In addition, we can consult Kenyon and Knott's *A Pronouncing Dictionary of American English* for regional pronunciations as well as other dictionaries that generally list several pronunciations arranged in order of popular usage.

Moreover, you will find much variation within the broad dialect patterns previously described—in New England, you find the Maine accent; in New York City, the distinctive Brooklyn accent; and in the Midwest, the Missouri accent. You will even find distinctive patterns of pronunciation in specific urban areas such as Philadelphia, Boston, and Chicago. Some of these dialect patterns reveal the geographical, social, economic, and ethnic backgrounds of the speaker.

Regional or area dialects are not always distasteful. They add color to speech patterns. However, there is a problem when the accent interferes with the communicative process.

Speech that is strange to the ear may sound like a foreign language. It can prevent the speaker from being understood by the listener. For instance, the New Englander on vacation in the South not only has difficulty comprehending southern speech but has a similar problem in getting the natives to understand his speech. Where the southerner elongates or drawls the vowel sound, the northerner places a flatter quality on these same sounds. In its own geographical location, each is acceptable, but in an unfamiliar surrounding, can cause interference with the exchange of ideas.

Some authorities who have studied regionalism have classified some regionalism as unrefined or sub-standard. There are many speech patterns associated with the uneducated or lower social classes. We chuckle at the sounds of the British cockney speech which some Englishmen consider unrefined. The Brooklyn accent is also amusing and is imitated by many comedians but it too is judged by many to be a poor quality of speech. In such instances, the attitude of the listeners toward the speaker may be influenced by the nature of the speech sounds.

To determine if regionalism is your problem, you must do some self-evaluation. You must listen carefully and objectively to your own speaking characteristics. However, you may think you will be unable to recognize anything wrong with your own speech. Some will insist that since no one has ever criticized their speech, it must be acceptable. Both reactions are partially correct. For example, in a particular environment most people conform to the norm of the group; therefore, the speaking of the group is rather uniform in characteristics and quality. It is only natural than an individual's speech will not be considered *different*.

To hear your own regionalism, you must learn self-listening. In the years you have been speaking, your speech has become a learned *habit*. For the most part, we do not consciously think of speech. We simply say words as we have learned them. It is while learning to speak from others in our environment that we unknowingly adopt local accents. For instance, if the word bird is pronounced boid in your surroundings, which will you learn? Obviously the second, which is a regionalism.

Speech learning begins at infancy when we have no discretionary powers. First, we imitate parents, then the peer group. As a result, we sound just like everyone else in our smaller social group. The ability of the ear to become accustomed to any reasonable sound only compounds the problem. If we habitually distort the sounds of words, our hearing accepts them as natural. Thus, a person does not hear his own speech pattern.

However, simply because we become accustomed to a particular accent we should not think we cannot sensitize our hearing once again. If an individual awakens his hearing and actually listens to the sound of words spoken in the environment, the first clue to his own speech is revealed. He must then turn his listening on himself.

Listening becomes the key to self-evaluation. Listen to others. Listen to yourself. It is not an easy task. As in learning to play a musical instrument, time and practice are needed to hear the proper notes and be able to play them.

Let the listening habit grow. In this society of mass media, we have examples of generally good speech immediately available. Listen to the newscasters on national television and radio. Notice their speech. Compare your speech with that of these professional speakers. Compare the speech of companions and associates with that of these trained speakers. By doing so, you are re-learning the sounds of speech. You will learn to judge the speech of those around you and your own speaking characteristics. At first, you will hear little difference. Gradually, you will notice certain distinctions between the speech sounds of the group and of the professional. Keep listening and the gap between the two will become more obvious.

Once you recognize specific words and vocal mannerisms of the environment as different from those of the professional, it is time to begin self-analysis. Imitate the selected words of the professional, even if you must sit next to the television or radio to do so. Eventually, you will hear the difference between the speaker without a strong regional accent and yourself. Correction has then begun. Progress may be slow at first but it will quicken with experience and a refined sense of hearing.

Animation

Even while concentrating on the improvement of voice and articulation, you must still think of the entire effect of the speech. It must be *animated.*

Animation is the giving of oral color, vitality, and feeling to a speaking performance. Monotonous, lifeless, or drab-sounding speech is boring for listeners. This is inanimate delivery. No one wants to listen to a mere mechanical mouthing of words. Moreover, it is extremely difficult to listen attentively to such a speaker. Inanimate delivery can cause a failure of communication.

Actually, animation while speaking is natural. Inanimation is artificial. Listen to others in conversation. Listen to yourself. Is there life in the manner of speaking? Of course there is! It is perfectly natural for a person to speak with feeling. True, the degree of animation will vary with the subject of the speech, the purpose of the speech, and the personality of the speaker. There is no one who naturally speaks in a monotone or without feeling.

We are all born with lively speaking voices. Listen to children talking. They have no problem with animation. However, if these same children are given a piece to recite, the situation suddenly changes. What were normally animated young speakers become stiff-lipped robots spouting words. The problem stems from a concentration upon remembering the pronunciation of all the words. There is no thought to the communication of ideas. The child can be excused but what about the adult who speaks in the same manner?

The effective deliverer of a speech is interested in his subject and the listener. He *wants* to tell the listener about the subject. Therefore, he becomes involved in the communication of ideas. To the animated speaker, there is no difference in delivery for a *speech* or for *conversation.* In both instances, he feels the full meaning of the ideas and

113

the words, and then lets his emotions carry this same sensation to the listener through an animated delivery.

The animated speaker will have a variety of normal speaking qualities. *Emphasis* is present to accentuate words and phrases of importance. *Volume* increases on vital thoughts. *Pitch* will raise or lower to indicate urgency of ideas, believability of content, or seriousness of attitude. *Rate* of speaking will quicken with excitement or slow with contemplation. Throughout the entire process of speaking, natural vocal *inflection* will let the voice change at will. This is a stimulating speaker. This is the normal, natural animation of everyone.

Animation is most often affected by the style of presentation. Conversational and impromptu speaking usually present no major problem in vitality. They are both conducive to a natural method of speaking. Extemporaneous speaking should be no more difficult, since it is simply planned conversation. However, the manuscript speech and the memorized speech usually have the poorest delivery. The lack of *thinking* about the speech content while reciting is the cause in both cases.

The typical manuscript speaker thinks only about the reading of the speech without mistake. Such a speaker does not think of the content. The memorized speech presents a similar problem. The speaker tries to remember the words that were written and committed to memory. Again, no thought is given to content. If you concentrate on the content of the speech, there should be little difficulty with animation.

One final class of ineffective speakers is the extemporaneous-manuscript-memorized speaker. This class of speakers pretends to be giving an extemporaneous speech. Some even deceive themselves into believing the same thing. Actually, the speech is completely written but more like a composition than in the proper manner of a manuscript speech. To make matters worse, the script is hidden on cards used for extemporaneous speaking. The speaker has been forced to memorize because it is practically impossible to use cards for such an abundance of notes. At the time of delivery, the speaker tries to combine all delivery methods into the one presentation. The resulting method of delivery is not only confused but leads to an inanimate presentation. Indecision has led to a failure of communication.

Animation is essential to delivery. The listeners want to enjoy a speech just as they do conversation. Therefore, you should show the same vitality in the more formal forms of speaking.

Hｏw should you sound? Articulate, correct, pleasant, and animated. Only by concentrating on all aspects of vocal production and vocal style will you be able to sound as effective as you want.

Step 2 | Exercises ～ Assignments

1. Listen to several radio and television announcers. Describe their use of variety of pitch, loudness, tempo.

2. Write a detailed description of your own vocal characteristics.

3. Practice relaxation of the neck muscles by allowing the head to fall forward. Try over-tensing the neck muscles and then let go, relaxing the muscles. Phonate a series of vowels with tight, tense muscles. Try the same series with relaxed neck muscles.

4. Practice variety of tempo, pitch, and loudness using the alphabet.

5. Read the following aloud, paying particular attention to phrasing and pausing:

LINCOLN'S GETTYSBURG ADDRESS

Fourscore and seven years ago our fathers brought forth on this continent a new nation, conceived in liberty, and dedicated to the proposition that all men are created equal.

Now we are engaged in a great civil war, testing whether that nation, or any nation so conceived and so dedicated, can long endure. We are met on a great battlefield of that war. We have come to dedicate a portion of that field as a final resting place for those who here gave their lives that that nation might live. It is altogether fitting and proper that we should do this.

But in a larger sense we cannot dedicate—we cannot consecrate—we cannot hallow—this ground. The brave men, living and dead, who struggled here, have consecrated it far above our poor power to add or detract. The world will little note nor long remember what we say here, but it can never forget what they did here. It is for us, the living, rather, to be dedicated here to the unfinished work which they who fought here have thus far so nobly advanced. It is rather for us to be here dedicated to the great task remaining before us—that from these honored dead we take increased devotion to that cause for which they gave the last full measure of devotion: that we here highly resolve that these dead shall not have

115

died in vain; that this nation, under God, shall have a new birth of freedom; and that government of the people, by the people, for the people, shall not perish from the earth.

6. Read the introductory section of several dictionaries. Prepare a report for the class on "Dictionary Makers as Reflectors of Usage" or "Dictionary Makers as Standard-Setters."

7. Practice variety of pitch on the following:
   Up-up-up it goes—out of sight.
   Down-down-down it goes—out of sight.
   It's a beautiful day.
   My pitch gets higher and higher and sometimes it gets lower and lower.

8. Practice shifting emphasis in the following:
   You come here now.
   You *come* here now.
   You come *here* now.
   You come here *now*.

9. List those vocal qualities that annoy you as a listener. Do you have any of the same qualities as a speaker?

10. Practice the following statements or questions trying to carry the meaning indicated in parentheses.
    How do you feel today? (sympathetic)
    How do you feel today? (humorous)
    We are glad to see you. (friendly)
    We are glad to see you. (relief)
    Report to your superior officer. (anger)
    Report to your superior officer. (disappointment)

Step 3

How is stage fright managed?

THE time for you to give the oral report approaches. You try to review. Suddenly, you seem to have completely forgotten everything. The moisture in your mouth mysteriously evaporates. Your tongue becomes a sandpaper base in an oral desert. Swallowing is impossible. How can you speak this way? Impossible! You just know you will make a fool of yourself by stammering and being incoherent.

Now you feel ill. Why does your stomach have such a queer tremor? Or is it tense? You do not know which. Yet, you do know there is a creeping feeling of sickness strangling your insides.

Now your hands and forehead begin to perspire. You taste the tart saltiness of the tiny beads trickling down your face. How did you ever get into such a terrible situation? Never again will you take on any responsibility which includes public speaking. You seem unable to hold the speech notes steady. Failure is imminent. There can be no doubt about it. You will make a complete fool of yourself.

Then your name is introduced. You rise, step forward, and begin to speak: "I, Cicero, come before you. . . ."

Here we have a typical speaker. A speaker facing a group of listeners does what is natural. You are simply going to talk. Yet, the fear racing through your nervous system makes one think you were about to leap from a thousand foot platform into a basin of water.

Stage fright is a common experience. Those butterflies in the stomach are felt by almost every speaker when appearing before an audience. Pre-speaking nervousness has been consistently recorded in history. Speakers are no different today. We all experience some trepidation before speaking. Even those people who frequently talk before others find the same tingling anticipation. Some persons appear more composed than the infrequent public speaker simply because of the repetition of exposure. Many will become more accustomed to speaking situations and gain a greater degree of control over emotions and appearance. Yet, for some, stage fright will always be present.

Recognize the natural existence of pre-performance excitement. If you are *prepared,* then its cause is relative to the situation. There is the normal concern over listener evaluation of the performance. You want to do your best. Thus to cope with the situation your concentration becomes intense. You unconsciously activate all senses and put them on the alert. Now you are ready. The entire mental and nervous system is in high gear, ready to meet any situation that may arise during the speech.

For many speakers, the butterflies leave shortly after the speech is begun. Therefore some individuals believe the most frightening moment of speaking comes just before actually talking. This is a misconception, however. Those jitters do not leave once the speech is under way. But they are not as noticeable because the speaker has put them to work by speaking.

Following the speech, the speaker feels relaxed and even slightly tired. This clean, comfortable feeling is simply the return of the senses to their normal state. It is somewhat like the relief one finds when relaxing a muscle which has been held taut for several moments.

Many experience the same tingling high-key excitement before the speaking occasion. The *prepared* speaker may accept it as an asset of nature. The *unprepared* speaker is different. This individual *should* feel fear. He has little to say. He is not ready to speak to the listener. Instead of merely being concerned with normal stage fright, the unprepared speaker must worry about what to say. No speaker is confident entering a situation under such conditions.

You are asked to spend a night alone in an uninhabited house on a lonely island. You might react with a strong sense of apprehension. You may develop a sense of fear. In order to minimize these reactions to this adventure, you might prepare yourself with several flashlights, a strong baseball bat, and, if possible, a change of attitude. Stage fright can also be minimized by taking proper steps.

Stage fright an asset

BY NOW, YOU probably suspect that stage fright is looked upon as an asset to speaking. If so, you are quite correct. Although the novice may doubt the validity of such an assertion, some quick thought on the matter can produce a similar conclusion.

What are the responsibilities of a speaker? He must be aware of presentation and content. Simple? Not so when one remembers the many components of effective speaking. Presentation consists of physical appearance, bodily movement, gestures, vocal quality, vocal animation, eye contact, language, and audience adaptation. Content involves introduction and conclusion, organization of the main body, logical reasoning, explanatory examples, supporting proofs, summaries, and clarity of thought. These are just some of the concerns of a speaker.

How then can a speaker divide his attention over all these individual aspects while giving a speech? It is impossible. So he must allow some to be controlled by habit or instinct. This is where that overactive nervous system shows its value.

While a speaker puts his conscious thoughts on certain selected aspects of speaking, the rest are put under the charge of the autonomic nervous system. For instance, when the voice of a speaker rises in volume and excitement, the hands gesture dramatically while the words make a vital point. It is not necessary for the speaker to think of vocal volume, animation, or gestures. His thoughts simply center on the idea. Habit, whether natural or practiced, takes charge of the delivery and fits it to the thought.

Stage fright is really the awakening of the nervous system.

Stage fright in practice

THINK FOR A MOMENT of the many instances where nervous tension plays an important role. In most, it is accepted as normal.

For instance, the athlete experiences stage fright before a contest. At the track meet the mile runners are seen pacing, jogging, and exercising before the race starts. Butterflies invade their stomachs. They wait nervously and impatiently for the signal gun. All senses are tuned for one moment, toward one aim. This keen sense of inspiration and

119

competition gives the athlete that extra something needed to accomplish his objective—victory.

The actor suffers from similar anxiety. Before curtain time, a creeping nervous feeling comes over him. As performance time nears, the inner excitement mounts. All senses watch the clock and, with each passing moment, the butterflies become more active. All those learned lines, movements, reactions, and interpretations flash through the mind in a jumble. The senses are simply tuning up for the performance. Although the keyed-up feeling seems to leave on stage, all stage actors recognize that it enables them to give their best.

Even the businessman experiences stage fright although he does not call it that. Whether selling an idea, product, or investment, he finds himself sparkling with mental acumen. He is excited about the selling situation. This can give the seller the advantage over the buyer, who is not similarly stimulated. Therefore, the businessman's chances for success are greater because of his stage fright.

The student has that before-final-exam feeling. He finds sitting relaxed difficult. Everything seems to be charged with energy under the surface. Comments to others make little sense. Thoughts narrow down to a specific hour and room. In the examination room, impatience reaches a climax just as the test is distributed. Then, self-control takes over as the questions are scanned and answers flash through the mind. All mental and emotional resources have joined into a unified effort to achieve success.

Stage fright plays an integral part in our daily lives. Whenever we strive for a superb performance, a type of stage fright becomes our greatest aid. This is true whether the occasion is occupational, social, extracurricular, or the most common of all—speaking.

Avoid exaggeration of stage fright

THE ONLY DANGER in this normal excitement comes from its exaggeration. The only way to control this nervous energy is to recognize it as inherent within man and accept it as an asset. Let it work for you by allowing it to exist.

The only time a problem can arise is when the individual attempts forcibly to prevent the nervous reaction.

First, the physical delivery of a speech can be hampered. The person who tries to force the nervous feeling away only invites trouble. The physical exertion of the attempt heightens the tension and may cause additional muscular spasms. Hence, the physical discomfort is increased. Panic then grips you. Additional effort is made to stop the intensified physical strain. Further tension is forced upon the body. By now you have probably turned yourself into an inanimate, frozen slab of flesh. Movements are stiffened and gestures are lost. The listener no longer sees a human being but rather a wooden object.

The second consequence follows as a direct result of your self-attention. With all thoughts directed toward your physical exposure, you can forget your ultimate purpose of communicating ideas. Therefore, the listener is not compelled to be attentive. Without listener rapport, there is no communication and you have failed.

There could possibly be a further complication. You may lose all thoughts of content. With ideas slipping away, words become meaningless symbols and panic becomes complete.

If you had only accepted stage fright as natural, all might have gone smoothly. You should not interfere with the stimulation of the situation any more than you would attempt to stop breathing.

A speaker has only one purpose: to transfer thoughts to others. You should concentrate on this goal.

The best advice for the neophyte is:

1. *Understand* what you are talking about.
2. *Want* to convey your thoughts to the listener.

Neither of these points can be solved with an easy formula. You must realize your responsibilities and attempt their resolution through an intelligent approach to the speaking situation.

Ways to reduce tension

ALL THIS PHILOSOPHIZING over the good of nervousness is fine but we also have some more practical suggestions. At the moment of speaking, the most immediate thought of any speaker is how to reduce the actual physical tension. Who has the time to be objective about the fear? Now is the time for doing something about it. Here is the clue— *do something*. Do something *physical* as an outlet to that excess of energy.

Before speaking

What is the normal desire before entering a formal speaking situation? Most of us would probably like to run away. Unfortunately we cannot. As an alternative, we pace back and forth—back and forth. Why? Simply because excess energy is put to use. Alas, pacing does not really solve the situation because it is too much like running away. It can lead to an increase in anxiety rather than have a relaxing effect. Moreover, how often does a speaker have a private area in which to do his pacing? Not too often. Your running in a conference room, a waiting room, or on a platform might not create too favorable an impression on the listeners. Therefore, try some other form of action.

One method of relaxation is the stretching of the muscles. Extend arms, firmly. Hold them in the stretched position for a couple of moments. Relax. Stretch again. Hold. Relax. The tension is relieved. You feel more at ease. Do the same thing with the fingers and even the legs. This, too, helps. If you are tactful, these little exercises can be done while you are sitting behind a table in the presence of the listening group. In fact, you can effectively practice them even without having a table to hide your movements. The secret is the tightening, holding, and relaxing of the muscles. You do not have to throw your arms or legs in the air to do this. Try the stealthy exercise in private and find how easy it is to do. It is just like an isometric. No one can see the action but you can feel the results.

The neck muscles and the corresponding spinal area can also be sites of annoying tension. This can cause a twitching head, a rather disconcerting reaction in some speakers. Again, the way to alleviate the strain is muscular exercise. Roll the head around—slowly. Exert pressure on these muscles as you follow a wide circular movement. This is a particularly good exercise since it tends to relax the entire body.

This exercise is easy to do in private, but how can you get the benefits in the presence of listeners without appearing as a head-rolling fool? Just use your imagination a moment. The answer is really quite simple. Instead of staring straight ahead, at the table and floor, or at your hands—look around you. Look around and in doing so turn the head not just the eyes. It is perfectly normal for you to glance around the room. You can do the exercise at the same time. Look at those to your right and to your left. Look up in thought. Look down in contemplation. Do not fix your head in one position. Let it move! Although you are exercising, you are still an alert individual.

A final technique to relieve tension involves breathing. Surely you have not let the excitement of the approaching speaking situation stop you from breathing. You can add a controlled breathing exercise to your repertoire of relaxers. Take a slow, deep breath. Pause for a fraction. Let it flop out. It is simple—inhale slowly and deeply—pause—flop. The advantage of this particular relaxer is that it can easily be done at any time. It can even be done without being noticed just before you begin to speak.

The three ways of easing tension before speaking can be used separately or in combination and the pre-speaking tensions will be considerably reduced.

While speaking

Upon beginning to speak, you should immediately use relaxers because at this point nervousness is high. These relaxers also consist of physical movements that supply an outlet for excess energy. They are merely variations of those used prior to speaking. In addition to relaxing a speaker, they also improve his appearance as an effective speaker.

Remember the breathing relaxer? Use it when looking at the audience just before your introductory comments. Take the slow deep breath, pause, and let it flop out. Do this as you rise to speak or move to the speaking position. Repeat it again as you look around at the listeners. Be subtle and no one will notice. It makes you feel more comfortable and adds an effective moment before you deliver your speech. It also prevents you from rushing into the talk, thus giving the hearer time to focus his attention on the business of listening.

Next, use head movement to continue the relaxing procedure. As you begin to speak, look around at the listeners. Not just with the eyes but with the entire head. Turn the head with deliberation and look at the different listeners. See their faces and if you do, you will know the head movement is positive. Tension of the neck and spinal area is removed and you remain physically relaxed. Meanwhile, the listener is treated to direct visual contact right from the beginning.

Why not keep up the appearance of a practiced speaker and, at the same time, relieve any nervous tension that may remain or arise later? Keep the head movement, pause occasionally for a breath-relaxer and add gestures. Move the arms, the hands, and even the whole body if circumstances permit. Listeners like to see a physically animated speaker, and you remained controlled.

There is really little to all the fears of speaking before a group of listeners. We know that all of us have the jitters before a speaking situation. It is an advantage and there is no way to prevent the feeling. All we need to do is to eliminate the excess energy and speaking can be done comfortably.

Preparation for speaking is essential. You need to understand the elements to be faced in speaking. You need a procedure to follow. Without both, the path to speaking is tangled with indecision. With both, the specific speaking situation can be met.

Now you are prepared to move to the construction of the two basic forms of oral communication—the speech of explanation and the speech of opinion.

Step 3 | Exercises ∾ Assignments

1. Research the problem of stage fright. Each member of the class selects three speech texts from the library. Report to the class the authors' explanations of stage fright and their recommendations for overcoming it.

2. Interview someone who has frequent occasion to speak before an audience such as a politician, teacher, clergyman, or salesman. Ask him about his experiences with stage fright and how he managed it.

3. Practice using a tension-relaxation sequence while reading aloud to the class.

4. Research the suggestions by the psychologists for reducing fear situations.

5. Report to the class on the most frightening speech situation that you have ever faced.

6. Prepare a short talk on the usefulness of fear.

7. Prepare a speech using maximum physical action as a means of using up excessive physical energy.

Part IV

Speeches of
explanation

TODAY, as a speaker, you are on the spot. Before you can safely face a modern listener, you must give careful consideration to what you are going to say. You must have something intelligent to convey and must do it with clarity. If either is missing, the communicative process breaks down. Therefore, our examination of oral communication will now concentrate upon the intelligent expression of ideas.

We first examine the speech of explanation. As stated in Part I, explanation is basic to all communication. We explain information. We explain ideas. We explain opinions. Every time speaking takes place, there is explanation. It is essential to communication. Therefore, the following steps are the guiding procedure toward developing greater clarity through exposition.

Step 1

Analyze the speaking situation

DURING the discussion on speech presentation, we observed that you, the speaker, must necessarily concern yourself with the circumstances under which the speaking process takes place—the physical setting, the reason for speaking, and the listener. When speaking to explain, you should give attention to particular matters while making the usual examination:

1. Determine the *state of information* of the listener.
2. Then consider this information in light of the particular *purpose* of explanation.

Since a speaking situation involves a listener and a speaker, the speech joining the two must be relative to both parties and satisfy the purpose of the communicative form.

Informative needs of the listener

WE KNOW all listeners are not identical. There are differences in personality, intelligence, education, occupation, age, and numerous other characteristics. When explaining, you must have some idea of the *state of information* of your listener. With this knowledge, you can adapt the content of the speech to meet the listener's interests and needs.

Well-informed listener

If the listener is particularly knowledgeable on the speech subject, you must adjust the level of content to satisfy this advanced state of information. To spend much time with fundamental details would only prove boring to this listener since he already knows them. Would you hire an experienced secretary and then explain the operation of a typewriter to her? Or explain the basis of techniques of selling to a sales manager of fifteen years' experience? Or tell a truck driver how to drive an automobile? All the instances illustrate a poor use of time for both the speaker and the listener. There is no need to explain something that is already known.

To maintain the interest of the well-informed, you must provide thought-provoking details. The speech should contain materials which add to the knowledge of the listener. It may be information on a *new aspect* of the subject or *new information* on a known aspect. Perhaps it may be a *new* or *different approach* to the subject. Or it could be a discussion on a related area of interest. Whatever the case, a speaker is responsible for providing the knowledgeable listener with *advanced* content.

Uninformed listener

While the well-informed listener demands a high degree of information, there is another group of listeners presenting a different challenge to a speaker. The *uninformed listener* has little, if any, knowledge on the speech topic. The speaker, therefore, needs a simplified approach to the process of explanation.

As a beginning student of the piano, would you understand a teacher who immediately explained the techniques of playing a selection by Liszt? Could you be expected to understand an explanation of statistical equations if you were unfamiliar with algebra? Or make out a double entry ledger knowing nothing about accounting? In each instance, the obvious answer is a firm "No." Before there can be understanding of the complicated, there must be a foundation for comprehension.

Take for instance, the college football player who attempts to explain the game to a younger sister or a girlfriend who knows nothing about football. It would be pointless to begin describing strategy or maneuvers. There is no basis for understanding by the girls. The speaker needs to deal with elementary matters. First he must explain the simple facts—the purpose of football, the organization of teams, and the general procedure of play. After he takes particular care to define all special terminology, he lays a foundation for later technical detail.

When speaking before uninformed listeners, the speaker must have a positive adaptation to the needs of his audience. The content is kept reasonably simple and deals only in *fundamentals*. There should be no attempt to cover too much material too quickly. That you find the elementary details easy to understand does not mean that this is also true for the listener. Remember, you already know the subject in detail, and therefore have no trouble understanding the review of elementary points.

The speaker's main aim is clarity of explanation while maintaining the attention and interest of the listener. You should be on guard against talking down to the hearer. This is equally as detrimental to effective speaking as lack of clarity. Unless otherwise classified, the listener is regarded as intelligent but simply unfamiliar with the speech topic.

Generally informed listener

Somewhere between the two extreme states of the knowledgeable and uninformed listener is found the generally informed. This type of hearer is probably the most common. With the other two types, the techniques of a speaker were rather well defined—detailed content or elementary content. There is need for a combination of materials with the average listener. Some fundamentals plus some details make up the substance of the speech. The problem is to determine how much of each is necessary.

You would not explain how to use a checking account to those who have had one for some time. You could, however, review the use of the personal checking system and its place in the banking system.

131

Similarly, it would not be necessary to restrict a talk on the federal government to its organization when speaking before the average citizen. Instead, there might be a review of the system of government with emphasis upon the specific departments within the federal branches.

As mentioned earlier, the problem before the speaker is to find a balance between the basic and the advanced. Only the speaker faced with the specific situation can accurately determine the best approach. However, you should be aware or two possible conditions. First, a speaker may have a tendency to underestimate the capability of the listener and be overly elementary in the explanation. The listener recognizing this may not only lose interest in the subject but even lose respect for the speaker. Second, there are some listeners who incorrectly consider themselves better informed on a topic than they really are. To circumvent this problem, the speaker needs to muster all his talents of listener adaptation. Never let the hearer feel that as the speaker you have any attitude of superiority. A fairly safe approach is to state that you are reviewing certain points merely to establish a common ground of recognized information. Another approach is to identify the review as necessary for those few listeners who may have forgotten certain points but will recall them as a result of their mention. Either of these techniques should solve the problem.

The speech of explanation before the generally informed audience, therefore, does present more of a problem than any other. The speech content must be:

1. simple enough to be understood,
2. detailed enough to give new information or provoke thought,
3. presented in a way that compliments rather than offends.

The state of information of the listener is important to the success of your speaking. Examine your particular listeners to determine their type. After doing this, you can move on to the selection of a specific purpose in speaking.

Purposes of explanation

WHILE CONSIDERING the type of listener, you should remember the *purpose* of your explanation. You need to decide whether the informative state of the listener has any bearing upon the special purpose of the speech. To be able to do this, a speaker must be aware of the possible specific purposes of explanation.

Although all explanation has the general purpose of increasing knowledge, you have additional rhetorical objectives. This aim varies with the topic of the speech and can have an effect upon the approach. Keeping the specific purpose of explanation in mind while analyzing the listener aids you in selecting an approach to the communicative situation.

Purpose of describing

A common type of explanation is that containing a stimulation of the hearer's imagination through description. The subject may be original with a speaker or may have come to his attention through a secondary source.

Instances of descriptive explanation occur every day. We create a vacation experience, describe a movie, relate an experience or event, describe a scene or object. When the purpose of speaking is to convey imagery, use descriptive explanation.

For instance, if you tell about a conducted tour of the United Nations, there is explanation with the purpose of describing what took place. Similarly, the art connoisseur describes the Mona Lisa by explaining the image on the canvas, the technique of the artist, and possibly the effect upon the viewer. The historian verbally retraces events with descriptive explanation. The newspaper reporter constantly uses descriptive explanation. Think of the many times you have used this form of explanation. Notice the great number and variety of descriptions you come in contact with every day.

In description, you need vivid details that will transfer to the listener the same image you have seen or felt. Therefore, if you know the listener's familiarity with the topic, you are better able to select the point to begin the description. In some instances, because of the less-informed listener, a speaker must restrict the explanatory process to general material. With the more specifically-informed listener, however, the description may be carried to greater detail.

Gaining skill in effective description can be of great value to the speaker. The ability to recreate for the listener is a tool that is used quite frequently in explanation.

133

Purpose of informing

There are speeches which have the specific purpose of communicating information. This is the process of informing by explaining the selected details on a subject. While the descriptive purpose was to excite the imagination, the aim of informing is to convey to the listener *facts* increasing knowledge or awareness.

For instance, the teacher spends much of his time practicing informative explanation. The classroom lecture on history, geography, English, sociology, or the many other subjects of education can be taught by informative explanation. When the businessman presents his report on the results of a new advertising campaign, he is informing the listener as he explains the outcome. The student who presents an oral paper on a science study is another example of speaking with the purpose of informing.

It can be rightly concluded that the informative aim of communication is a rather common purpose of speech. In a single day a person could compile a very long list of instances containing informative explanation at home, at work, at school, or at play.

When presenting information, an effective speaker is particularly concerned with the state of the listener's knowledge on the subject. To be successful you must select the precise points of beginning and concluding. You must determine the degree of detail for content, ranging anywhere from the general to the specific.

Purpose of demonstrating

When a speaker explains how to do something or shows the composition of something, there is demonstration. Demonstration explains *by doing* or *by showing*. It is a combination of the visual with the oral.

The speaker of demonstration proceeds to explain by following a logical progression of steps or points, which clarify the elements of the topic matter for the listener. When showing how to do something, the speaker gives directions while putting them to actual use. Have you ever seen the department store demonstrator of the "marvelous machine" which grinds, scrapes, slices, cubes, and shreds? While expounding upon each of the wondrous capabilities of the machine, the professional demonstrator actually puts his machine to work. Step-by-step, he does what he is saying. The listener can *see* the claims of the speaker, thereby learning how to do through the oral and visual.

On a less commercial level there are many who teach by demonstrating. The instructor of athletics shows how when teaching basketball. The art instructor, the music teacher, the mechanical arts teacher, the science professor, and the professor of surgery explain through demonstration.

Sometimes the truth of the topic is revealed through demonstrative explanation. A famous illustration of this took place when Galileo demonstrated gravity on the Tower of Pisa. Perhaps it could be said that Columbus used demonstration to exemplify the theory of a round earth. The scientist, the mathematician, and the engineer often make use of demonstration to substantiate the correctness of an idea. Whether it was yesterday or thousands of years ago, demonstration is often the only conclusive means of establishing the truth of a topic.

While analyzing the listener, you should consider the advisability of employing demonstration. If you decide in favor of it, you will then determine the degree of demonstrative explanation and choose the viusal aid to be used when speaking. The level of demonstration will vary depending on the state of the listener's information. For the well-informed, complex explanation and visual aids may be advisable. For the less-informed, the relatively simple is more suitable.

The speech of explanation makes special demands upon a speaker. First you analyze the speaking situation. You need to give special attention to the level of the listener's knowledge on the speech subject. Then, you consider this information in light of the type of the explanation—describing, informing, or demonstrating. With this step completed, you are ready to move on to the construction of the speech.

Step 1 | Exercises ∽ Assignments

1. Select a topic that you will use for a speech of explanation. Analyze your informative needs for the immediate class listeners. Make a listing of what you think they know and do not know on the subject. Present this list to the listeners to determine your accuracy.

2. Using a subject on which you have specific knowledge make up a list of informative points. Next, for each point write an adapted statement which gives greater meaning to your listeners. Test them on the listening group.

3. Select a speech from a book of collected speeches found in the library. Learn to whom the speech was given. Now, examine the speech for the speaker's analysis of the speaking situation. How did he show this in his speech?

4. Explain a situation with which you are familiar. Use the same subject for each of the following listener types:
   a. informed listener
   b. uninformed listener
   c. generally informed listener

5. Have the entire class listen to the same lecture or speech on television. Evaluate the speaker's analysis of the speaking situation. Was he successful in his communication?

6. Using the following topics show how you could describe, inform, or demonstrate:
   Our Space Program
   Air Pollution
   Safe Entry onto a High-speed Highway
   Good Posture and Public Speaking
   Using a Splint on a Broken Arm

7. Prepare a questionnaire to determine the level of knowledge of your audience. Prepare a speech adapting to that level after you have compiled your data.

Step 2

Classify collected materials into speech forms

SIMPLY collecting the particular materials to be used for the speaking process is not quite enough. Further refinement must take place. That is, the materials chosen for the speech need to be identified as individual ingredients to develop speech content. The classification of speech materials according to their particular type makes it easier to construct the speech. Merely to regard each of the selected materials as something going into the expression of thoughts does not lead to the orderly presentation of ideas. Therefore, before proceeding to the organization of a speech, you should recognize each of the materials as a special type. You thereby permit its systematic distribution throughout the content.

Each of the selected materials is a means to an end—the clear, intelligent expression of ideas. The materials of content are the tools a speaker uses to reach this end. However, not all tools are the same. Each serves a different and essential function. The constructor of intelligent speech must recognize his tools before he can put them to effective use.

Materials to support ideas can be classified first into the broad categories of fact or opinion. Then you can assign speech materials to the classifications of examples, testimony, or statistics. You will improve your communication ability by gaining skill in using varieties of speech materials.

Types of speech materials

SPEECH MATERIALS COME in an assorted variety of forms. Some stimulate the intellect while others affect the emotions. Basically, however, there are only two types of speech materials—fact and opinion.

Fact vs. opinion

What is a fact? Before answering, decide which of the following statements qualifies as a fact:

1. In 1965, New York City was the largest active seaport on the east coast.
2. New York City is the most exciting city on the coast.

Have you made a choice? If you selected the first as a fact you were correct. The second statement is an opinion. What is the difference?

A fact

A fact is that which is certain. It is indisputable. It exists without doubt or objection for it is unquestionable. It is irrevocable. It is permanent. It is verifiable. A fact is accepted as truth by all men.

Before you begin to object and point to the possibility of factual change, make the following observation. A fact remains as such so long as it has been proven with all the resources of man. However, it is realized that throughout history there have been occasions when that which had been commonly accepted as fact was later shown to be incorrect. It has been so in the past and, undoubtedly, will be in the future.

You should submit a fact to the following tests before using it in speaking:

1. Is it indisputable?
2. Can it be verified?
3. Is it consistent with other facts?
4. Do authorities recognize it?

If you can get all affirmative responses for your fact, you can use it in speaking as a reality. However, if any one of the test answers is negative, the specific item cannot be held up as factual since there is a question as to its validity.

Applying the sample statements on New York City to the tests for determining a fact, we can see the difference between a fact and that which almost qualifies as a fact. In the first alleged assumption, that New York is the largest eastern seaport, the answers to all test questions are positive. The first statement is indisputable, verifiable, consistent, and recognized. Here we have a fact. However, in the claim that New York is the most exciting city on the coast, there is some question. It may be verifiable and consistent with other facts, but not all authorities necessarily agree, and residents of other locations will dispute it. Although you have some evidence to prove that New York is a most exciting city, it cannot be considered conclusive. Therefore, it is not a fact.

Be on guard against the indiscriminate use of alleged facts. Test them first. If they meet the requirements of a fact, use them as such. If, however, there is any doubt, do not use them as fact. Instead, you can include them as qualified pieces of information. You would jeopardize listener respect for you if you did otherwise. The speaker who is caught passing off questionable material as fact will have a difficult time in regaining the confidence of listeners. Though a listener may not be well-informed on a subject or a topic, this does not mean that he cannot distinguish between fact and non-fact. Why take the risk? Maintain self-integrity by using provable material as fact and questionable material as qualified information.

An opinion

An opinion is a considered judgment or conclusion reached after examination of available information but still lacking in positive knowledge. In short, an opinion is that decision meeting *some*, but not all, of the tests of fact and is, therefore, not absolute in certainty. A fact is indisputable. An opinion is disputable.

When you offer *your* opinion on a certain matter, others may take exception to it. If you recall the two statements about New York City, it was decided that the city *may* be considered the most exciting city on the coast, but it would be impossible to prove this conclusively. There may be certain information which *indicates* that this is true, at least to some people, but it could always remain in dispute.

This is also true when you use opinions from other sources as a means of developing the content of a speech. Recognize the difference between fact and opinion, both in the selection and use of materials in speaking. Simply because you find certain material in printed form, do not assume that it is fact. It may be the opinion of the author. The statistician, for instance, collects specific information, examines the material, and then draws a conclusion. This judgment is not always fact, however; often it is only a considered opinion. Another expert may examine the same data and reach a different conclusion. The competent speaker, when using his selected materials in speech construction, is careful to distinguish between fact and opinion.

The opinions of others are valuable to the development of your own ideas and can be used as desired. However, be on guard against an unsound opinion. First, consider its source. If the source is reliable, there is usually reason to respect the opinion. To be on the safe side, it is wise to examine the opinion further. Analyze the opinion for its basis. Is the opinion founded upon sound information and logical reasoning? If so, then it is probably an intelligent opinion and can be safely used in your speech content. Never use indiscriminately the beliefs of others and remember your speech content reflects upon you as an intelligent individual. If there is criticism, it is always directed toward you, not toward the opinionated source. Therefore, protect yourself by carefully investigating the source and basis of other opinions before adding them to your speech.

As a simple review test, decide which of the following are fact and which are opinion.

FACT OR OPINION TEST

1. Two cars to a family are a necessity today.
2. Public utilities are legal monopolies.
3. Public health medical teams are dedicated people.
4. It is safe to say most people own a television set.
5. The Federal Reserve system protects the bank depositor.
6. Life insurance is easy to sell.
7. A mother's place is in the home.
8. Speeding is the cause of automobile accidents.

9. Hawaii and Alaska are the only two states not attached to the mainland.
10. Common stock is more speculative than preferred stock.

Remember. A fact is a fact. An opinion is an opinion. Recognize them as separate types of speech materials and use them accurately in the construction of your speech.

Forms of speech materials

FACTS OR OPINIONS may appear in your content in three major forms—example, testimony, and statistic. Each is valuable in the complete development of any speech. You should be familiar with each one and make an effort to use a variety of forms when speaking.

Example

An example explains or supports a speech point through the use of a specific instance or illustration. It may be designed to stimulate the intellect or the emotions or both. The example adds interest to speaking by allowing the listener to use his imagination while understanding the ideas of the speaker. Use the example frequently to maintain the listener's interest and increase your effectiveness in the communicative process.

SPECIFIC INSTANCE

The specific instance is a brief means of giving an example. It cites a particular case without going into elaborate detail.

Military leaders have become President of our nation. For instance, there was Washington, Grant, "Teddy" Roosevelt, and Eisenhower.

∽ ∽ ∽

Examples of self-made men are Presidents Harry Truman and Lyndon Johnson, baseball's Ted Williams and Casey Stengel, and businessmen Charles Percy and Jackie Robinson.

∽ ∽ ∽

141

A number of weekend activities our P.T.A. group could sponsor are drag-racing, dressmaking, landscaping, painting, or carpentry.

This form has the advantage of being brief, concise, and to the point. No elaboration is needed. The message gets across without details. The listener knows exactly what the speaker means. The speaker has not only added content stimulation but the speaking time saved can be directed to other matters.

ILLUSTRATION

An illustration is a detailed form of example. If you decide a speech point requires specific concentration, you use elaboration to promote additional clarity. Although you center the listener's attention upon one particular point, the illustration returns greater listener stimulation through its elaboration of vivid detail.

Let us suppose, for example, that you were speaking to a group of new junior executive trainees just joining your company. You have been discussing the matter of promotions—the how's and the who's. To give added impact and clarity to your comments you may illustrate.

To show the type of man our organization most appreciates, and this appreciation is shown through promotion, let me tell about two young men who joined our staff a number of years ago. Both had equal qualifications the first day on the job. Both made a equally fine initial impression. Both had top level executive ambition.

Following company policy, both began in the sales department. Now it was up to them.

The first young fellow found the sales part of big business rather difficult. He had no college courses to teach him the complicated and delicate problems of selling. Assigned to an experienced man, he observed the procedure for a couple of weeks. Everything seemed to be a jumble of faces and talk. Conferences followed each sales experience. Conferences with lots of advice but little meaning. He knew that any day it would be his turn and he nearly panicked at the thought. Then he stopped and thought about the whole problem of sales. He clearly analyzed the needs of a sales person. It was merely a matter of a commodity and a buyer. Now he knew what had to be done. Each night for two weeks he stayed on at the office. First, he studied our files on present and prospective buyers: who they were, what they had, and what they needed. Next, he digested our product reports, present and future, and even took a private inspection tour of the company, stopping to talk with each department head. Then, he examined the company's information on the competition. He was now ready to take the initiative. He was ready for sales.

No, he wasn't successful in his first attempt. It didn't matter though. He was now a professional businessman.

Oh yes, the second fellow. Well, he didn't especially care for doing homework. I have no idea where he is today.

Incidentally, our student of sales is now president of our company. Furthermore, he still does his homework.

A speaker does more than present information to the listener with illustrations. He breathes life into matter. It comes alive. It finds meaning.

When do you use an illustration? Whenever you desire to:

1. Give clarity to a point which may be difficult to understand.
2. Draw listener attention to an important point.
3. Capture listener interest.

Why lecture when you can tell an illustrative story? Which would you rather hear? Which would have the greater meaning to you? It is a procedure as old as the history of man and as successful as man. Why tamper with a proven method of communication?

Next let us look at two variations on these forms of example.

REAL EXAMPLE

The *real example* is founded upon facts. It follows the truth without deviation. It does not come from the imagination or creative spirit of the speaker. This does not necessarily restrict the speaker to a verbatim repetition of every detail of an example. This requirement may be an imposition upon both the speaker and the listener. However, there can be editing of the specifics to fit the needs of the speaker, the listener, and the situation.

A political campaigner reports regularly to headquarters on his one-day whirlwind tours of the local political circuit. The campaign managers want to know what happened and what it was like. Therefore, the speaker uses a real illustration.

Saturday at six a.m. Joe Dikes and Harriet O'Connor picked me up at home in the campaign car. The "whirl" was on and plenty of "wind" would follow.

143

Two hours later, we arrived relaxed at the high school auditorium in Harristown. Over a thousand people cheered at our entrance, our slogans and our attack on the opposition. It was the best breakfast I've ever had. I thought I'd have some seconds but the efficiency experts, Joe and Harriet, pushed me out the back door and away we went. Just for a moment I began to suspect what lay ahead. There wasn't much time to think about it though. At nine o'clock we were standing in the town square in Rochester orating happily and enjoying the cheers. Then just like in an old vaudeville act the hook came out and I was back in the car zooming toward East Town. Although we were only about ten minutes behind schedule at this point, you could already begin to feel the importance of time.

Here we were at East Town. Leaped out of the car. Skipped up the steps. Talked to our supporters. Welcomed the cheers. Had the hook put to me again and off to a luncheon talk before the P.T.A. of Hadley Center.

Did I say luncheon? Maybe for everybody but me. I talked. They ate. Meanwhile, I was "whirling" to the next stop. Now I began to recognize the real meaning of a quick campaign tour. My lunch convinced me. Ever eat two cold, dry hamburgers with no salt, no ketchup while rocketing along in a car? Discussing the next stop? Taking down notes? Memorizing names?

The pattern has been set. Ride—Talk—Ride. Waterville. Marblehead. Exeter. Pittsfield. Meredith. And all the others.

The results? Exhaustion for me. Success for our campaign. I'm sure we came home a winner.

In this example, the actual details of the situation fulfill the listener's need for information and stimulation. The amount of detail was neither understated nor overwhelming but just right. There is an impact upon the listener because it is the "real" story. It is best to use real examples, whenever possible, for living reality is generally much more interesting than fiction.

HYPOTHETICAL EXAMPLE

There are times when the real details are not available or not suited to the purpose of a speaker. Under these circumstances, you can create a hypothetical example.

The hypothetical example comes from the imagination or the creativity of the speaker. However, the speaker does not intend to deceive the listener. He uses this type of example openly as fiction and makes sure it is recognized by the listener as such. Its purpose is to assist the hearer in understanding the ideas or feelings of the speaker. Therefore it may be used either to advance clarity of comprehension or to arouse the emotions of the auditor.

For example, a person in a social rehabilitation project speaks before a group with the hope of gaining their cooperation. His message must reach the listeners. Sociological causes, statistics, and philosophies may not be enough to carry the full impact of understanding. Therefore, the speaker turns to the hypothetical example.

> Sometimes those of us working with the so-called underprivileged forget that people, like ourselves, are humans and have understanding. And are trying to understand. But what do we do? We throw around sociological phrases and slogans. All of which don't really make much sense. They are just the technical jargon of the trade. Our main slogan is "Socially disadvantaged equals social stagnation." Well what does this mean? No, I'm not going to give a definition. Instead let me explain with an example. An example—not about any special person but applying to everyone in the group which concerns us.
>
> Let us consider a young boy. We'll make him about thirteen or fourteen years old and call him Jake.
>
> Jake lives in the poor part of the city. We call it the slums. Jake has always lived here. It didn't make much difference for many years but now Jake is becoming old enough to understand the reality around him. Those alleyways he used to think were wonderful playgrounds for hiding and hunting now come into focus for what they really are. Cesspools of trash, rotting garbage, crumpled beer cans, smashed whiskey bottles. A place fit only for flies, roaches —and kids.
>
> Take a look at Jake's home. What do we see? A place of comfort? No! It is a loathsome den decorated with rat holes, roach-infested walls, and decaying plaster. All you can hear are screaming women, cursing men, and wailing babies. A young boy can't take this! He escapes to the street.
>
> Where to now? The poolroom where the bookies hang out? The cafeteria with the junkies? The corner drug store where the sharpies smack little kids? The school yard is closed and besides that's someone's territory.
>
> Suddenly Jake feels trapped, like a caged animal. Inside or outside he is cornered by the slums. He has got to fight back, but how? Nobody cares about him. Everyone is against him.

145

But Jake does find others who care. Others just like himself. The gang. They swear allegiance to each other and fight against the cage that birth and society has placed around them. Jake and his friends have an escape now. However, it is with knives, zip guns, chains, iron pipes, and most important—territories.

All this because we stood by and condemned rather than understanding and helping.

Although the illustration is not an actual case, it does convey the idea of the speaker with clarity and imagery.

Hypothetical examples are useful aids to speaking. However, you should use both actual and fictional examples. Too many hypothetical illustrations can make your speaking appear to be sustained only by the imaginary. Avert this impression by blending the real with the hypothetical.

Examples are probably the most important means of developing your speech content. Examples, facts, and opinions can make what you say more interesting and comprehensible instead of just a series of dry factual statements. Think of your hearer as a live, vital individual and exemplify all your main and secondary points. It is not only easier to listen to a speech which "tells a story" but it is also easier to speak if you have interesting "stories to tell."

Testimony

Testimony develops content by using selected materials—information, ideas, or opinions—from a source other than that originated by you, the speaker. The listener realizes that you as a speaker can seldom do all the original research and all the original thinking on the topic. It is understandable that you will turn to other sources for much of your material. Few speakers do differently. Therefore, the use of testimony in a speech is an accepted practice. All the listener really asks of a speaker is that he *identify the source* of the testimony. How can a hearer have respect for a speaker who pretends he originally conceived all his materials? It is difficult to fool the average listener. Even an authority on a particular subject must turn to other sources for materials. There is generally no problem with an expert because he usually identifies his sources automatically. It is usually the speaker who is not an expert who attempts to present himself as more knowledgeable than he really is. As a result, the listener loses respect for the speaker and the effective flow of communication is blocked. Thus, it is important to identify all testimony and, thereby, maintain a favorable rapport with the listener.

Testimony may come from any source—books, essays, articles, speeches, magazines, films, radio, and television programs. There should be a valid reason for using testimony regardless of its source. Such purposes may be:

1. To present original material.
2. To introduce new concepts, information, or opinions.
3. To clarify points under dispute.
4. To substantiate points within the speech.
5. To give authoritative support to ideas of the speech.

Two methods of presenting specific points of testimony are quotation or paraphrase. The quotation is the exact repetition of words of the testimonial source while a paraphrase is a restatement of the thought in your own words. In each instance, you must be accurate.

QUOTATION

Quotations can be effective if the speaker uses them strategically. Use them when what you want to convey has been particularly well phrased by another source:

> Men, today is our day to break all department sales records. Today is our day to show loyalty to our profit-sharing store and, in particular, to Men's Wear. Remember those inspiring words of our president, Mr. Bigness, when he said, "Bigness buys big! Bigness sells big!"

You may include the view of a specific source as part of your content development:

> Medical experts have long recommended that both the husband and wife have separate activities as one means of keeping a freshness in their relationship. Typical of this attitude is Dr. Fisk Butterfield who, as chief psychologist at Family Relation Centers, has often stated, "I cannot stress too strongly the need for a personal

147

activity for each. Simply getting out on one's own, thinking, and doing by one's self, enables each partner to return to the marital relationship with refreshed mind and emotion."

In each instance you will note the quotation was rather brief. It should be. Long quotations may become bogged down and result in the loss of listener comprehension. Avoid this situation by keeping your direct quotations as brief as possible.

PARAPHRASE

To paraphrase, a speaker takes the essence of the testimony and puts it into his own words. Although some of the quotation's impact is lost, paraphrasing does have its particular advantages. Involved, complicated, or lengthy material can be easily condensed. A speaker is free to mention only the part significant to the speaking situation:

> During the five-hour Board of Education debate Friday evening, Chairman Russo attacked our educational system on a number of matters. Those charges that directly applied to us were lack of classroom stimulation, poor academic counseling, and a deliberate lack of parent-teacher rapport.

The freedom to condense gives paraphrasing another advantage since more than one testimonial reference can be used in a compact package:

> There is no question that governmental experts endorse the Civil Service system. Professors Hagood and McClaren of the State University have just published a study which places it above any foreign system. Ambassador Copeland obviously agrees with this as he has often remarked that he sorely missed the Service when on assignment abroad. Even political rivals, Representatives Longstreet and Engelman, were in agreement when each spoke of its efficiency and equity at the last Civil Service ceremonies.

No elaboration was used here because none was needed. And yet, testimony was used. The speaker achieved his purpose without the use of the more specific and often difficult quotation form. It is for this reason that many speakers find paraphrased testimony to be more satisfactory than direct quotations.

Statistics

Statistics are figures that summarize a number of items, show size, or indicate proportions. They can be used to clarify, exemplify, prove, or visualize points of speaking. In this age of computers, statistics are more important than ever in bringing clarity to a talk.

Generally they can be found in two forms—percentages and whole numbers. Both forms are acceptable and can be used separately or in combinations. In every election year, for instance, we hear a barrage of statistics—percentage of districts returned, numbers of votes cast, percentage of leading vote, and the amount of each candidate's vote. Statistics have become part of life and talk and we should be prepared to make use of them.

When should statistics be employed? If more meaning can be brought to a particular point in the course of content development, use them.

We engineers are often thought to be a group of specialists all doing the same thing—building something with a slide rule. This picture isn't quite accurate because not all of us have the same job. In my company we have quite a variety of "slide-rule" specialists. We have over 200 engineers on the payroll and I doubt that any of us could swap positions. When the total number is broken down, we find about 25% are chemical engineers, another 30% are mechanical engineers, still another group of nearly 20% are quality control specialists. This covers approximately three quarters of the staff. The remaining fourth is a mixture of electrical, research, physical, safety, and administrative engineering personnel.

In this sample we see whole numbers, percentages, and even fractions being used as statistics. But notice how they are used. The speaker did not present exact figures. Instead he spoke in terms of "approximates." Furthermore, he avoided statistical complexity by summarizing numerically when it was appropriate and convenient. Here, then, are the keys to successful statistical usage.

First, use statistics with discretion. Too many figures clutter a speech and can result in clogged meaning. Some speakers will use statistics piled upon statistics in an attempt to impress the listener.

Gentlemen, 13% of our production is devoted to increasing the 23% quota increase compared with 26% of our sales increase for the comparable period while our efficiency dropped 19% over the projected figures of 31%.

Second, use statistics possessing immediate meaning. Involved statistics can clog meaning in the same way as the overuse of statistics. If the exact figure is not necessary, it will be easier for the listener to comprehend the meaning when you round off the statistics. It is easier to understand "over 10,000" rather than the number "11,264."

Incidentally, the speaker must recognize that statistics are not always self-explanatory. Therefore, examine your figures as though you were hearing them for the first time. Would you understand them? Would your listener understand them? If you think there might be some confusion, interpret the statistics as they are presented in your speech.

Gentlemen, our sales record for this quarter has shown a remarkable leap above our success for the first quarter. During the last period's meeting, I congratulated you for a 28% sales increase. At that time, it meant each of you averaged a noteworthy sales of 6 units a day. But today, I am at a loss for words of praise. The sales statistics reveal a 55% increase. Each of you has sold the incredible number of 12 units every day this quarter.

To improve your use of statistics, use the following list as a guide:

1. Be sure you know the meaning of all figures used in speaking.
2. Be sure all statistics are truly representative and have significance.
3. Round off statistics when possible.
4. Express statistics in terms of numbers instead of decimals.
5. Interpret the meaning of statistics for the listener.
6. Always use with discretion.

Statistics are not impressive merely because of their sound. To have value, they must have meaning to the topic under discussion. Use them only when they add to the listener's understanding.

In a speech, fact or opinion may appear in the form of examples, testimony, and statistics. Each contributes to the development of ideas in communication. Often during our daily conversations we make use of one or more of these forms. We "tell about" things done at work

150

or at play. These are examples. We "tell about" what someone said or what someone wrote. This is testimony. Furthermore in this age of computer and ratings, we may even use numbers to give meaning. This is statistics. Use these forms of opinion and fact consciously, and purposeful speaking takes place.

Step 2 | Exercises ∾ Assignments

1. Select a column by a news commentator. Analyze it for facts. Separate the fact from the article, remembering to make sure the fact is fact. Read each factual statement to the class. Are they all fact?

2. With the same article, take out the statements of opinion. Now, take one further step. As you remove each opinion make specific note of the fact which is the basis for the opinion. How many opinions do not have supporting fact? Are there any with a weak factual basis?

3. Compose a list of ten statements, some fact, others opinion. Test them on your friends and report on their proficiency in recognizing fact from opinion.

4. Giving examples impromptu can be a challenge. From the following sample list give an impromptu example—specific instance, illustration, real example, hypothetical example. Have someone else give the word and the type of example.

warmth	love
excitement	trust
success	fear
eagerness	helpfulness
uselessness	aggressiveness

5. From an article or a speech take two pieces of testimony that are about a paragraph in length. Paraphrase each. Read one as a quote then give it in the paraphrased form. Have the listeners decide which they prefer and their reasons.

6. Develop a talk including a real example and a hypothetical example to explain one of the following:

   An Educated Person *vs.* An Intelligent Person
   A Liberal Education *vs.* A Practical Education
   A Fine Art *vs.* A Liberal Art
   Propaganda *vs.* Persuasion
   Liberalism *vs.* Conservatism
   Dictatorship *vs.* Despotism

7. Create a hypothetical illustration to support one of these statements:
   Haste Makes Waste.
   Waste Not, Want Not.
   Charity Begins at Home.
   All's Well That Ends Well.
   The Early Bird Catches the Worm.
   Don't Count Your Chickens Before They Hatch.
   One Rotten Apple Spoils the Barrel.
   Too Many Cooks Spoil the Broth.

8. Analyze a speech for the forms of support used. Report on the frequency of use and give illustrations of each type.

9. Locate statistics and testimony to support one of these statements:
   Cigarette Smoking May be Injurious to the Health.
   Seat Belts Save Lives.
   Stage Fright Is a Common Fear.
   Higher Education Is "Big Business" Today.
   The Junior College Is Growing in Importance in Higher Education.

Step 3

Convert selected materials into patterns of clarification

IN addition to the forms of support materials, you also have the opportunity to use some originality in the clarification of the speech. With the following procedures, you are able to mold the materials of content to satisfy the speech topic, the speech situation, the listener, and your own method of communication. The procedures for clarifying content are definition, comparison, contrast, repetition, and restatement.

Definition

AS A SPEAKER, you must always be positive there is no misunderstanding of the meaning of thoughts or language. Nothing constructive can be accomplished if the listener interprets your words differently from what you intended. Moreover, such a situation can lead only to confusion or possibly hostility.

It is often necessary to use definition to gain unity of comprehension between you and the listener. Definition is important to effective communication and is often found in speech. Therefore, definition is considered a means of developing content. In the selection of materials for speaking, it is always wise to be aware of the need for some means of defining unclear terms or items.

There are two instances in which definition is most commonly warranted—abstract words and unfamiliar terms.

Nearly all *abstract words* should be defined. Even though the abstraction may be commonly used, there is still a possibility of various interpretations. Therefore, use definition to acquaint the listener with your particular meaning. Often a speaker will turn to a dictionary for a universal definition. Though this is quite acceptable, do not use the direct dictionary quotation in your speech. Its phrasing is often too concise or pedantic for oral communication and might lead to confusion. You should instead rephrase the definition to give it greater clarity. Compare the following definitions for clarity. The first is a typical quotation from a dictionary while the second is a rephrasing of the same definition.

> Socialism is a "theory or system of social organization by which the means of production and distribution are owned, managed, or controlled by the government (state socialism) or by associations of workers (guild socialism)."
>
> ◇ ◇ ◇
>
> For our purposes of discussion, we shall consider socialism to be a political system in which a nation's economy is regulated by the government.

The second definition has more immediate clarity and has the "sound" of oral communication.

Whenever *unfamiliar terms* are used in the course of speaking you should give a definition. Simply because you understand the terms, you cannot assume the listener does. Although some of your listeners comprehend your language, it is still advisable to use definition. Never assume that all auditors have the same understanding as you, the speaker, do.

It is not always necessary to use the dictionary when defining terms. Sometimes you may be able to present a better explanation. In addition, there are some special terms not found in a dictionary.

> When I speak of the two-platoon system in football, it is not military talk. It is football jargon. Quite simply, the two platoons are

just two groups of eleven players on the same team. They alternate playing the game. One group attempts to score points. The other tries to prevent the opponent from scoring points. It's that simple.

For speech purposes there are several methods of definition that are useful.

Negation

Definition by *negation* means clarification by telling what something is not.

Bravery does not mean foolhardiness.

Freedom does not mean that one can yell "Fire" in a crowded place to create a panic.

Discussion is not casual exchanges about the weather or about one's health.

Classification

You can define by placing the word or concept in a *classification* and then showing how it differs from others in that classification. For example:

A dictatorship is a form of government (classification) that does not permit free expression of opposition or open elections (differentiation).

～ ～ ～

An automobile is a form of transportation (classification) that contains its own power-generating and propelling system. It is usually used for transportation of not more than nine passengers (differentiation).

Synonym

As a speaker you may find that a set of *synonyms* is your best means of definition. This method is quick and sometimes is all you need.

Another word we might use for "vitality" is "enthusiasm" or "liveliness."

❧ ❧ ❧

Rebellion of youth may be labelled as dissatisfaction, disenchantment, and disaffection.

Example

You can classify a concept or word by *example*. The following illustrates this pattern of definition:

What does "conservation" mean to me? I always think of my first view of the Grand Canyon. Here is an example of nature preserved not only for our pleasure but for generations to come.

❧ ❧ ❧

When I speak of "skilled manpower" I mean the man who *knows* he knows what he is doing. The automobile mechanic who quickly and efficiently solves the problem of the broken automobile horn is "skilled manpower."

Analogy

Sometimes you can clarify by using *analogy*. The comparison of the confusing concept or term to an idea already familiar helps you to communicate the unfamiliar.

You may think of democracy as a raft. It is true that the raft is not always comfortable or fast but it can weather storms. The same is true for a democracy.

❧ ❧ ❧

Think of insurance as an umbrella of protection. You don't use it every day but when the weather is bad you will be glad to have its protection.

❧ ❧ ❧

Listeners can enjoy a speech far better if they understand everything you say. You, as a speaker, can avoid many problems if definition is part of your content development.

Learning to speak effectively may be that *spark* that skyrockets your career toward that distant objective.

156

Comparison

COMPARISON IS USED to examine the *similarities* between a known and an unknown. In the comparison the unfamiliar elements of a speech are classified by noting similarities with something already known.

The degree of detail in a comparison depends upon its purpose. If you wish only to arouse quick recognition, it may be brief.

> When I saw the new design for the proposed library, it reminded me of a tea cup turned upside down on a saucer.
>
> ∽ ∽ ∽
>
> Our new home is shaped just like a match box sitting on four stiff legs.
>
> ∽ ∽ ∽
>
> What is a mailman's life? It's like walking from here to Hong Kong and back each day.
>
> ∽ ∽ ∽
>
> This year's car styles resemble rockets with wheels.

If you wish to use comparison to further understanding of some important point, there may be need for elaboration.

> A bank is composed of men with varying ranks comparable to those used in the army. At the top of the scale is the president, who is the army general. Second in rank is the vice-president who is the colonel of the organization. Third ranking is the treasurer who has a position similar to a major in the army. Fourth, there is the army captain of the company, the department head. Finally, we find the junior executive, the lieutenant among the banking "brass."

In using comparison, the main point to remember is to be sure the statement of known fact is actually familiar to the listener. Therefore, an analysis of the hearer is necessary before designing the comparison. Comparisons are extremely useful in definition. As you will see in a later section, the comparison can be extended to form the entire structure of a talk.

Contrast

IN METHOD, CONTRAST is similar to comparison. Two items are observed side-by-side for the listener. However, the purpose, unlike that of comparison, is to note the *differences* between the known and unknown.

> For those of you who have never seen a so-called beatnik, let me give you an idea of his appearance. Unlike most young men, who are clean and wear tailored clothing, society's rebel sets his own fashions. Instead of being well-groomed, his intention is to appear just the opposite: unshaven face, uncombed hair, and unclean shirt and trousers. The female version of the beatnik is no better in appearance. No curls or dainty starched blouse are found here. Oh no! What we see is a sweatshirt and dungarees, both splotched with paint and food stains and frayed from excessive wearing, and blackened feet partially covered by sandals of rotting leather.

Just as in the use of comparison, be sure in your use of contrast, that the known statement is truly familiar to the listener. Of course, the two items of contrast should be similar enough to give some reason for this technique.

Repetition

REPETITION CONSISTS OF stating an idea or point over again in the same words. Repetition gives the listener more than one opportunity to hear and remember your statement. If you use repetition for your main points throughout your speech, the hearer is more likely to remember them. This is just what you want. Therefore, when you say something important, feel free to use repetition immediately or a little later in the speech.

> The most important part of driving at night is to stay alert and don't drive when sleepy. Remember these points. Stay alert and don't drive when sleepy!

෴ ෴ ෴

Peace and prosperity. Peace and prosperity are the aims of our government.

～ ～ ～

There is only one way for a person to advance today. Work. Work. And more work.

Of course, you should use discretion. If you spend too much time repeating points, the listener may become immune to this means of emphasis. Therefore, carefully consider the reason for employing repetition before you use it. For emphasis? As a reminder? If these are your purposes for using repetition, it should be effective.

Restatement

RESTATEMENT IS NOT only similar to repetition, it is a form of repetition. The difference occurs in the manner of expression. Repetition uses the same wording while restatement rephrases the comment and presents it again. Restatement not only repeats an item but also provides a variety of wording.

Today's students live with much stress. They are under pressure constantly. Pressure to do well. Pressure to satisfy their teachers and their parents. This stress is constant and with them twenty-four hours a day.

～ ～ ～

The seat belt provides an additional margin of safety. It may save your life. When you have the seat belt firmly fastened and not sitting alongside of you unused, your chances of remaining alive in an auto accident are much better.

Like its half brother, repetition, restatement amplifies the content of speech in addition to providing clarity. It gives emphasis. It gives impact. And it gives a touch of the dramatic.

Procedures for the clarification of content are valuable. Definition helps clarify words, concepts, and ideas. Primarily comparison and contrast are means of presenting speech material in an interesting and effective manner. Repetition and restatement serve the listener by reviewing essential items within the discourse. Using all five makes your speech more interesting and stimulating as well as serving to increase clarity.

With the materials of your speech classified for use in communication, it is time to move on to the next step in construction—selection of the materials to meet the specific speech situation.

Step 3 | Exercises ∽ Assignments

1. Take a number of specialized or technical words with which you are familiar. Taking into consideration the class audience, define them. Present them to your listeners. Then have one of the listeners give the definition back. Is the definition of the listener accurate?

2. Prepare a short talk, taking "definition" as your primary aim. Use an abstract concept. The following list will illustrate the types of talks that are acceptable:

Honesty	Courage
Democracy	Communism
Duty	Fairness
Beauty	

3. Analyze several speeches and locate samples of:

A. Definition	*D*. Repetition
B. Comparison	*E*. Restatement
C. Contrast	

4. Use a proverb as the theme of your speech. Use all of the methods of clarification in explaining the proverb.

5. Select one of the following for a short talk. On your outline indicate the methods used in clarification.

Democracy	Welfare State
Communism	Socialism
Nationalism	Colonialism
Imperialism	

6. Prepare and deliver a talk in which you clarify your concept of one of the following traits:

Dogmatic	Brave
Animated	Trustworthy
Courteous	Honest

Kind   Sincere
Arrogant   Reverent

7. Prepare a talk in which you clarify one of the following:

Realism   Pragmatism
Romanticism   Idealism
Existentialism   Rationalism

Step 4

Select the materials

for the specific

speech situation

AS we mentioned earlier, the speech of explanation has three major purposes—description, demonstration and information. You need to select the general purpose first. Next we suggested that you select a specific purpose based on your interests and your analysis of the audience.

After the specific purpose of the speech is identified, you then select the particular details to be included. If you remember, when we discussed the preparation of a speech, we advised that you should have more information on a topic than is required by the specific situation. This provides you with a cushion of additional information. Therefore, you need to choose only the most important of the materials collected for your actual speech.

Preliminary considerations for content selection

THERE ARE TWO preliminary considerations governing the selection of specific materials—the speaking situation and the needs of the listener.

Both should be regarded as having a direct bearing upon the success of the communicative process.

Speaking situation

What is the reason for the meeting of speaker and listener? Why are you speaking to this audience? The answers to these two questions will give the speaker a beginning for content selection.

The speaker and the listener are together for some reason. If, for example, the speaker has called a meeting of the neighborhood men to organize a bowling team, the substance of the speech will be selected to fulfill this purpose. Undoubtedly, the first matter to clarify would be the reasons for calling the meeting. Here you could state the availability of team members and their amount of free time. Next, the speaker might give details on elementary matters—the organization of a team, the operation of a team, a review of bowling as a sport, the entering in local competition, and the costs of membership. Although the speaker may be well-informed on the subject of bowling, the situation calls only for a specific type of detail. The speaker chooses the material satisfying the immediate needs of the moment.

> Gentlemen, as you know, we are meeting tonight because there seems to be some interest in forming a bowling team in our neighborhood. Before we go any further into the actual organization of a team, let me explain just what a bowling group will involve on your part. There are three essential factors which each of you must consider when making a decision: first, a bowling team is a competitive sporting group and will enter contests; second, there are expenses involved for equipment, practice, and league contests; and third, time is required. Now let me give you the details on each of these points and then we shall have a mutual understanding for further action.

Whatever the reason for speaking, a speaker is guided in the limiting of the scope of content materials by knowing the *what* and *why* of the occasion.

If the listeners are novice bowlers, it would be appropriate for the speaker to explain the basic fundamentals of the sport. The intricacies of bowling can come later. If, however, the listeners are bowlers but have never been members of a team, the selection of speech materials would be designed to satisfy questions on team bowling. For a mixed group of beginning and experienced bowlers, the speaker selects materials to meet the differing needs. Neither group of listeners should be neglected. Combine elementary materials with advance materials. This way both can be kept interested while both needs are being satisfied. Always remember, a speaker has the obligation to select speech materials to meet the needs of the situation and the listener.

Special considerations in content selection

FOUR FACTORS ARE given *special* consideration when selecting speech materials. Each is important to maintain a high degree of speaker-listener rapport throughout the speaking occasion. Listener analysis is now put to practical use.

Is it relative?

In answer to the question of relativity, a speaker chooses content on the basis of its meaning to the particular listener before him. If the listener realizes there is no personal significance to the speech materials, the process of listening may cease. Think of the audience as being composed of individuals and use those details which have meaning to every one.

It would be pointless to compare a union to a college fraternity if you were speaking to people who have never been to college. There would be no basis for understanding a collegiate fraternal organization. The comparison must be founded upon a basis relative to listener *interest, experience,* and *knowledge.* At least one of these three factors must be present.

You must be careful to ensure the relativity of the selected materials. No matter how strongly you believe materials are meaningful there is no guarantee the listener feels the same way. Think of the listener objectively. Think of his interests. Think of his special needs. Think of his values. Then make your selections.

The following selection illustrates this factor:

164

It seems that someone is always appearing before business groups and social organizations asking for their support—just as I am doing tonight. And I am sure that you were sympathetic to their cause. But that is not my purpose. I *don't* want you to support my interest for the advancement of nursing. I don't want you to become supporters of the National League of Nurses. You are busy people. You have your professional life, your home life, and your personal life to occupy all your time and energy. Your "life" is far more important than any organization or its cause. And it is your "life" that I want you to support—your life and its health.

Do you remember the teacher who attempted to arouse your interest in bicycling when you had just become old enough to drive an automobile? Or the aunt who wanted you to spend the holidays at her house when you had just made the first team in baseball? Or the boss who insisted on your membership in the departmental bowling team when you preferred to spend your free time participating in the local community theater? Were they successful?

You probably remember a number of incidents in which the specific substance of the talk had little, if any, relation to you as an individual. What was your reaction in each case? Was there a high degree of speaker-listener rapport? Or was there complete lack of interest?

Is it familiar?

To achieve complete understanding of content, a speaker should strike a balance between familiar and new materials. It would be rather dull to listen to a speech composed of details already known. On the other hand, to hear too much of the unfamiliar only clouds meaning. A general guide for the selection of materials for familiarity is to use the familiar to provide understanding and the unfamiliar to provoke interest.

If a speaker was explaining the operation of a teletype machine to a group of secretaries, a meaningful foundation for understanding would be gained through a comparison of the unfamiliar teletype machine with the familiar electric typewriter. Here, the familiar material provides a means to comprehension. The unfamiliar details bring interest through learning. Since the aim of explanation is understanding or learning, the goal of the speaker has been achieved.

165

Is it not easier to understand a subject when a key to understanding is provided? This is true in the classroom when the instructor introduces a new topic by drawing upon the knowledge of the student. The same is true in the training program. The trainee is given keys to accomplishing the new task by referral to previous experience. "Remember when you used to . . . ?" says the trainer, "Well, this new procedure follows a similar system." Thus, the student is given a basis from which increased understanding can be drawn.

Furthermore, the use of unfamiliar information is equally important to the speaking situation. If a speaker merely reviews that which is already known, the listener may quickly lose interest. Therefore, new material is introduced to catch the interest and to provide substance for thought. The effective speaker stimulates the listener's mind with the unfamiliar.

Just a word of caution—always be positive that the listener is *really* familiar with the material designated as "familiar." The fact that *you* are does not necessarily mean the hearer is. In addition, recognize the degree of familiarity. Sometimes, a listener may be *acquainted* with it but not enough for it to be considered as *familiar.* Thus, such detail could not serve as a foundation for understanding. For instance, it might be pointless to explain the new turbine automobile engine to many laymen by drawing a comparison with the piston engine, since they may know little about the piston machine even though all have cars. Such listeners could become confused by this comparison.

Finally, the speaker needs to determine the *degree* of familiarity. In the above example, we noted that all listeners were automobile owners. But this does not guarantee that there is any detailed knowledge of the mechanical operation of the piston engine. The speaker must either select different materials or use that which is the *more* familiar for the explanation.

Is it acceptable?

No effective speaker wants to lose his hearers due to the presentation of offensive materials. Therefore, you should avoid materials which clash with established listener morals, mores, ethics, or customs. Because many matters have deep-seated significance to people, it would be foolish for a speaker to alienate his listeners by treading on sacred grounds. Although he did so unintentionally, the results could prove detrimental to the purpose of speaking.

The task of a communicator is to offer an explanation intelligently and successfully. There must be effective listening by the auditors to do this. A wise speaker will select materials to keep others listening.

This is not to imply that a perfectly harmonious relationship should always exist between you and the hearer. Much of the time there may be disagreement. Often this is the case between politicians and voters, salesmen and consumers, employer and employees, officers and enlisted men, and teachers and students. Such conflicts are so common they go almost unnoticed. Purposeful disagreement is not a primary concern with a speaker when considering the acceptability of materials.

What you need to avoid is *offending* or *insulting* hearers. It is occasionally necessary to shock an audience and this can be done with a clear conscience. However, to offend is inexcusable and only serves to alienate the listener.

The speaker can easily detect the potential objectionableness of most speech materials to all listeners or special groups. These present no problems. The content that is used in clear conscience but results in an alienation of auditors is what causes the trouble.

The only real safeguard against this problem is a thorough analysis of the speaking situation. Be aware of the makeup of the listening group. Know the tastes of the listening group. Finally, when choosing materials, put yourself in the position of the listener. Remember the selected materials can be controversial, if you wish, but never offensive.

Is it stimulating?

All listeners find speaking more enjoyable when the contents are stimulating. The two classes of stimulating materials you should use in selecting the specific content for speaking are intellectual and emotional.

(1)   There is content which brings *intellectual* stimulation. Since it has substance, such material makes the listener think. It promotes new learning or greater understanding. It may be a statement of fact, testimony, statistics, example, or any form of content detail which allows the listener to think. It puts information before the listener for

contemplation. This, therefore, stimulates the mental capacities of the hearer and makes the speech more enjoyable. Notice the following example:

> What are the facts in the situation? These are our principal considerations now. First, the area in question is owned by a local business group but they are prepared to sell the mining rights for two and a half million dollars. Second, our exploratory tests indicate a mineral deposit estimated at eight million tons. Third, the mineral quality is 63% pure. Finally, at today's market price the ore is valued at a half million dollars.

You may stimulate the intellectual *curiosity* of the listener. Here, several types of controversial material enter into the speaking event. It can raise questions in the minds of the listener. It can imply or interpret, thereby provoking the listener to do some critical thinking.

Curiosity draws the listener closer to the speaking event. He is interested and wants to hear more. What better situation could a speaker want? Listeners who desire to hear more are the ideal in audiences.

> Two time-study experiments have been conducted in the assembly lines during the past three months. The purpose was to learn if periodic shifting of specific assembly duties really improved the quality and quantity of production. The results were most surprising and most disconcerting. In fact, so much so, that we have found it necessary to formulate several new policy changes.

The stimulation of intellectual curiosity sets the listener to thinking. He follows the words and thoughts of the speaker and perhaps evaluates the materials and ideas. As the speech progresses, the listener falls into the thinking process of the speaker. The speaker has his complete attention. The logic and substance of the oral reasoning become those of the listener. The speaker is master of the situation!

(2)   There are materials that stir the *emotions* of the listener. Here a speaker chooses details designed to effect the imagination. The hearer "sees" or "feels" the words of the speaker.

Such materials may be of many types. They may have any number of effects upon the auditor. Some may provoke humor. Some may excite the passions—anger, fear, disgust, or horror. Some may awaken the memory. Emotional content is illustrated in the following paragraph.

> These facts were brought most vividly to mind last week when during the P.T.A. meeting an English teacher was confronted by both parents of a senior girl. Now, this alone was enough to raise the suspicions of any teacher. What was the father doing at P.T.A.? If he was forced to come, why hadn't he escaped to the coach's office? But here he was, adamantly defending the quality of his daughter's homework compositions. Suddenly, after nearly twelve years of schooling for his daughter, Dad rushes to the defense of "homework" compositions. Interesting, since he didn't show the slightest indication toward wanting to discuss her classroom compositions. However, Dad wasn't so lucky this time. The teacher, not in the mood for parental abuse, calmly and quietly suggested a solution. If Dad would attend the regular class as a student, then, perhaps, the quality of "homework" compositions would be lifted to twelfth grade level. Flushed and stammering, our concerned father made a hasty retreat.

Because the emotions and the minds are so closely connected, a speaker can use emotional situations to a high degree to direct the thinking of an auditor. For every main point of expression, there can be some degree of emotionalism. If a speaker were explaining the Normandy Invasion, he would not need to restrict the historical facts. A vivid description of the tension, the fears, and the trepidation of the landing forces might be included. Both mental and emotional details are combined to raise the level of stimulation within each listener. He may thereby realize the point of explanation more clearly and more emphatically because his attention has been specifically drawn to a point of information within the speech. As a result, the listener accepts each element of the speech.

Man is an emotional creature and the effective speaker makes use of this fact. Emotional stimuli are, therefore, an integral part of communication. Through it, people are compelled to listen, to be attentive, to learn, and to accept. However, emotionalism is no substitute for intelligent content.

The selection of the materials to be used in speaking are determined by the topic, the purpose, and the situation. In fulfilling this essential step to speech construction, you need to weigh each choice with care. What remains after the final selection becomes the content of communication. If communication is to be successful and effective, speech materials must be effectively arranged.

Step 4 | Exercises ∽ Assignments

1. Select a speech subject which could be presented to a number of different groups. Discuss with the class what specific materials you would use for each of the following listener groups. Give the basis for your selection.
    a. Union members
    b. American Banking Association
    c. Parent-Teacher Association
    d. High school seniors
    e. Ladies club

2. Interview a salesman. Ask him how he approaches different listeners— businessmen, professional people, housewives, retired people, etc. Report your investigation to the class.

3. Select a speech from *Vital Speeches* magazine. Note to whom it was presented, then examine it for selection of materials for the specific listener.

4. Using a specialized periodical (i.e. *Beekeepers, Public Relations, Electronic Engineers*) find advertisements that illustrate use of material that is relative and familiar for that group.

5. Collect a series of advertisements that use curiosity as a key feature.

6. How would you adapt materials for the topic of "Unidentified Flying Objects" to the following audiences:
    a. High school science students
    b. Professional football players
    c. Professional photographers
    d. Farmers
    e. Commercial artists

7. Show how you would select materials that are (1) relative (2) familiar (3) acceptable (4) stimulating for the topic of "Cheating in the Academic World" for the following audiences:
    a. Clergymen
    b. College administrators
    c. College students
    d. Foreign students

Step 5

Organize the speech materials into purposeful speech

NOW that the speech materials have been selected and recognized as special forms, what are you going to do with them? They are to be arranged into an orderly pattern to serve your purpose of explanation. The organization of the speech is designed to produce an effective balance between the *materials* and the *reasons* for speaking.

Generally, a speech has three major divisions—introduction, body, and conclusion. Each is significant in accomplishing effective communication. No one part can be considered lightly as they all combine to make the whole speech. Therefore, we shall consider them separately.

The introduction

FIRST, THE FUNCTION of the introduction is to gain the *attention* of the listener. What good is a speech if no one listens? Or if the hearer tunes in late? The opening words should center all attention upon you and your speech.

Second, an introduction establishes a *speaker-listener rapport*. From the minute the first words are spoken, you are on trial. Immediately, you are being judged by the auditors. Listeners are not so objective that they make their final evaluation at the conclusion of your speech. Many even reach a decision by the end of your introduction. Therefore, you must consider intelligently the organization of your introduction.

Third, early in your speech, give your listener some idea of the topic to quickly capture his *interest*.

The introductory materials are organized by various methods to satisfy all three of these aims. Study the following types and decide which pattern or combination of patterns fit your speaking needs best.

Statement of central idea

A most common method of organizing the introduction is merely to reveal the central idea of the speech. It is simple and uninvolved in style. There can be no doubt as to what the topic is going to be.

Today, I am going to explain the procedure for producing home movies.

◇ ◇ ◇

There are two possible routes to take on a cross-country trip from San Francisco to New York. Let us consider each one before making any recommendations.

This type of introduction can be effective because of its simplicity.

Rhetorical question

The rhetorical question is a variation of the simple statement. Here you ask the listeners a question containing the central idea of the speech. However, you expect *no* response from the listeners and, furthermore, the hearer does not feel inclined to respond. Both you and the listener understand that the answer will be supplied during the speech.

The advantage of the rhetorical question is that it not only reveals the central idea but it tends to arouse listener curiosity and to start him thinking about the question.

How many of you ever wonder how beer is brewed?

∽ ∽ ∽

A question came to my mind the other day. Possibly you have also been curious about the same thing. Just how is an image transmitted from a television studio to our sets at home?

Your listener waits for an answer. You have their attention.

Partition of main points

Sometimes your subject may be more readily understood if you review its main points before actually developing the speech body. Thus, the introduction takes the form of partition. Here you state or list each main point of the speech in the introduction for the hearer.

There are three particular matters that need explanation at this time: first, the history of our organization; second, the structure of the group; and third, the future of the club.

∽ ∽ ∽

Our construction plans for this recreational center show a progressive sectional layout: the north section for pre-school children, the east section for school children, the south section for adults and, the west section for family outings. Now, let me explain each in detail.

The advantage of this partition introduction is the placing of the basic outline of your speech in the minds of the listeners. They know what specific points are to be covered. Then as you develop the speech body, the hearers can easily follow its direction.

Background information

At times the listener may be unfamiliar with the general subject from which you have drawn your topic. In order to give your topic complete meaning or full significance, it may be important for the hearer to have a background knowledge of the subject. If this is the case, your introduction should give the necessary background information.

173

Ten years ago, a group of our townsmen got together to attempt to spur the state legislature into voting the establishment of a state-supported community college in our area. During the first six years of this private campaign, all seemed hopeless. Then our number of college-age youngsters increased. In fact in the past four years it has tripled. This situation plus the crowding of the state university has forced the legislature to accept our idea. Now, before submitting any final plans to them, let me explain our proposals and then you can give us your thoughts on the matter.

∽ ∽ ∽

Thirteen weeks ago, I would not have suggested the need of a new advertising campaign for Simpson Machines. For three years, everything has been fine. Simpson was first in sales. However, in the middle of July, a new competitor came on the market and, subsequently, sales have been slashed. Yes, I know this comes as a surprise. Simpson has dropped to third in national sales in the past three months. With this in mind, I have called you to this emergency meeting to evaluate my new advertising program.

The purpose of background information is to *acquaint* your listener with a subject or to arouse a feeling of appreciation for your speech. It prepares the hearer for the main body of your speech. For more effectiveness, keep the background information as brief and concise as possible.

Dramatic statement

The dramatic statement can be used to gain listener attention quickly. It sets an immediate atmosphere of drama by its very phrasing. It stimulates the emotions of the listener and focuses the attention on you, the speaker.

We human beings are butchers of our fellow men and we enjoy it. Each of you is a killer. You know it. (Speech on capital punishment, war, careless driving)

∽ ∽ ∽

I want to tell you about the most senseless and useless habit that can infect us. It is a waste of precious time. It takes away from our television, our gardening, our card parties. It only serves to make us different. (Speech on reading, music appreciation, painting)

∽ ∽ ∽

Some moan: Stupid! Ridiculous! Absurd! Others cry: Marvelous! Sensational! Magnificent! Why the difference? Nobody knows! (Speech on critics, modern art, clothing styles)

Dramatic introductions are useful in presenting overexposed speech topics. The listener, having encountered the subject before, may not have much interest at present. Although you may have new ideas on the matter or, at least, a new approach to it, the problem of a lack of attention does exist. However, knowing the listener would be interested if he would only give you a chance, you use the dramatic introduction to shock the listener. You capture attention because of the difference and unexpectedness. Sound dramatic and fulfill your promise of a stimulating speech. No barrier to gaining listener attention is insurmountable.

Striking facts

While dramatic statements play upon the emotions of the listener, you may want to go further and spark the mind of the hearer. This is the place to use an introduction employing striking facts. The facts, presented crisply and with little elaboration, speak for themselves. Let the listener feel the impact of truth.

Ten thousand babies are born and within weeks over 250 are dead. One hundred thousand babies will die this year without even celebrating their very first birthday.

～ ～ ～

One million students quit high school last year. One million will quit this year. And one million will quit next year. Ten years equals 10 million dropouts. A hundred years equals 100 million dropouts.

～ ～ ～

The present world population is so large that if genius were the result of numerical quantity, there would be as many geniuses alive today as there have been in all the centuries of human history preceding this one.

Striking facts are useful under conditions calling for the shock of reality. When listeners are nonchalant toward a matter requiring their concern, you must use the dramatic combined with truth. Fire home the facts and let the listener be startled. Then, you have their attention and more.

175

Personal experience

To give a personal flavor to speaking, you can present an experience, directly related to the subject of your speech. The pointed experience tends to draw the listener closer to the speaker and there is a more intimate relationship. Thus, better listening can occur.

If the personal experience can advance the effectiveness of your speech, use it. Never tell a story simply to amuse or interest just for the moment. Without an immediate purpose, it only postpones the actual introduction. Sometimes relating a meaningless experience works against a speaker. For instance, the speaker who begins "A funny thing happened to me . . ." only announces that a dull speech will probably follow the "funny story." The listener gives some attention to the beginning and then prepares to fall asleep.

Consider explaining the reason for the story to give your personal experience complete meaning and to prevent misinterpretation. Do not assume its significance is obvious to all listeners. You had the experience. Tell the other fellow how you found it meaningful.

When I was a young boy, the hospital was an important part of the school summer vacation. It seems that one or two weeks every summer were spent in the town hospital, mending the bones of a young cowboy, baseball player, or explorer. Furthermore the youthful mind of a boy of eight or ten accepted it as normal. During one of these visits for recuperation, I made a friend. We had a grand time together in the ward trading comics, comparing experiences, and sharing goodies brought from home. On the day for my release, we signed each other's casts and pledged continued friendship.

I never saw that fine fellow again because the world outside the hospital wouldn't allow it. My pal was of a different race.

How confusing it was to a little boy who saw no difference between buddies. However, it wasn't a world of little boys. It was an adult world. They made the rules and gave the orders. Little boys had to obey and not ask questions.

I wonder if we adults recognize the problems we impose upon our children. The situation is no different today than when we were youngsters. We still give the orders. They still are not permitted to ask questions. Just for a few moments, let's consider some of the problems we have passed on to the children of all races today.

Although you can use the personal experience introduction at your discretion, a most appropriate time is when you know the listener has an interest in you as a person. The hearer may know you personally or by reputation. Whatever the case, you, the individual, give greater significance to the experience.

Quotation

You may use a quotation as a method of introduction. A quotation is best and has fuller meaning if it is placed in a setting of your own words. It is not enough merely to repeat the words of another. The listener usually does not catch the significance or implication of the quotation. Therefore, when you present a quotation complement it with your own introduction.

> We hear much about the improvement of speech. Sometimes we may wonder why there seems to be so much fuss about speaking. Maybe it would be better to go back to the good old days when supposedly there was little talk and lots of action. For an answer, we have to go way back to the old days, about 2500 years back. Around this time there was a rather perceptive scholar, named Aristotle, who had many thoughts on the subject of talk versus action. He said, "It is absurd to hold that a man ought to be ashamed of being unable to defend himself with his limbs, but not of being unable to defend himself with *speech and reason,* when the use of rational speech is more distinctive of a human being than the use of his limbs." In other words, man is the only creature with the power of speech. Why doesn't he, therefore, use it effectively?

An introductory quotation does not need to be very long. In fact, a single sentence may be more satisfactory:

> Sometimes students ask the value of studying so many subjects which seem to deal always with the past. Whoever gave the first answer to this problem is long forgotten. However, we do have the thoughts of the brilliant Englishman Disraeli, who said, "The more extensive a man's knowledge of what has been done, the greater will be his power of knowing what to do." Thus, we can more accurately decide what to do now by knowing the mistakes and successes of our predecessors.

In each of the foregoing examples, the quotation was woven into the introduction. It was not left standing alone but instead was given a background setting or interpreted for the listener. The reason for its use was clearly transmitted to the listener. Set the scene for the quotation. Give it. Then, interpret the quotation.

We have reviewed the various types of introduction. Now you, the speaker, will select the best method or combination of types to gain the attention and interest of your auditors. Above all, be sure you have a positive approach to the beginning of the speech regardless of the type of introduction used.

The body

THE BODY OF A SPEECH is the most important part of effective speaking. This is where the main points and their corresponding materials are organized to guarantee clarity of expression. The body contains the material you want to communicate and, therefore, you should develop it with special care.

In Part II, Step 3, we discussed outlining and revealed the function of each part of the Speech of Explanation.

Main Points: The major parts, ideas, items to be covered in the explanation.

Secondary Points: The actual explanation for the corresponding main point.

Specific Points: The exemplification of a secondary point.

With these functions in mind, we now turn to the various patterns of *arranging the main points* of explanation.

Chronological organization

The first type of arrangement for the speech body we will review is *chronological order*. In this organizational pattern, the main points of your speech are arranged by the *calendar* or the *clock*. Often you will find that the principal parts of a topic naturally follow a pattern of hours, days, years, or some other time arrangement. This is the place to use the time order of organization.

Historical subjects often fall into a pattern like that of a calendar. Why disturb the chronology? Simply make it more precise and adapt it to your speech topic.

SUBJECT: THE HISTORY OF MY TOWN

    I. Founded in 1648 with the greatest difficulty.
    II. In 1763, the Revolutionary War caused political chaos.
    III. Industrialization of 1900 brought many changes.
    IV. By 1950, the future of this industrial city was established.

The calendar time order does not necessarily mean an arrangement by the year or century. A smaller period may be used.

SUBJECT: A WEEK AT MARINE RESERVE SUMMER CAMP

    I. **Monday**   Two hundred miles in a military convoy.
    II. **Tuesday**   A Marine's life begins and a civilian's ends.
    III. **Wednesday**   Hiking for fifty miles is not pleasure.
    IV. **Thursday**   Military instruction is a re-awakening.
    V. **Friday**   War games are serious business.

SUBJECT: A FRESHMAN'S EXPERIENCE
            DURING COLLEGE ORIENTATION

    I. **Sunday**   Travel, move in, get acquainted.
    II. **Monday**   Speeches, speeches, speeches.
    III. **Tuesday**   Registration for first classes.
    IV. **Wednesday**   Meet the upperclassmen.
    V. **Thursday**   Begin classes.

The following pattern illustrates a chronological arrangement by hours.

    I. **7:00 a.m.** Begin the day with breakfast and cleanup.
    II. **10.00 a.m.** Swimming and athletic instruction.
    III. **1.00 p.m.** Quiet creative work in arts and crafts.
    IV. **4:00 p.m.** Free period for all activities.
    V. **7:00 p.m.** Conclude the day with the nightly campfire.

To ensure clarity of organization, each main point of the time order must be specific. State the time division to make sure the listener definitely knows your patterns of arrangement.

Space organization

You can use *space organization* for topics having a definite physical arrangement to their main points. The physical positioning of each item is found in a *positive* order. Irregularly arranged or isolated points are not included in this particular pattern of organization.

Space order may take different forms—east to west, north to south, left to right, top to bottom, or inside to outside. Any number of specific and orderly arrangements is possible. However, remember the elements of the speech topic should have a natural placement as illustrated in the following two examples. The first shows a space pattern of "bottom to top."

SUBJECT: THE MODERN SKYSCRAPER

I. Below Ground:	Maintenance centers and parking.
II. Ground Floors:	Auditoriums.
III. Main Floors:	Offices.
IV. Top Floors:	Restaurants and observation towers.

The next example of organization follows a geographical arrangement.

SUBJECT: THE PROPOSED PLAN FOR THE NEW CAMPUS

I. Western Section:	Dormitories for men and women.
II. Northern Section:	Athletic fields and clubhouse.
III. Eastern Section:	Classrooms for all departments.
IV. Southern Section:	Library and administrative buildings.

For effective space organization, the listener must mentally place each main point in its proper place. It should have a natural order which the listener can anticipate. If this occurs, the organizational arrangement is effective.

Comparative organization

Comparative organization is used to explain similarities or differences between items. In this method, the speaker introduces two items for examination. It is your obligation to explain each item and the points of comparison for the listener. Plan it carefully.

There are two variations of comparative organization. In the first, the comparative points of the items are discussed immediately and the listener is given a step-by-step examination of each detail. In the example, the initial item would be a comparison of the basic cost of two types of cars followed by the comparison of their safety features.

SUBJECT: ENGLISH CARS AND AMERICAN CARS

    I. Initial cost.
       A. English car.
       B. American car.
   II. Safety features.
       A. English car.
       B. American car.
  III. Comfort.
       A. English car.
       B. American car.

Another approach to the comparative organization would explain fully each item as separate points. Then you make the comparison. In this method, the speaker gives the listener an understanding of a complete item before proceeding to the comparison.

In the following illustration, the English game is explained first, then the American game, and finally the comparison is made.

SUBJECT: ENGLISH FOOTBALL AND AMERICAN FOOTBALL

    I. English football.
       A. Objectives and rules.
       B. Techniques.
       C. Spectators.
   II. American football.
       A. Objectives and rules.
       B. Techniques.
       C. Spectators.
  III. Comparison of the two games.

It is essential that the structure be obvious in any version of the comparative organization. Clarity is important. The speech should preview the pattern for the listener.

Procedural organization

For some topics, you will find that the main points follow a natural order of appearance. There is a step-by-step arrangement inherent in the subject. Usually it cannot be altered. For such topics, the speaker uses a *procedural organization* to place the main speaking points in their natural order.

Many things follow a sequence of points or steps—cooking, first aid, building, dressmaking, or manufacturing. Whenever we give directions, they usually are in a sequence. When we learn, there is generally a procedure of steps to follow as we move toward our goal. This arrangement gives both a starting and a finishing point. In between, certain steps are completed.

When organizing the procedural topic, you may give numerical classification to each step.

SUBJECT: THE MAKING OF WINE

    I. First   Grapes are grown on special farms.
   II. Second Ripe grapes are processed.
  III. Third   Grape juices are fermented.
  IV. Fourth Resulting wines are graded and bottled.

SUBJECT: PREPARING A SPEECH

    I. Choose and narrow a topic.
   II. Collect and select materials.
  III. Organize content.
  IV. Present the speech to the listener.

Procedural organization is particularly effective when preceded by the partition form of introduction. The listener, given the outline of the procedure in the introduction, then hears an elaboration of each point during the body of the speech. The combination of the two patterns helps the listener to remember each element of the topic in proper order. As seen above, procedural patterns of organization generally follow a chronological sequence. However, the major units of the talk are not time units but are the steps to follow.

Topical organization

In topical organization, the main points are arranged in an order most convenient for presentation and understanding. That is, each specific main point of your speech is discussed in that position allowing the greatest degree of effectiveness. Examine the following examples of topical order. In each instance, only the discretion of the speaker determined the arrangement.

SUBJECT: U.S. FEDERAL GOVERNMENT

    I.   Legislative branch
   II.   Judicial branch
  III.   Executive branch

SUBJECT: HOW TO FIGHT JUVENILE DELINQUENCY

    I.   Make more part-time jobs available.
   II.   Expand organized extracurricular activities.
  III.   Enforce driving and drinking laws.

SUBJECT: THE RESPONSIBILITIES OF A TEACHER

    I.   A teacher should be a vitalized educator.
   II.   He should be a practical guidance counselor
  III.   Most important, a teacher must understand youth.

Use topical organization when logically justified. However if this cannot be done, one of the other patterns will undoubtedly serve your purpose much better.

The organization of the body of a speech is most important for effective communication. Consider your choice wisely. Only use the arrangement best satisfying the speech topic and the speaking purpose.

The conclusion

THE CONCLUSION SERVES a most important function to effective oral expression. A speaker should give as much thought to the conclusion as he did to the introduction. The speech of explanation conclusion has two major purposes—to summarize and to highlight.

Summary

Probably the most familiar method of concluding is a formal review of the main points of the speech. It is, in effect, a restatement of your main points.

Therefore, we can conclude that three main considerations are given to all applicants. First, the usual matter of specialized experiences in the field. Second, the applicant's ability to adapt to our particular operation. And third, the capability of the applicant for putting new ideas into practice. If we keep these points in mind during the forthcoming interviews, I'm sure that we'll choose the best man for the job.

The value of the review-summary is easily seen. It refreshes the mind of the listener while bringing the speech to a close. This form of conclusion is highly recommended for its practical value to effective speaking.

Highlighting

If a speaker wishes to have a more stimulating ending, he can have the highlighting conclusion. In it, you exemplify the essence of your speech through its application.

These new advances in medical science now give new hope for a more healthy world. No longer will the majority of children of Asia, Africa, and South America die before their fifth birthday. No longer will man struggle with the paralyzing deformity of muscular disease and disorders of the nervous system. No longer will there be a blight upon men over fifty. Instead, we can look into the future and see an age free from pitiful pain and dreaded death.

Although there is no formal summary of the main points, the listener is stimulated to recall the essence of the speech.

With these two principal methods of conclusion, you can adapt a speech ending to fit your specific needs. A smooth and purposeful conclusion is essential.

Transitions to unify

THERE IS ONE FINAL DETAIL to consider before leaving organization. As you know, the organizational structure consists of three parts—introduction, body, and conclusion. If they are left as separate parts, the listener hears only blocks of unattached words and information. However, he should hear a continuous progression. The obvious way to gain unity is to bridge the organizational sections with *transitional* phrasing.

Between the introduction and the body, the speaker can use any number of familiar expressions as transitions:

Moving on to the various reasons . . . .
Now let us examine the first point . . . .
Here are the reasons . . . .
Starting at the bottom . . . .
Before giving the causes, let me . . . .

For connecting the body and conclusion, you can use equally familiar transitions:

And what does this all mean . . . .
In summary, it can be seen . . . .
It can be concluded, therefore, that . . . .
What can be done . . . .
Now what has been said . . . .

These are only sample transitions used to join the three units of your organization. The materials in each unit will virtually dictate the obvious wording of these transitions.

One final reminder—transitions are also needed to unify the main points in the body of the speech. You want the main points to build into completeness rather than remain a series of items. You also want to avoid jumping from point to point. In other words, you need a smooth transitional flow. There are expressions of various lengths to serve this purpose.

> In the next instance . . . .
> Bearing this in mind we move on to . . . .
> Following this . . . .
> The next obvious step . . . .
> Tracing this process further . . . .
> However, we now find . . . .
> But, what about . . . .
> Resulting from this . . . .

As noted before, there are no standard transitions to link points or any other of the elements of organization. As you develop content, natural connectives will come to mind. These are generally the best for they relate specifically to the subject-matter. Transitions bring together the units of the speech into a unified whole.

In summary, you see that it is necessary to arrange all units of the talk in an effective order. You must have an introductory section to serve as a "lead-in" for the body of the speech. The major part of the talk must be arranged in the most productive order for the specific topic and the particular audience. Your conclusion should summarize and highlight. In addition, you need to provide smoothness and clarity by meaningful transitions.

Step 5 | Exercises ∾ Assignments

1. After you have chosen your next speech subject, experiment with the different types of introduction. Arrange an introduction for each of the forms suggested in this section. Test them for effectiveness on your class. Which does the class prefer? Discuss the reasons.
2. Examine the introductions from several speeches of explanation found in *Vital Speeches* magazine or in a speech collection. What are the types used? Does the speaking situation or the listening group seem to be a determining factor?

3. Prepare a series of three minute speeches of explanation. Use a different pattern of organization for the body of each. Does the listener know which form of organization you used?

4. Again examine explanatory speeches in *Vital Speeches* magazine or a speech anthology. Report on the organization most frequently used in several randomly selected speeches.

5. Prepare a fifteen minute speech of explanation. Incorporate all of the steps of explanation. Do not forget the steps of "Preparing for Speaking." Make this a polished performance.

6. Take one of the following subjects and prepare brief outlines using at least three different patterns suggested in this step:
   Our Space Program
   Automobile Safety
   The Problems of the City
   The United Nations

Step 6

Preevaluate the speech of explanation

THE true effectiveness of speaking can only be determined after its conclusion. Whatever the speech subject, it is the final performance that decides the degree of success or failure of your presentation. The conscientious speaker will realize this fact and will attempt to evaluate a speech *before* presentation. By doing this, he can refine the planned speech to increase the possibility of achieving the highest degree of effectiveness.

The following check points can be used as an aid in self-evaluation:

1. Has the speaking situation been intelligently analyzed?
2. Has the purpose of speaking been clearly defined?
3. Is the speech topic specifically determined?
4. Have you gathered all materials relevant to the topic?
5. Were only the best materials selected for the speech?
6. Do you know more on the topic than you are presenting to the listener?
7. Did you carefully follow each step in the construction of the speech?
8. Is the organization of the speech clearly outlined?

9. Does the introduction form an immediate rapport of attention and interest with the listener?
10. Is the central idea of the speech topic quickly revealed?
11. Is the speech body fully developed while following the most appropriate organization?
12. Does the conclusion really add effectiveness to the speech?
13. Have you practiced the presentation of the speech?
14. Can you express all thoughts fluently?
15. Will you use appropriate visual aids wherever possible?
16. Will the listener understand the speech?
17. Will the listener gain from the speech?
18. Does the speech have significance for the listener?
19. Would you enjoy hearing the speech if you were the listener?
20. Will you enjoy presenting the speech?

If the speaker and the speech satisfy each of the check points, then there can be confidence in entering into the communicative situation.

Speeches of explanation are fundamental methods of communication. All speaking is born in the explaining process. Therefore, mastering the steps of explanation is essential to all effective communication.

Part V

Speech of

opinion

As humans, we have the power to think and to speak and we do both often. Much of our time is spent in explaining the multitude of subjects that are part of our complex world. There are times, however, when we are not satisfied to limit our speech to the presentation of objective information. We like to express our attitudes or beliefs and, in doing so, we give opinions.

Opinions are personal judgments covering a wide variety of subjects from the quality of pipe tobacco to the possibility of life on other planets. How does one go about forming an opinion? Supposedly, we consider all known details on a subject, both favorable and unfavorable, logically weigh this information for its significance and implications, and then form an intelligent belief about the matter.

The expression of opinion occupies much of our speaking and, therefore, it is important the speaker does it with *intelligence* and *effectiveness*. The steps within the speech of opinion will assist you, the thinking speaker, in the formation and expression of opinions based on *specific knowledge* and *sound reasoning*.

Explanation as a prerequisite for opinion

WHEN YOU HAVE an opinion and present it to a listener, you must necessarily use explanation. How else would the hearer understand your complete opinion? Since explanation is involved in the expression of opinion, we can conclude that there must be clarity of explanation to have effective presentation of personal judgments. One is basic to the other. Thus, before you enter a situation requiring an intelligent speech of opinion, you must first be at ease with the speech of explanation. The speech of opinion is, for the most part, an extension of the explaining speech.

As we progress along the steps of the speech of opinion, you observe that you will be concerned with certain matters necessary for this complex form of communication—the psychology of the speaking situation, the basis for judgment, and the reasoning process used in reaching the conclusion.

To achieve the successive aims of the speech of opinion, the speaker will find the following matters essential:

1. *Consideration* of the opinion as sound in fact and reason.
2. *Agreement* with the opinion.
3. *Action* upon the opinion.

With these objectives in mind, we shall now move on to the specific steps included in the speech of opinion.

Step 1

Analyze the listeners
for attitude

WHEN presenting an opinion, you need to know much more about the listener than when you are giving an explanation. You want the listener to do more than understand. You want the hearer to accept and, possibly, to act.

You should know something of the background of the listener. You should also be cognizant of his level of information. The analysis does not stop here, however. You should also know the listener's attitude toward your subject because you are proposing a specific opinion. Unless you have some definite ideas of the possible reaction of the auditor to your opinion, how can you present it effectively? Know your listener's attitude and you can adjust your presentation to gain the most satisfactory results under the particular circumstances. In other words, you need to know more about your listener in the speech of opinion. Information level knowledge is important but you also need to know the listener's attitude.

To simplify this analysis, you can first assign one of three general classifications—friendly, indifferent, or hostile—to the listener. Knowing the listener belongs to one of these three groups will assist you in meeting the speaking situation. Second, you must evaluate the state of knowledge of each classification as follows:

LISTENER ANALYSIS
SPEECH OF OPINION

Listener Classification	State of Knowledge		
Friendly	Uninformed	Informed	Generally Informed
Indifferent	Uninformed	Informed	Generally Informed
Hostile	Uninformed	Informed	Generally Informed

Is the friendly listener *uninformed, informed,* or *generally informed?* You also ask this same question about the indifferent and hostile listeners. Thereby, you will be better equipped to adjust to each different circumstance.

Friendly listener

THE FRIENDLY LISTENER presents the least difficulty to a speaker. The listener is already amenable to the position of the speaker, and, therefore, acceptance is generally assured under such circumstances. No unique barriers exist. However, this does not mean you can be lax in the preparation and presentation of the topic. You must still fulfill the requirements of effective communication. Just because a Republican speaks to Republicans on Republican matters does not ensure success. As always, there still is the matter of the state of information of the listener.

The uninformed-friendly listener requires special attention. You need to explain the topic to pave the way for a true appreciation of your opinion. Even though there is no objection to your opinion, it can only be fully understood and really accepted after you have imparted the background details. You only waste your opinion on a listener who has no comprehension of the subject.

> Someone once referred to a union as a brotherhood of working men and this is so true. We are much like a family. We live together Monday through Friday. We eat together five days a week. And most important, our family fights together for the good of all our brothers. However, something has been happening to our family and we have not been fully aware of it. If we don't take immediate action today, our union will cease being a family of brothers and instead become a group of distant cousins.

The problem began five years ago at the Chicago convention. . . . (review background)

The informed-friendly listener usually alleviates the need for detailed explanatory material. Therefore, it is a prudent speaker who always interprets and defines his position to ensure complete understanding. After doing this, he can proceed to the opinion by maintaining the interest of informed auditors with stimulating content and logic.

Poverty exists among our people. Poverty is apparent in our city. We don't like what we see. We are all concerned with this most urgent of social problems because we know that poverty is like a decay and can destroy our city economically, socially, and morally. We must act immediately to prevent a blight upon our city. But, the question is—Where do we begin? Well, we can begin by examining the specific forms of poverty and their causes. Then, and only then, can we plot a direct course of action.

For the past year I have worked with the Social Welfare Department in the poverty areas. During this period a number of rather unique situations presented themselves and have become the basis for our new plan of attack on poverty. . . . (interpret the problem)

The generally-informed friendly listener calls for a review of the subject before you reveal the opinion. Refresh listener knowledge on the subject, correct any misinformation, add new details, and then, you have the hearer prepared for the opinion.

We need a new high school. We are in complete agreement on this. For forty-five years, we have lived with our present high school. Our fathers went to this school. We attended the same school. Now our children are forced to study in an archaic building unfit for modern education. Let us reminisce for a moment by taking a mental tour of our old school. How does it compare with the educational needs of today? . . . (refresh listener knowledge)

Although you are speaking to a friendly listener, there is little point to present ideas they have already accepted. However, you may have a new or different approach to the subject and, perhaps, your expression of the opinion can strengthen its soundness. Whatever the case, you should make an effort to present an intelligent, logical speech if

195

for no other reason than to reflect upon your ability as a thinker and a speaker.

In this speaking situation, you can make greater use of an emotional delivery than is often possible. It is a homogeneous speaker-listener relationship and a spirited presentation is usually welcomed. The listener does not suspect you are trying to sway him with clever eloquence. In fact, a highly animated presentation with vivid language usually heightens the effect. Your analysis of the speaking situation will determine what degree of animation is permissible.

The friendly listener generally offers a pleasant speaking situation but because all agree to the same opinion there can be the danger of oversimplification. Therefore, the truly effective speaker prepares his speech to interest and to stimulate the listener.

Indifferent listener

A SPEAKER DOES NOT ALWAYS have the opportunity of addressing supporters of his opinion. There are occasions when the listener is indifferent to the subject, the opinion, or both. If this is the situation, you have problems which require adaptation.

First, a lack of interest for the subject poses a challenge. The listener must be stimulated immediately. It is essential for you to emphasize the significance of the topic to the listener. Otherwise, the lethargy of the hearer will remain. In effect, the listener says to himself: "Who cares?" You must give him the reasons to care. If you have none, perhaps the listener is justified in having an indifferent attitude. If this is true, there is no need for you, the speaker. However, you are making an address and undoubtedly you have a reason for speaking and a cause for the listener to hear. It is up to you to activate listener interest before moving on to an opinion.

Two nights ago, a young fellow and his girl friend were speeding home from a late date. Suddenly, as they rounded a corner, there was another car moving much slower ahead of them. There was time to slow down but the young man's reflexes were numbed from drinking. In a flash, the morgue had been given two more broken bodies. Last week it was the same story. Drunk driving and the death of four young teenagers were chalked up on the scoreboard.

So far this year, we have recorded a dozen deaths and thirty-seven injuries among our sons and daughters.

Our sons and daughters? No, not mine. He's a good boy. He'd never drink and drive. And so, in a couple of quick words, you dismiss the whole sickening matter. You, the parents, turn your backs on teen drinking. And yet, some night when the death patrol rings your bell you'll sob: "Why me? Where did I fail?" I'll give you the answer. You failed because you don't care right now!

Second, any indifference toward your opinion obviously does not advance effective communication. Therefore, you must state reasons for listener interest and concern with the opinion you are presenting. In most cases, you cannot be subtle and you can never expect the listener to awaken his own interest. Your role as the speaker requires you to show cause for listener attention. Be specific and direct. Break down the barrier of indifference by pointing to the value or importance of your opinion and its significance to the hearer. If you give the hearer reasons for listening to your opinion, he will be attentive.

If I were to announce that I wanted to give my views on space travel, you would probably say: "Who cares?" Furthermore, I wouldn't blame you. Or if I wanted to tell you what I thought about the future of mankind, you would be bored. I don't blame you. Suppose I gave you my thoughts on how to make our town a better place. Again your reaction would probably be indifference. But, this time I do blame you. I blame you for the very indifference that has caused our home to become a decadent village of the dark ages. A feudal town of "Who cares?"—of boredom and of indifference. We yawn at suggestions instead of listening earnestly for ideas that can become keys to a modern future for our home. . . .

Third, it is still important to consider the degree of familiarity of the listener to the subject. If there is a lack of information on the subject, you must provide it. If the listener is only generally informed, give specific details. In either of these two situations, it is possible the hearer "thinks" he knows more than he really does. This could be the cause of his indifference. Be on the lookout for this when analyzing the speaking situation. If you find it, prepare your speech to correct it.

Another difficulty can arise with the well-informed, indifferent listener. He may consider both the subject and the opinion to be commonplace and no longer worthy of his attention. This is particularly true if the subject has been discussed a great deal. You need a fresh approach or new materials to combat this type of indifference. You should draw a direct line between the matter under discussion and the listener. First, re-awaken the listener's concern with the topic and then direct his interest toward the opinion.

> "How to sell." "How to be a top salesman." "Selling can be easy." "Tricks to selling." Selling! Selling! Selling! How many, many times have we been told how to do our job. We are lectured on selling. We are told to read about selling. All kinds of expert advice is thrown our way. And yet, who actually does the selling? We do! Not the experts. Why do we bother to listen? As one of those "experts," I must admit that there is a good argument here. But, then again, how many of you are completely satisfied with your record? Are you 100% successful? Can you sell anything? To anyone? Maybe there is something to all this advice. Maybe there is a point or two that can be learned from an "expert," particularly if this expert can really sell his own product—selling.

In confronting an inanimate listener do not be inanimate yourself. This is the time to have a stimulating delivery. You must have a vital presentation to give impact to your thoughts. This, alone, can do much to capture the interest of the hearer.

The indifferent listener does not always present a hopeless situation. Specific adaptation and stimulating presentation are the keys to effective communication here.

Hostile listener

FINALLY THERE IS the hostile listener and he presents the most difficult situation for a speaker. He opposes your opinion, possibly your subject, and probably even you, the speaker. This is a real challenge. Therefore, your primary goal must be to determine the direction—the opinion, the subject, or the speaker—of the listener's hostility.

When there is hostility toward your opinion, concentrate first on gaining respect for your opinion. If the listener accepts your opinion to be an intelligent one, you have, undoubtedly, been as successful as possible. If a listener has his own firmly-set opinion, there is little you can do to change it. Only the individual listener himself can alter a predisposed belief. All a speaker can hope to achieve under such circumstances is to have the listener recognize an opinion as being well-founded.

Not too long ago a neighbor and I were chatting about the new baseball season just ahead. In the course of our casual discussion, I mentioned that I thought the Giants would win the National League pennant. Well, I knew my friend was a Dodger fan, but I still wasn't prepared for what followed. He immediately jumped to the defensive. With face flushed and eyes blazing, he proceeded to tell me how stupid I was to have such an opinion. For nearly fifteen minutes he attacked my comment. Fortunately a phone call broke up our discussion. Did I say discussion? I had given one simple opinion while he did all the rest of the talking. He hadn't even bothered to inquire about the why's of my opinion. Maybe if he had, he would have had a better understanding of how someone could reach a conclusion different from his own. Possibly, he may have even found additional reasons for his own beliefs.

Well, we are not here to discuss baseball. However, by hearing the reasons behind *my* opinion, you may possibly add to *your* collection of reasons for the other side.

Trying to force acceptance of an opinion will only increase hostility. You should instead present the substance of the speech with clear logic and with rationality. Moreover, you may even plant the seed of change in the listener.

On the other hand, if the listener directs his unfriendly attitude toward the speech subject, you should find the cause before starting your speech. Often such hostility stems from listener prejudice toward the subject. Since prejudice usually arises from a lack of knowledge and sound reasoning, you can circumvent the problem by doing for the listener what he has not done for himself. Informative explanation presented as a 'matter of intellectual concern can slip by listener hostility. Therefore, lay a foundation of information before going on to an opinion. By then, the listener may be ready to hear your thoughts on the subject.

All of us are vitally involved in the success of our corporation. Therefore, I am sure the financial report which I am about to present will be most impressive. First, total sales for the company during the second quarter were nearly $300,000. Second, sales during this period were up 16% over the record sales of the first quarter. Third, the research department has developed a new process of packaging which will save the company nearly $50,000 each year in labor costs. Fourth, stock value has risen $38 a share in the past eighteen months.

Quite a financial record isn't it? No, it is not the report of our company. It was that of Miller and Sons, the company which you have refused even to discuss for possible merger.

Finally, when the hostility is directed toward you, the speaker, patience is needed. You immediately introduce the speech subject as a purely academic matter needing consideration from all points of view.

Today, among the complexities and problems of the nuclear age, a single man is a rather insignificant creature. One man in a world of involvements is merely a speck of sand slushed around by the surf of a tumultuous time. Remove that speck of mankind and nothing is lost. Throw him into the tide of humanity and he passes unnoticed. Today, it isn't the man that is of concern. It is the ideas of the man. Right or wrong, sound or unsound, it is the thinking of each single man that shapes the future of the mass of men. Take away one man's thoughts and you lose from every man. One idea from one man is the cornerstone to progress, for as the single idea sifts through the minds of others we ultimately reach a course of action which is best for all men. And so it is that I come before you, not as a single man, but as an idea. An idea from which you will do the sifting.

Let this be your guide for establishing an image of objectivity. Be specific in detail. Be sound in reasoning. Make these two characteristics evident to the listener. In this way, you try to lessen personal hostility and gain respect.

When confronted with any hostility, a speaker should immediately determine the state of the listener's information. A difference here has a direct effect upon the approach to the situation.

Hostility from the uninformed and, often, the generally informed is usually emotional. Since this listener has limited knowledge of the subject, it is virtually impossible for the unfriendly attitude to be intelligently founded. If you can pierce the emotionalism of this hearer with logic and information, your chances for successful communication are increased. Although this is often quite difficult, you must make the attempt by revealing to the listener your complete process of reasoning from the substantial information available. Lead him through your thinking process, step by step. Avoid leaving anything to the listener's imagination. *You* do his thinking. It is like a teaching situation. You are the instructor and the listener is the student. Let him see how you thought through the subject and reached a conclusion. If all goes well, the listener will be enlightened by your teaching and may possibly accept your opinion.

Hostility from the well-informed listener presents a more challenging problem. He has reasons for an opposing opinion. You, the speaker, must discover the specific points of conflict causing the hostility. Furthermore, you must do it before entering the speaking situation. Failure to do this could be most unfortunate for you.

Once you know the main points of conflict, your presentation can be adapted to resolve the problem. Use an objective approach. Openly recognize the opinion of this hostile listener and the reasons for it. Let the listener know you are familiar with his thinking on the subject. However, instead of launching into your reasons for a differing opinion, continue the objective method and review the entire subject from the very beginning. Show overt impartiality to any particular view. Simply lead the listener through a re-examination of the issue. You are then free to explain the means by which your opinion was reached. Be specific and interpret all main points leading to your belief.

The demonstration of objectivity in the formation of your opinion may help the well-informed listener to recognize its qualities. This method can gain respect for you, the speaker. When the hearer views you in this light, he will listen attentively and probably even respect for your opinion will follow.

In this situation, your delivery should obviously be restrained, employing only quiet animation. Emotionalism would only seem to indicate the subjectivity of content. Your main concentration should be clarity of expression.

To face a hostile listener is difficult but there is hope of effective communication. Do not fight hostility with more hostility. Use the opposite approach. Emphasize sound, knowledgeable ideas which point clearly and logically to your opinion. Be confident, be objective, and be intelligent.

E xpressing an opinion goes beyond the usual bounds of communication. It often involves the sensitivities of your listeners. Therefore, the need for precise adaptation to the hearer is greater. By careful listener analysis, the basis for the effective communication of the speech of opinion is achieved.

Step 1 | *Exercises ⁓ Assignments*

1. Listen to a speech on television or attend one in person. How did the speaker analyze his listeners for attitude? How do you know? In what way did he adjust his speech for these listeners?

2. Select a controversial subject which you might want to discuss before a group. Discuss how you would adjust your speech for the hostile, the friendly and the indifferent listener.

3. To determine if your listener-approaches in the preceding exercise will work, test them on the class. Let the class overtly react as the friendly, then the hostile, and finally the indifferent listening group on your instructions.

4. Just as an impromptu exercise before differing listener attitudes, have a member of the class leave the room and contemplate an opinion for presentation. During this time the class decides their reaction as listeners. Let the speaker enter and make his listener adjustment while speaking.

5. Prepare an "in-depth" survey of your class to discover their attitudes toward two controversial topics. The following list will serve as a guide to topics:
    Capital Punishment Should Be Abolished.
    Working Mothers Are Unfair to Children.
    World Federation Should Be Our Goal.
    Legalized Gambling Is a Cure for Crime.
    Censorship of Books Should Be Abolished.
    The Roots of Crime Are Found in the Home.
    Education Is "Wasted" on Too Many People.

Step 2

Recognize human motives

TODAY, we hear much about the "organization man," the "lonely crowd," the "status seeker," and the "pyramid climber." These phrases suggest man is susceptible to certain inducements to action. These inducements are variously titled motive appeals, human wants, human motivations, and psychological appeals. Since these factors do affect the thinking and actions of individuals, it is important to use them in the speech of opinion. Why? Because through motivational appeal, you may bring the listener into direct relationship with the special subject. You adapt to listener interests and thereby answer the question, "What does it have to do with me?"

After collecting background information on your listener, consider the appeals to human motives you can use to heighten the acceptability of your opinion. The choice depends largely upon the speech subject and the results of your listener analysis. The speaking situation, if adequately examined, should indicate the potential effectiveness of certain motive appeals. Make your selections carefully then use them for *each* main point. Take full advantage of your listener adaptation. The motivational appeal must continue throughout the communicating process and the listener must be fully aware of the significance of each main point.

Let us review the various types of human motivations. The ones listed here seem to satisfy the principal needs of most listeners but there can be others. Using your own discretion, think of other *specific* means of appealing to your particular listener. We will discuss the ones that are most common and have the greatest usage.

Self-preservation motive

THE URGE for self-preservation is a strong motive. We can see the evidence of this in the millions of dollars spent every year for health and safety. Vitamins and medicines fill the homes and stomachs of society. Schedules of medical practitioners are endless. Hospitals are filled to capacity. Television health programs are part of the daily routine. Athletic clubs have thriving membership lists. Manufacturers emphasize the safety of their products.

We are rarely allowed to forget the constant threat to life and limb. Holiday warnings predict the slaughter of human life. Summer bulletins warn of the dangers of swimming, boating, and camping. Winter brings more admonitions regarding driving, skiing, and hunting. Signs appear everywhere pleading for caution in everything we do. Is it any wonder we are concerned with self-preservation?

How is this human motive used in the speech of opinion? Be direct and point to the specific value of your opinion for maintaining self-preservation. For instance, a vitamin company advertises that one pill a day will keep you sound of health. Failure to swallow 365 tablets a year can produce some mysterious and dire consequence. The vitamin company is of the opinion its product is beneficial to the public. However, it knows the mere listing of ingredients does not insure acceptance. Therefore, a specific appeal is made to the listener's concern with self-preservation.

In voicing the need for increased town expenditures for snow removal, you could include self-preservation as one of your reasoned appeals:

What is it like driving home from work in a snow storm? Is it safe with our present limited snow removal situation? Of course it isn't. Several inches of snow cover the roads. Even with snow tires, our cars continually slide about the street. Speed up the car and you skid broadside into the oncoming traffic. Apply the brakes and you skid helplessly straight into the rear of the next car. Steel crashes against steel. Flesh and bones are thrown hopelessly about the interior. Shattered glass and jagged metal mix with spilled blood and cracked bones. At any moment, any one of us could be that victim in the ambulance with the wailing siren. We always think it only happens to the other fellow. To the other fellow! Are we going to condone needless pain and grief just to save money on snow equipment? How would you vote if you *were* the other fellow?

Anyone who has an opinion involving the well-being of the listeners uses the same approach: "Accept my opinion and self-preservation will be maintained." This is the underlying thought behind an appeal to the human motive of self-preservation.

Social acceptance motive

WE LIVE in groups, and as gregarious individuals, we naturally seek the approval of our fellow men. As a result, what is considered acceptable controls our thinking and our actions. This human motivation directly affects our social activities, the purchases we make, the ideas we have, and our behavior. Obviously, it is an important consideration for the speech of opinion.

Our standards are set not only by society-at-large but also by the smaller, more intimate, immediate group. We want to be accepted, and therefore make an effort to avoid offending the standards of our associates. We do and think as the group dictates. If our "special" group belongs to the country club, we join too. If the group drives a medium-priced automobile, so do we. If the group supports the Republican party, we become Republicans. If the group favors federal aid to farmers, we follow suit. To oppose the norms of the group makes us outsiders. The degree, of course, depends upon the seriousness of the infraction of acceptable action. As the group changes, we change.

When an individual moves from one group to another, there is concern with new standards. We see this in the case of the businessman moving up through the ranks. His behavior differs with each new promotion. He adopts the ways of the new group. He originally belonged to the company bowling team but then came a promotion to executive status. Bowling was no longer accepted. It was time to become a member of the athletic club for professional persons. Times and groups had changed.

In the preparation of the speech of opinion, you must take into account the social acceptability of the ideas you will express. This applies not only just to you, the speaker, but more importantly to the listener. Will the listener recognize that your opinion meets the approval of his peer group? You need to consider this. You need to explain this.

> Twenty years ago we believed a woman's place was only in the home. A girl began learning the duties of a housewife while practically in the cradle. If she happened to graduate from high school, she was expected to marry almost immediately and settle down to a life of dishes and diapers. Our society accepted this as a natural way of life. Although it doesn't seem like such a long time ago, we all know times have changed considerably.
>
> Today, our daughters go away to college, attend graduate and professional schools, enter business and professional occupations, and go to foreign lands for the government. Today's young woman thinks on international terms instead of just dishes and diapers. What we must always remember is that our modern society accepts this active woman-of-the-world. Our society expects our daughters to play an integral part in the nation's activities. Our complex society needs our daughters. One of the places our daughters can serve our nation honorably is in the Women's Army Corps.

Once you have examined the speaking situation, determine the group norms of the listeners and then adapt your content to meet their requirements. Explain how *each* main point of the opinion satisfies the group and, thereby, is socially acceptable. Before the hearer can agree with your opinion, you must make it clear that no breach of acceptability exists. This is the speaker's responsibility.

Prestige motive

Do WE seek prestige? To become someone special? To do something special? If we were to judge by the advertising we hear and read, it would appear so. Smoke a certain cigarette and turn into a "real" man. Drink a special beverage and become a movie star. Drive a super sports car and become the hero of the block. In effect, what the advertiser is really saying is that the listener will gain prestige by using its product. Truly a tempting offer!

Amid all the accusations that man tends to conform and settle within a group, there is still the urge to attain some special status within the chosen group. There are prestige schools and colleges, neighborhoods, shopping areas, and organizations. Pages could be filled with a listing of the prestigious. Because it is significant, you must take the prestige factor into account when presenting the speech of opinion.

Offer the listener a reward for accepting your opinion. Describe the type of return whether it is a simple feeling of kindness or increased recognition among others. The charitable organization gives no concrete return to those who lend but only offers the prestige feeling of doing something worthwhile. The university promises no special reward to contributing alumni other than the knowledge that they have helped. There are other cases, however, which give special prestige recognition ranging from citations to the overt admiration of the group members. In all these instances, the individual finds reward in prestige The following speech, asking for a cultural center, demonstrates the appeal to prestige.

> Just think what a cultural center would bring to our community. A symbol of our interest in the arts—ballet, opera, and theater. A reality to prove we do not merely talk of advancing our home but that we take constructive, positive steps for cultural development. An inspiration to our young people maturing in the atmosphere of the fine arts. An inspiration which will invade the entire community with its uplifting spirit. By constructing the cultural center, we would feel the reward of prestige for it is *our* center. Our city would gain prestige as the cultural center of the state.

In this illustration you can see that we are asking for a cultural center. However, we also hold out the additional reward of prestige for our city.

When planning the speech of opinion, you must consider if there is some element of prestige to offer the listener in return for his acceptance of your proposal. Will it make him feel more important? Will others look at him with greater admiration? These are the factors you must answer for the listener.

Power motive

THE URGE to exert influence over others is a compelling motivation. While prestige brings the respect or admiration of others, power means the ability to influence them. Children playing games squabble over who is to be the head of the cowboys, the father of the family, or the teacher. The same type of competition continues as these same children grow to maturity. Each strives for a position with authority. Similarly, many adults seek to satisfy their power motive.

There are compromises to this particular human motivation. Once it becomes apparent there is no further advancement in the power structure, the individual compromises by accepting the position which has the least frustration. The businessman settles for the managership of a department. The educator goes to a small college to find his position as a dean. The actor turns to supporting roles on television. The politician accepts the nomination of vice-president. Each has compromised for the best possible position available. They may have superiors but they also have subordinates.

If your opinion contains the possibility of a power return, let the listener know it. It may be the key to the acceptance of your opinion. The school guidance counselor appeals to the power motive of the students. For instance, he may have the opinion a certain student should enter a vocational training school following graduation. However, the trend is toward college. What should he do in this situation? As he explains the advantages of a skilled trade, he includes those factors that will put the individual in a position of authority. Possessing this knowledge, the student is more likely to accept the opinion.

The union advocate uses the same appeal to the power motive in his membership drives:

> There's no sense kidding yourselves. Just who do you think you are? *What* do you think you are? You're just one man out of hundreds. Do you understand that—one out of hundreds? What makes you think a single, lone worker can face the bosses on an equal footing? They are a united group with the money and the power to back them. How do you compare? One man, one voice, one job and probably only one dollar in the bank. Not much of a threat to anyone—except, maybe, to yourself. What do you think will happen if you go to the bosses alone and demand more money? Or longer vacations? Or better conditions? You might as well demand to be the president! You are just one!

Now what does a union offer you? The union offers you equality with management. Together it means hundreds of voices, hundreds of jobs, and hundreds of dollars. This also means the power to demand. The power to be heard and to be respected. It means the power to be a man! Your one vote can give you that power!

Although your listener may have already compromised the power motive, there is probably a spark still left. Strike it and watch the results. The thoughts of fulfilling the power drive, no matter how dim, can move a listener to acceptance.

Security motive

INSECURITY SEEMS TO BE a constant threat to man. It is like a trap door beneath him. There always appears to be some doubt about a completely secure life. We have banks to protect valuables, insurance to compensate for losses, unions to guard against unemployment, and pension funds to insure a comfortable old age. In these and other ways, we show our concern with security.

When a speaker can point to an opinion promoting the security of the listener, acceptance follows more easily. The insurance salesman has an opinion his insurance is best. In selling it, he emphasizes security to the buyer. The politician proposes legislation which, in his opinion, is beneficial to the security of the voter. The husband who wants to buy a new car meets the objections of his wife by stressing its greater security.

An appeal to the security motive can be worth a thousand words when seeking acceptance of an opinion.

Yes, what we propose is expensive. There's no denying that. But, what do we get for our money? Security! Security for the people of our city. The addition of special night patrols will mean we can rest more comfortably at night. No longer will we fear for our daughters' safety as they return home from the dance. No longer will there be fear for our sons after the night game. It will be safer for our wives to shop after dark. Men will be able to enjoy an evening stroll to the store. The adoption of a night patrol returns security to our lives.

Consider your listener. What forms of security would be most appealing to him? Think of your opinion. Are any of these items of security within the topic? When you find them, use them. Let the listener know how the acceptance of your opinion will ensure security, or increase it. The security motive is a strong drive among men. An effective speaker uses it to his best advantage.

Possession motive

THE DRIVE to acquire possessions is most common. The possession motive is especially apparent in an affluent society. Material wealth means comfort and achievement. If acceptance of an opinion means the acquisition of possessions, the speaker probably has listener support.

> Another justification for permitting the government to build a new airbase here is economic. And, I might add, perhaps the most important justification. Do you realize what the airbase can mean to our city—to us, in terms of financial gain! Who is going to construct the base? Our contractors using our supplies and employing our townsmen. Where will the military personnel live? In homes built by our town and apartments owned by our town. And where will these people spend their money? In our town! Who will service the base? Our town! What does all of this mean? Wages will go up. Profits will go up. In short, our town faces an economic boom!

Society has become accustomed to material possessions. To live comfortably in our society it is imperative that each individual have certain goods. We are used to the conveniences of many possessions. It would be difficult today to live without them. Man has an incentive to acquire all these so-called essential articles. Offer to satisfy a part of this drive in your speech of opinion and you gain acceptance more easily.

Material possessions also mean achievement. What successful person is without them? The possession of goods is a sign of accomplishment to many people. To be without them, therefore, is an indication of failure. Sometimes it appears the success of a person is in direct proportion to his possessions. Although this is obviously not true, there is some relationship between material wealth and achievement. When a person is successful, he is able to have more and better goods—providing success has also brought financial rewards. And though many successful persons are not fortunate enough to reap the benefits of a high economic position, material possessions still carry with them the idea of personal achievement.

The final significance of the possession motive is its importance for social status. Those who are socially prominent usually are rich in possessions. Therefore, to raise oneself socially, it is often assumed material goods must be acquired. Although wealth does not automatically bring social position, this implication does exist.

In the speech of opinion, you must decide if an appeal to the possession motive will stimulate or repel the listener. Either reaction is possible. Therefore, you must take particular care to analyze the listener for potential susceptibility to this specific human motive.

Pleasure motive

THE PLEASURE MOTIVE can be satisfied in any number of ways. It varies with the individual and the moment. It may be tending the flowers in a garden or simply sitting in a special chair. Then again, it could be climbing a treacherous mountain. Pleasure cannot be specifically classified. It can be anything and anywhere and, sometimes consume more energy than normal work.

A person looks for things that please him. If possible, he surrounds himself with all that is enjoyable. The pleasure motive, therefore, is stimulated by such promises. If a speech of opinion offers pleasure, who can resist? Of course, it must suit the particular listener. Remember, not all hearers have the same conception of this motive. Some like activity, while others prefer inactivity. To use this motive appeal effectively, you must channel the right motive to the listener. It is also wise to explain in some descriptive detail the specific pleasure resulting from the acceptance of the offered opinion. Let the pleasure palate sample the impending enjoyment.

> The addition of a swimming pool to your property does increase the real estate value. It does enhance a home's appearance. And it does add prestige. But, before thinking of these benefits there's one other reward. Pleasure!
> Creeping home in the sweltering heat of the afternoon rush hour, husbands, knowing that before too long they will be submerged in a cool, blissful pool, can forget their irritation. Wives will play at housework for they can renew their spirits by frequent

relaxing dips in their own backyard. The children will enjoy an endless summer holiday right at home. No more stifling trips to the beach. No more weekend sunburns. No more summer discomfort. Just cool fun in your own pool right at home. Summer will be fun again!

There are times when a listener might reject an offered pleasure. Not because there is a lack of appreciation or understanding, but because the listener believes there is no justification for his acceptance of it. Therefore, the speaker should include reasons why the listener should accept the pleasure.

Welfare-for-others motive

MAN IS a gregarious being. As such, he has concern for the members of his group. This is the welfare-for-others motive. The reality of this motive is seen throughout history. Man enters combat to safeguard the group. He supports with loyalty, time, and contributions the government of the group. He dedicates his life to advance the health of the group. He risks his life to further the group's knowledge. It is truly a powerful motive spurring many persons to action.

By an appeal to the welfare-for-others motive, the listener can be moved to make contributions. Think of the numerous charitable organizations existing in this country. They help the poor, the infirmed, and the orphaned. Medical research institutions, expecting no profit in return, struggle to solve the problems of all men. Social clubs spend much time making the community a more enjoyable place for the unfortunate. Case after case can be cited in which man gives of himself without thought of repayment. His only interest is the betterment of the whole group.

It is true that the flood has not affected us—at least not directly. We have had no damage to our city. Our homes are untouched. Our children can still go to school and play in the park. We go to work as usual. Our plates are full. Our clothes are warm. Our beds are comfortable.

But what about the flood victims downstate? What is it like to return to homes buried in mud? Clothing lost to the waters? Beds saturated with river silt? Schools and businesses closed? When will

212

they be able to enjoy a home-cooked meal again? When will they be able to laugh again?

No, we haven't been affected directly but we are involved. We know it is our duty to aid our neighbors in this crisis. None of us will be able to face another day of normal pleasures if we do not help those unfortunate families. That is why we are here tonight.

In the speech of opinion, the welfare motive can have a strong effect. Accurate description of how it affects the welfare of others can move the listener to quick recognition of the merits of support for your opinion.

Human motives are an integral part of the effective speech of opinion. Know your listener and, through an appeal to his natural inclinations, spur him to acceptance.

Step 2 | *Exercises* ∽ *Assignments*

1. As a discussion project, prepare yourself to agree or disagree with the contention that human motives are an important factor in gaining acceptance. Do you believe all of the motives in the preceding materials are realistic? As part of your preparation recall any instances that show the motives in action or disprove them.

2. Collect samples of the different appeals to human motives used in magazines and newspapers. Do the members of the class believe the appeals are effective?

3. Watch the commercials on television. Do they use human motive appeals? If so, carefully record the type and its use. Compare your findings with those of the class.

4. Discuss the use of human motive appeals with a salesman in your area. Does he use them consciously? When does he use them? How does he use them? Which does he find most effective?

5. Visit a sales training program in a department store, business concern, or school. Do they train their sales personnel in motive appeals? If so, which are dominant?

6. Select a cause or drive that is usually promoted in your town on a yearly basis (Community Chest, Heart Fund, Boy's Club, etc.). Prepare a short talk in support of the cause or drive in which you stress two major motive appeals.

7. Select an organization on campus. Study the appeals used to gain members. Report on this to the class.

8. Prepare a talk on the importance of studying speech. Use two major motive appeals.

9. Analyze several recent decisions that you made. What motive appeals were primary in influencing your judgment?

10. Select a specific product (automobiles, cigarettes, soap, gasoline, etc.). Report on the motive appeals used by the different manufacturers in trying to win your approval for their product rather than a competing product.

Step 3

Use psychological patterns

CONTENT development for the speech of opinion is basically the same as for the speech of explanation. However, because the objectives are different, the method of presenting content is slightly altered. When you were explaining, the basic aim was clarity of understanding. Now with the speech of opinion, you want, in addition, to stimulate the listener in a specific direction—consideration, agreement, or action. This you can do through selected psychological patterns of presentation.

The psychological approach is not really new. It is most apparent in the selling of commercial products when the advertiser appeals to us as "concerned persons," "special people," and sometimes even as "discriminating persons." The obvious aim of the seller is to give the potential buyer the feeling that he must purchase the item. By using psychological patterns, the advertiser brings about an atmosphere which increases the chances of listener acceptance of the product.

Generally, the same approach can be used in any speech of opinion. Your purpose is to gain at least consideration of the opinion. Therefore, you want to present the speech in a manner to bring about this end. It is the time to use the psychological patterns. If there is consideration, then the chances of intellectual acceptance are increased. Let us look at some of these patterns.

Common ground

THE POLITICIAN constantly uses the common-ground pattern. He talks as if he and the listener belong to the same group. They are equals. It is not a case of leader and follower, but rather of individuals working side-by-side for the good of one another. This effective politician speaks of common problems and experiences in common terms. He bridges the gap between speaker and listener with the personal method of presentation. As a result, each listener feels that the speaker is talking directly to him about their common problems. This is successful communication.

Just a few days ago my son came to me with his plans to attend the state university. He wants to be an engineer. He's not the best student in his senior class but his grades are good enough to get accepted. Naturally, I want my son to get a college education just as the rest of you want your sons and daughters to get the education they deserve. But, what can I say to him? What can you say to your children? We all know the situation at our university. No room! We pay taxes to support a state university for our children and when the time comes—there's no room!

Do you realize that over three hundred of our sons and daughters are turned away from the university every year? What can we parents say to these poor kids? Sorry! Better forget all your plans and dreams?

Well I'm not going to let it happen to my son. And I'm not going to let it happen to your children. I'm tired of all those campaign promises of expansion, then nothing is done. What we need in the legislature is someone who will make sure all our sons and daughters have the chance for a college education. If these politicians can't do the job, then let a concerned father do it!

Escape hatch

A SPEAKER PRESENTING a speech of opinion necessarily takes into account the possibility the listener already has a different view. This is determined by an investigation of the speaking situation. Although the listener may recognize the truth of your opinion, he may be reluctant to change his opinion to the one you offer for fear of being a hypocrite to his earlier conviction. The answer to this problem is the "escape hatch." With this method, *you* provide the listener with the rationale for changing his mind while giving him reasons why there can be an acceptance of a new opinion.

The Nazi leaders used the escape-hatch technique often during their rule in Germany. For instance, when they were re-arming Germany, they used the argument that Germany was being threatened by her neighbors. Thus, they established a need for a change in her anti-military expansion position. They had opened the hatch for a change of opinion.

Fortunately such extreme instances of the escape-hatch technique do not happen too often. However, quite frequently, we do find this method being used for more common matters. Take, for instance, the dealer in expensive automobiles. When the salesman approaches a customer who should purchase a more moderately-priced car, he carefully provides an excuse for buying the more costly car. He talks of quality, durability, and long range economy, and points out that the car would be an "investment." Nothing is said of the conspicuous extravagance of the automobile or of wanting to impress the neighbors since this would only support the buyer's original opinion. The rationalization of the purpose provides the escape hatch.

The psychology of escapism is important in the speech of opinion. Careful analysis of the listener can reveal possible opinions contrary to those in the speech. Even when none are apparent it is still wise to provide escape hatches.

Hindsight

HINDSIGHT IS THE ACT of looking back upon a completed act and criticizing it. When compared to offering a new idea, hindsight is easy. In reviewing a battle, anyone can find the "obvious" mistakes of the generals. One look at a recent political campaign and the causes for defeat are visible to all. After seeing a film of a championship boxing match, we wonder why the loser made such apparent mistakes. Everytime we look at something already finished, we are all astute critics.

In the speech of opinion, the speaker can use hindsight to good advantage. The political arena is an obvious place to find the technique of retrospection. A Democrat is in office. A Republican challenges in an election. How does the Republican campaign? He uses hindsight. He enumerates with elaborate detail the mistakes of the officeholder. He points to "obvious" errors in judgment. He "brilliantly" reveals how he would have handled the matters if in office. Before the Republican contender has completed his criticism, it appears that the man in office is far inferior to the challenger. Thus, without giving any positive evidence of his own capabilities, this office seeker has established himself as a competent man for the job. Hindsight has given weight to the opinion.

Hindsight draws listener attention to the failings or weaknesses of a completed act. Therefore, the soundness of a proposed opinion is automatically heightened. Although it should not be used in place of specific evidence, hindsight is a psychological device which can make a listener more receptive to your opinion.

Association

HOW OFTEN ARE conclusions reached from associated information rather than from specific facts? We have probably all known this to happen at one time or another. The young man who is judged by the company he keeps instead of by his own qualities. Or the idea that is evaluated by its source rather than on its own merits. You can easily recall any number of instances in which a decision was based solely on association. Association, because of its effect upon decision-making, can be a useful tool in the speech of opinion. The speaker can use it to imply a relationship. There are two principal versions of the pattern—word association and association by connection.

In *word association* you use selective language which *implies* a certain position. Examine the following three passages. Each contains the same substance but the meaning is changed through the use of word association.

First, the comment as it would appear with no effort to use any particular form of word association:

> The reason for presenting this committee with another suggestion from Mr. Williams is to further the efficiency and the productiveness of the group.

Now the wording is altered. Through the use of word association, the person offering the suggestion is placed in an unfavorable light:

The alleged reason for burdening this committee with still another unrequested suggestion from Mr. Williams is supposedly to correct the alleged inefficiency and unproductiveness of this time-established group.

Finally, the same passage can have its implication completely changed by favorable word association:

The sincere reason for assisting this committee with another contribution from Mr. Williams is to help in lightening the burden of our recognized efficient and productive group.

In each of the above instances, the meaning of the passage was decidedly changed by language. When a speaker is offering an opinion for acceptance, the effect of word association can be easily imagined.

In association by *connection,* the points of speaking are joined to those items having qualities you want to *imply* instead of stating directly. The listener transfers the characteristics of one to the other. Again, the implication can be favorable or unfavorable.

In the following instances, favorable and unfavorable qualities are given to three different items simply through association by connection:

INDIVIDUAL:

Favorable: The dignified behavior of the young boy was reminiscent of the age of aristocratic refinement.

Unfavorable: From the dictatorial attitude of the chairman one would think Hitler had been reborn.

IDEA:

Favorable: The proposed solution to our water shortage must have been the result of Socratic contemplation.

Unfavorable: My idea of an enjoyable pastime is that which strengthens the mind not the pagan worship of the muscles.

219

OBJECT:

Favorable: Our new floor tile is an anvil of strength and durability.

Unfavorable: My competitor offers to you a product which is a pigmy among giants.

Praise

JUST BECAUSE IT IS sometimes said, "flattery will get you nowhere," do not overlook its possibilities in gaining consideration for your opinion.

There is no need for me to appeal to your sense of patriotism. You are all devoted Americans. Your country comes before any personal considerations. I know that you are the type to respect any man's freedom to speak and to be heard.

If used with tact, praise can remind the hearer of his obligations as a listener. In the above illustration, the listener was reminded that the speaker should be heard. Depending on the listening group and the speech subject, you might appeal to such things as the hearer's intelligence, loyalty, love, objectivity, or community concern. You may appeal through words of praise to numerous listener attributes. You may, thereby, increase attention and gain greater consideration toward your speech.

Conformity

RELATED TO THE common-ground pattern, conformity appears in many forms. We all like to belong. Man is a gregarious creature and needs others.

One pattern, labeled "bandwagon," uses this need for conformity. This approach is used in the following:

The best seller this year is the X brand of car. Join the crowd in on the know. Buy the X and join the in group.

∽ ∽ ∽

More people are switching to Y cigarettes. Sooner or later you are bound to join those who enjoy a satisfying smoke. Why not join the switchers?

∽ ∽ ∽

We must consider the town-manager form of government for our town. Studies show that more than three-quarters of the towns of our size have adopted a town-manager system.

∽ ∽ ∽

Public opinion polls show strong support for our plan. Over the past three years more than 75 per cent of those responding have indicated agreement with our proposal.

Non-conformity

IN CONTRAST TO man's desire to be one of the group, to belong, and to be accepted, you also find that some respond to the call to be different, to be in the forefront of change, and to be exclusive. The following illustrates the patterns used in motivating such listeners:

Don't follow the crowd. Be different. This year vacation at Hideaway. This spot is uncrowded and off the beaten path. Come to the undiscovered vacation paradise. Be exclusive this year.

∽ ∽ ∽

This year we will produce less than 5000 cars of this type. If you are the kind of person who dislikes the ordinary, looks for the unusual, we are interested in you.

∽ ∽ ∽

It is true that only a few other colleges have adopted the pass-fail system of grading. Do we need to play the game of follow the crowd? I say no! Let us take a step forward and show the way.

∽ ∽ ∽

All great changes in thinking, in acting, and in producing have been the result of the few brave souls who said, "There must be a better way." I say that we must step out of our acceptance of the *status quo* and move ahead.

∽ ∽ ∽

Are you the man who always does the usual? Why not take the chance and step out of the group? Remember we recognize leaders because they are ahead, not with, the crowd.

No alternative

ANOTHER USEFUL psychological pattern is the "no alternative" system. In this case you show the listener that you have explored the alternatives and in your considered opinion there is no acceptable alternative. This pattern is sometimes identified as "all or nothing" or "do or die." Perhaps the most famous example is Patrick Henry's line of reasoning that ends, "I know not what course others may take, but as for me, give me liberty, or give me death!"

Here are other illustrations of this pattern:

> The opposition says the death penalty has a deterrent value. There is no evidence to support this opinion. They also say the number of murders will rise if we abolish the death penalty. The experience of states and nations which have already abolished it does not prove this out. I say that we have no alternative except to follow the path of enlightenment and abolish this uncivilized act.

∽ ∽ ∽

> If we withdraw from this program we will lose the support of those nations who are with us. If we diminish the program we cut its effectiveness. We have no reasonable alternative except to support our international commitment.

You need a word of caution here. Do not consider these psychological patterns as substitutes for reasoned, researched, and evidenced opinions. We are suggesting that an understanding of these patterns may help you motivate listeners in the direction of considering your opinion. These psychological patterns and the previous section on motive appeals are necessary for your understanding of human behavior patterns.

Psychological patterns are an integral element of the speech of opinion. Consideration of opinion is more quickly obtained from a listener who feels the urge to react favorably. We need to add a word of caution to those who would substitute psychological patterns for reasoning and evidence. Remember these patterns are useful in gaining consideration. You need to be sure that your opinion has the solid ground of reasoning and evidence.

222

Step 3 | Exercises ∽ Assignments

1. Bring in examples of the psychological appeals used in newspaper and magazine advertising. Do you think they are effective?

2. Make a special visit to a business which relies heavily upon salesmanship—auto, furniture, appliance, jewelry store. Act as a potential customer, but one who plans to buy later. Let the salesman do all the talking while you act hesitant. Make note of any psychological appeals used and report the experience to your own group.

3. Examine a psychology book on the use of psychological appeals to gain consideration or acceptance of an opinion. How effective does the author believe them to be? Does he have any others which can be useful?

4. Examine the speech of a political demagogue or propagandist. Report to the class the psychological appeals used. Would they be effective on the class?

5. Study several speeches by a single speaker and identify the major appeals used.

6. Prepare a speech in which you use one major psychological pattern. Redo the speech with another psychological appeal. Ask the class to rank the effectiveness of the two patterns.

7. Select a magazine that has wide appeal. Study the advertisements in a single issue and classify the types of appeal or psychological patterns used.

8. Select the psychological pattern that best fits one of the following speech topics and present a short speech using this pattern:

    We Should Withdraw from the United Nations.

    The United Nations Should Establish an International Police Force.

    Medicare Should be Extended to All.

    Public Speaking Should Be a Required Course of Study.

    Service in the Peace Corps Should Be Accepted as an Alternative to Military Service.

    Cigarette Smoking Should Be Prohibited by Law.

Step 4

Structure into organized-reasoned patterns

IN the speech of opinion, the organization is most effective if it follows a logical pattern of reasoning. However, you need more than just the specific items of content to gain listener consideration of your opinion. You must answer two questions in the speech of opinion. What is the basis for the opinion? How was the opinion reached?

The first question asks for specific items of content. Just as you did in the speech of explanation, you use example, testimony, definition, statistics, comparison, contrast, repetition, and restatement in the speech of opinion.

The second question applies *specifically* to the speech of opinion. You show how you analyzed the topic and reached your concluding opinion. In simple explanation, clarity of arrangement was sufficient. However, in the speech of opinion you must trace your method of thinking for the listener. You are actually thinking out loud before an audience. It is only by the organization of your materials into a reasoning pattern that the listener can understand how you formed the opinion. It also helps the hearer to think through the topic in the same way.

The introduction

USUALLY, THE INTRODUCTION for the speech of opinion employs the same methods used for explanation—central idea, rhetorical question, partition, background, dramatic statement, striking facts, personal experience, and quotation. Generally, the purpose of the introduction is also the same—to gain attention and interest. However, there is one situation imposing an additional requirement upon the introduction of an opinion speech. In speaking to the *hostile* listener, you will need to *conciliate.*

In your analysis of the speaking situation, you classified the listener as friendly, indifferent, or hostile. No unusual problem exists in the first two cases. However, the hostile listener demands special consideration. Since this type of auditor is unfriendly right from the very beginning, he is not listening objectively. Therefore, you must find a means of conciliation.

There are three approaches to introducing an opinion to the unfriendly listener—acknowledgment of hostility, comparison of attitudes, and review of listener opinion.

By acknowledging in your introduction the existence of the hostility, you appear both realistic and objective. You also satisfy listener demand for recognition and, thereby, may have a calming effect upon the hearer. Once the hostility is brought out into the open for all to see, you can then appeal to the more rational qualities of the hearer for consideration. In effect, you are saying: "I know you are opposed to me, but give me a chance to express my feelings on the matter."

If you compare the opposing attitudes immediately in the introduction, you quickly reveal your objective understanding of the problem you face. You are also able to explain your personal feelings on the subject under discussion while you emphasize the similarities with those of the listener. It may be possible to make the listener realize that although you and he have differing opinions you both have the same purpose.

You naturally gain interest by reviewing the main points of the opposing listener opinion in the introduction. No hostility will be shown when you state the opinion belonging to the hearer. The listener is being recognized for his specific ideas and since he is listening to his own opinion, his attention is directed toward the speaker. The

225

listener's urge to express himself is also satisfied. Therefore, he is more apt to continue listening even after the introduction.

Introducing an opinion to the unfriendly listener has its problems. If you do it with forethought and tact, however, you can overcome the situation and possibly turn it to your advantage. Handle the circumstances with dignity and patience. Set an example for the hearer. If your appearance, actions, and words show intelligent concern rather than emotional display for the subject, the listener may do the same. Remember situations where you as a listener have turned speakers off because of their initial statements. It is important for you to open and then keep open the channels of communication. If the listener has closed his mind as a result of your introduction, the rest of the speech will be of no value.

The body

SOUND REASONING FROM specific information is required for the formation of an opinion whether you do it in public or in private. Therefore, to present an intelligent opinion to a listener, you must reveal both the content and the logic upon which your judgment is founded. To do this effectively, a speaker should first be familiar with the basic processes of thinking and with those variations used to adapt to the speaking situation.

Basic methods of reasoning

The two fundamental methods for logical reasoning are induction and deduction. Let us review these before going further.

INDUCTION-GENERALIZATION

The process of examining a number of particulars and drawing a general conclusion is known as inductive reasoning. The inductive thinker says: "Let me look at the facts first, then I can reach a conclusion."

The process of inductive reasoning occurs frequently as we make decisions. When buying an automobile, you gather information and then select the model best satisfying your needs. This is simply induction. It is used everyday.

Subject: Should I Buy the XX Brand Car?

I.   The XX brand car is in my price range.
II. The XX brand car is large enough for my family.
III. The XX brand car has government-approved safety features.
IV. The XX brand car is a good buy.

Generalization: The XX brand car is a good buy.

Subject: Is the XX Brand Car a Dependable Car?

I.   Mr. Jones, Alaskan postman, has had no trouble with this car in the past ten winters.
II. Mr. Smith, race car driver, has had no breakdowns in the past five years of racing with this car.
III. Dr. Winters has used this car in answering emergency calls at the hospital for the past seven years without a single incident of failure to perform.
IV. Mr. Summers, snowplow operator, has been able to report to the maintenance department during all the snow storms of the past eight years.

Generalization: XX brand car is a dependable car.

Although there is no guarantee that inductive thinking is always correct, the chances of success increase when you have substantial information for generalization. The greater the specific detail upon which the induction is founded, the more conclusive is the final judgment.

DEDUCTION

In the deductive method, you move through three steps:

1. Begin with a generally accepted opinion.
2. Give evidence that your opinion is included within that which is already accepted.
3. Conclude that your opinion thereby qualifies for acceptance.

Apply these steps to thinking and you can observe the many times we use deduction in practical purposes. Suppose, for example, we believe that our friend, Timothy Jones, is equal to all other men

227

simply because he is one of them. How could we prove this deductively? Merely follow the three steps above.

   I. All men are equal.
  II. Timothy Jones is a man.
 III. Therefore, he is equal to other men.

This particular pattern of reasoning, as organized above, is called a *syllogism*. Formally, the syllogism consists of three parts. First, the generally accepted point is the *major premise*. Second, the specific point asserted is the *minor premise*. Third, the final judgment is the *conclusion*. Use these labels and you can see the following syllogism is the same as our unlabeled method above:

Major Premise: All American citizens must obey the law.
Minor Premise: Bill Williams is an American citizen.
Conclusion: Therefore, he must obey the law.

Just as induction is a common method of reasoning, so too, is deduction. Although it may not be recognized as deduction, we often find ourselves applying such reasoning when we present an opinion for consideration. For example, if you were to give an opinion on the need for civil rights legislation for the American Indian, you might begin with a generally accepted principle, move on to a point of question, and then draw your conclusion. This would be deductive thinking as can be seen in your outline:

Subject: Should There Be Legislation to Protect the Civil Rights of the American Indian?

Major Premise: **I.** All citizens of the nation are given equal civil rights under the Constitution.
                  A. Constitutional provisions.
                  B. Legislative action.
                  C. Judicial decisions.
Minor Premise: **II.** The American Indian is a legal citizen.
                  A. Subject to laws of the community, state, and the nation.
                  B. Responsible to the same compulsory taxes and military service as everyone.

> **III.** However, the Indian does not have complete benefit of civil rights protection.
>   **A.** Economic unfairness.
>   **B.** Social injustice.

Conclusion: Therefore, Congress should pass that legislation which would enforce civil rights for the American Indian.

In using deductive reasoning, you must be sure to have correct premises. The major premise must be a true generalization. You must prove that the major premise qualifies as being within the major generalization. The conclusion most definitely needs to be accurate.

Most often errors in deduction result from a false major premise because it may be thought to be generally accepted. Notice how the following logic is twisted due to a fallacious major premise:

Major: All tall men are good basketball players.
Minor: Sam is a tall man.
Conclusion: Therefore, Sam is a good basketball player.

Actually, Sam might be too clumsy for basketball. It is best to substantiate each premise to be sure of your reasoning. If you are going to use deduction intelligently, use it honestly.

Induction and deduction are the essential means of reasoning through a subject toward a conclusion. In a speech of opinion, you may use either method when presenting your opinion to the listener.

Organizational patterns

Special circumstances call for the use of special organizational patterns. You will need to select the most appropriate method for organizing your *main points.*

CAUSAL ORGANIZATION

Causal organization is the process of showing an *alleged cause,* or a *probable effect.* Often called "cause and effect," the procedure is really quite simple. The speaker either expresses an opinion as to the cause of a situation or on the resulting effects of a situation. A diagram of the causal process might look like the following:

CAUSE
↓
SITUATION
↓
EFFECT

As a speaker, you have the choice of giving opinions on cause, effect, or both.

The following is a sample outline of main points which express an opinion of the causes of a situation:

SUBJECT: THE CAUSE OF INCREASED AUTO ACCIDENTS
IS INADEQUATE LICENSING LAWS

   I.   Few states have practical physical and mental requirements to obtain a license.
  II.   States do not require re-examinations.
 III.   There are no revocations due to old age.

Each main point in the outline is an opinioned reason for the *cause* of the situation.

Reversing the procedure, the next example shows the effects or results of a situation:

SUBJECT: THE SOLUTION TO THE DELINQUENCY PROBLEM
IS A BOY SCOUT TROOP

   I.   Young people would receive vocational training.
  II.   They would learn and practice good citizenship.
 III.   There would be programs and activities for physical fitness.

Whether you are expressing an opinion on the causes of a situation, the effects of a situation, or both, the speaker still has the requirement of sound reasoning. You must clearly prove each point of reasoning is related to the situation.

COMPARATIVE ORGANIZATION

When in the comparison of two items, you note the significant similarities between them and then assume there will be other likenesses, you are using a comparative organizational pattern. Comparison is based on the concept that if something exists under certain circumstances it will repeat itself under similar conditions. However, there must be evidence that the similarities do exist.

In the organized camparison, the main points of speaking satisfy each of the expected steps found in this particular form of the thinking process:

SUBJECT: LEGALIZED GAMBLING WOULD SUCCEED IN OUR STATE

    I. Our state and XYZ state are very similar in size, population, and economy.
    II. State XYZ has a successful program of legalized gambling.
   III. Therefore, our state could also have a successful system of legalized gambling.

In this example, the comparison was drawn from the similarity between two similar states. Naturally, there must be no doubt that the two states do have *significant* similarities having a direct bearing on the opinion.

The use of comparison in organization may prompt the hearer to make further comparisons and inferences himself. Although this can be advantageous, you should proceed with caution. If emphasis is placed upon an emotional or an unconfirmed basis, an opponent could easily refute your opinion. Therefore it is always wise to give stress to substantiate specific, relative details.

PROBLEM-SOLUTION ORGANIZATION

The problem-solution pattern of organization is often used in speeches of opinion. Although it appears simple, it does involve more than merely stating a problem and giving a solution. Like the Dewey system mentioned below, there are a series of steps the speaker must include to make the process sound.

Problem-solving had a series of specific and practical steps for John Dewey:

   1. Recognize the need.
   2. Define the need.
   3. Consider possible solutions to the need.
   4. Select the best solution.
   5. Put the solution into practice.

Although the Dewey procedure is stated in terms of needs, it can be used to present an opinion. Rephrasing the Dewey system shows how it can be used to fit the broader scope of the speech of opinion:

1. We should have an opinion on the subject.
2. Here are the reasons for having an opinion.
3. Here are the choices of opinion available.
4. Here are the reasons for the selection of one.
5. Now accept the opinion.

The following series of steps provides you with an organizational structure for the problem-solution speech:

1. Establish the existence of the problem under consideration.
2. Offer an opinion for a course of action which should be taken.
3. Give evidence that the proposed opinion will solve the problem.
4. Finally, establish the workability and practicality of the proposed opinion.

You employ these same steps when you are stating that the other solution previously offered is not satisfactory.

The following example illustrates the problem-solution steps to *propose* a "new" opinion:

SUBJECT: A STUDENT CENTER IS THE ANSWER
TO OUR STUDENT PROBLEMS

    I. The students of the college waste free time on activities that are not conducive to an academic atmosphere. (Step 1)
   II. A student center would solve the problem by providing a supervised place for social and recreational activities which are of a college caliber. (Steps 2, 3)
 III. The student center would use available land and funds while adding to the campus appearance. (Steps 4, 5)

The following sample outline shows the arrangement of main points used to *oppose* a solution previously offered. Here, the opinion of the speaker is negative rather than positive:

SUBJECT: INCREASING THE COST OF TEENAGE DRIVING LICENSES
WILL NOT SOLVE THE PROBLEM OF DRIVING ACCIDENTS

I. The driving habits of teenagers are no worse than those of adults. (Step 1)
II. Increasing costs of their licenses does not improve skills in driving. (Steps 2, 3)
III. The proposed addition of license cost will only serve to add more tax burdens upon the parent while penalizing the careful teen driver.

Remember, just as in all forms of organization, you must have substantial detail in support of all contentions.

THEORY-APPLICATION ORGANIZATION

Occasionally, the speech of opinion will propose a theory. If the theory is unfamiliar or unknown to the listener, the speaker has a twofold problem—explanation and opinion.

First, the theory must be clearly explained.

Second, you need to show how the theory may be applied. If you were able to prove the theory conclusively, there would not be a need for an opinion. However, since the theory is not a fact, it is important that you make the application as meaningful as possible.

The following example of theory-application thinking uses the method of comparative assumption to give credibility to the opinion:

SUBJECT: LIFE EXISTS ON OTHER PLANETS

I. The earth does have conditions which are amenable to life.
II. There are places on the earth supporting life when it would seem impossible to do so.
III. These same unlikely places are quite similar to those on other planets.

The speaker who presents an opinion using the theory-application organization usually falls back upon supported assumption to gain acceptance.

REBUTTAL ORGANIZATION

The rebuttal organization is useful when voicing an opposition opinion. There is a two-step procedure for an effective rebuttal organization.

First review, without going into a detailed development, the main points of the opposing opinion. Thus, you not only show the listener you are aware of the thinking of your opponent but more importantly, you remind the listener of the opposing points without benefit of rhetorical expansion. Therefore, your task of refuting is much easier.

Second, move on to the development of your own opinion. You now answer each of those opposing main points you reviewed earlier. Point-by-point you present your opinion in rebuttal. By doing so, you disprove or discredit each major contention of your opponent. Notice how the following example uses the same order, which appeared in the opponent-review, to present the rebuttal:

SUBJECT: THE GOVERNMENT SHOULD NOT IMPOSE
HIGHER PROTECTIVE TARIFFS ON IMPORTS

Review **Introduction:**	I. My opponent has claimed three benefits of higher protective tariffs: A. Protection of smaller business. B. Protection of the labor force. C. Maintaining the gold balance.
Body **Rebuttal:**	I. However, small business will be ruined for lack of inexpensive foreign goods for themselves. II. Contrary to my opponent, labor will see unemployment increase. III. Instead of the gold balance being maintained, we will experience an unfavorable shift.

You will note that the review of the opposing points is included in the introduction as background information. This is done in order to use the main body of the speech for the sole purpose of developing your own opinion.

The organization of the body of a speech of opinion along the lines of logical reasoning is essential. It permits the listener to follow your thinking on the subject in an orderly step-by-step manner.

The conclusion

THE TYPES OF CONCLUSION used in the speech of opinion include those used in an explanation speech—review-summary and example-application as well as three types specifically designed for an opinion speech.

Appeal for action

If the opinion is aimed at motivating the listeners to take a specific action, the conclusion is the place to give directions. Whether the action is to take place immediately or in the future is immaterial. By the time you reach the conclusion, the listeners should be expecting your directions. Satisfy both yourself and the listeners by doing this—*specifically.*

Ask your listeners to:
   Support the Red Cross.
   Write their Congressman.
   Use their litterbaskets.
   Fasten their seat belts.

Application to listener needs

When the purpose of your speech has been to present an opinion intending to satisfy a need of the listener, you finish by explaining specifically how this is accomplished. During the speaking process, the listener may have forgotten this purpose of the speech. Or he may not be quite sure what specific satisfaction is to be gained from acceptance of the opinion. Therefore, a speaker must clearly make this explanation to prevent a loss of purpose.

Ask your listeners to:
   Buy Brand X and be safe.
   Vote for Bill Blair and save our club.
   Support the Art Center and bring prestige to our town.
   Join our yacht club and enjoy your summers.
   Learn to speak and be more socially acceptable.
   Donate blood and help your fellow man.

Prediction or implication

If acceptance of your opinion promises some future happening or implies something that may come to pass, use the conclusion to make either of these matters clear. It is your opinion. You have thought it through. It is your responsibility to leave the listener with a clear understanding of its significance.

Ask your listener to:

Support my plan and our town will prosper.

Move to Arizona and improve your health.

Invest in U.S. Savings Bonds and guarantee your future.

Learn to speak effectively for a future leadership role.

Whatever form of ending is used to the speech of opinion, it should serve the ultimate purpose of any conclusion. Let it announce to the listener the speech has come to an end. Furthermore, let the listener realize that what he has heard was significant.

In the speech of opinion organized logical thinking is the essence of effective communication. Combine accurate listener analysis with an understanding of human motives and adapt selected organizational patterns. Build this talk on the substructure of soundly researched evidence.

Step 4 | Exercises ∾ Assignments

1. Choose one subject on which you have a knowledgeable opinion. Using an abbreviated outline form as found in this section, organize your opinion into four different patterns.

2. Put the four patterns of No. 1 on the blackboard. Discuss the merits of each with the class.

3. Prepare a series of three-minute speeches each with the same opinion. Arrange each into one of the organized reasoning patterns. Deliver them to the class. Are the arrangements clear? Are they effective?

4. List several opinions which deal with current issues on the blackboard. Let the class suggest methods of organized reasoning to use. Justify the suggestion.

5. Listen to the recording of a recent Presidential inaugural address or State

of the Union speech. What methods were used in content development, listener appeals and arrangement?

6. Prepare a ten minute speech of opinion. Incorporate all the elements of speaking. Have the class vote on their reaction to the speech.

7. Prepare introductions for the following "hostile" audiences:
   Audience: Conservationists.
   Topic: We Need to Fill in Our Marsh Lands.

   Audience: Automobile Manufacturers.
   Topic: We Need Additional Safety Features in Automobiles.

   Audience: Parents.
   Topic: Teenagers Need More Freedom.

   Audience: American Medical Association.
   Topic: Extend Medicare to All.

   Audience: College Administrators.
   Topic: All College Courses Should Be Elective.

8. Prepare one speech with three different conclusions. Rank them in your estimation of effectiveness. Try them on the class and ask for their rankings

Step 5

Preevaluate the speech of opinion

HOW does a speaker know if his speech of opinion will be effective? There is no sure answer to this question, but listener reaction is a fairly accurate gauge. However, the following questions can help you to judge the possible effectiveness of your planned speech:

1. Has the type of listener been determined?
2. Is your central idea clear?
3. Has the speech purpose been selected?
4. Have human motives been considered?
5. Does the speech contain psychological appeals?
6. Does the introduction capture the attention and interest of the listener?
7. Does the introduction establish a favorable rapport between you and the listener?
8. Is the line of reasoning used truly applicable to the topic, purpose, and situation?
9. Is your reasoning fully and clearly outlined?
10. Are the main points sufficient for the presentation of the opinion?
11. Has each main point been completely developed?
12. Have you used sufficient evidence to prove all points?

13. Can the listener rationally and logically accept your opinion?
14. Does the conclusion clarify and motivate?

The speech of opinion is actually a thought process, even though it is in the form of oral communication. It not only reveals the ability of an individual to express himself fluently, but opens the way to an understanding of a person's capacity for logical thinking. The speech of opinion provides an insight into the reasoning processes of the speaker which is directly related to the degree of respect to be given to him by others. Let your opinions be the result of specific information and sound thinking.

Part VI

Group

communication

I N the place of a single speaker, there may be a number of *contributing* speakers and often the listener doubles as a speaker. When these conditions exist, there is *group communication* in a discussion or a conference. Differences exist between solo speaking and group speaking. However, the aims of the speaker are the same—explanation or opinion. This section presents a review of the essentials of discussion and conference. Parliamentary procedure, a more formal group process, is also included.

Discussion

DISCUSSION CONSISTS OF A number of people working together cooperatively to consider a question. Usually there is a chairman or leader to assist in maintaining a smooth and orderly discussion. There is often a general procedure to guide the discussion. For example, the following guide is an adaptation of the Dewey problem-solving pattern:

1. Recognize the specific question.
2. Determine the elements of the question.
3. Consider possible solutions.
4. Select the best solution.
5. Apply the selected solution to the problem.

Although these steps are a tentative guide for the discussion, there is generally no demand to complete the entire process or to have a strict time limit in effect. Discussion usually proceeds at its own rate to a point satisfactory to the participants.

Questions for discussion

Three types of questions for discussion are fact, policy, and value.

Questions of fact are accepted for discussion if there is need for *interpretation*. Unless this need exists there is no basis for discussion. Thus, in interpreting fact the discussion procedure remains the same but the objective becomes to answer questions concerning the meanings of fact.

Question-of-fact discussions are attempts to remove questions from the category of opinion and place them in the category of fact. Sample discussion questions follow:

Who was the author of the works attributed to Shakespeare?

Does driver education reduce automobile accidents?

Is there life in outer space?

Are unidentified flying objects from outer space?

Do fraternities aid scholarship?

Does television contribute to juvenile crime?

Questions of policy involve making a decision pointing to a course-of-action. That is, the object of the discussion is to solve a question or problem. Sample questions of policy are:

Should public school teachers have the right to strike?

Should the college adopt an unlimited cut system?

Should voting rights in all elections be extended to the eighteen year old?

Should all states adopt uniform examinations for drivers' licenses?

Should the United States modify its policy in Southeast Asia?

Questions of value deal with the merits of a subject. The evaluation may involve a program, person, or idea. The following are questions of value:

242

Is the trimester plan educationally sound?

Is our safety program worth the cost?

What was the best play on Broadway last year?

In a democracy is conformity more dangerous than non-conformity?

The question to be considered by a discussion group should be specifically determined and clearly stated before beginning the discussion. This permits each discussant to prepare fully and thus make the event more productive.

Types of discussion

The type of discussion depends upon the speaking situation and its purpose and the discussants are free to make their own arrangements. You are familiar with several types of discussion. The following outline form is a method of classifying discussion types. It is merely meant to be illustrative, not comprehensive. However, we can use it to examine the size, purpose, set-up, and degree of formality.

SIZE

Duo	*Small Group*	*Public*
2	3-15	16 and up

PURPOSE

Information Exchange
Problem-Solving
Contrasting Positions

SET-UP

Round Table	Panel	Debate-Forum

DEGREE OF FORMALITY

Less formal	← ⟶	*More formal*
"Buzz" sessions		Symposium

243

ROUND-TABLE DISCUSSION

The round-table group discussion is a common form for this communicative process. Although there are *no prepared speeches* in this form, there are certain times when prepared introductory statements are made by the participants. Group discussion is similar to the family circle talking about a common matter and is principally for the benefit of the participants. Therefore, the arrangement is designed to invite open informal speaking among the members. However, the number of discussants in any one group should be limited. It is much better to have two small workable groups than one large uncontrollable group.

ROUND TABLE DISCUSSION ARRANGEMENT

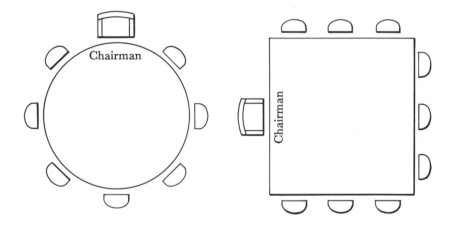

PANEL DISCUSSION

The format of the panel discussion is used when there will be an audience, since the round-table style would be obviously inappropriate. Therefore, the discussant must compromise some of the intimacy with his fellow members to allow the audience to hear and see the proceedings.

There are two possible arrangements for the panel discussion. The first is best for a group with a relatively large number of participants.

ARRANGEMENT FOR PANEL DISCUSSION

(large group)

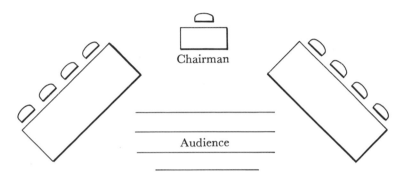

The second arrangement is more suitable for a smaller group of discussants.

ARRANGEMENT FOR PANEL DISCUSSION

(small group)

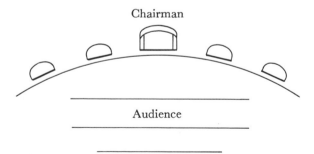

The panel discussion proceeds essentially the same as in the round-table discussion. While there are usually prepared introductory remarks, the primary method is informal talk on the subject among the members. Frequently a period for listener questions follows the conclusion of the discussion.

SYMPOSIUM

In the discussion form called the symposium, each participant presents a *prepared speech*. The specific topics are assigned to or selected by each discussant. Following the presentation of the prepared remarks, there can be a more informal exchange of comments by the symposium members and an audience question period. A symposium is held primarily for the audience and the seating arrangement is similar to the one used in the panel discussion. The speakers face the listeners and address their remarks to them.

The symposium is not merely a series of prepared speeches. Much of its success depends on the lively and informal interchange of opinions taking place following the presentation of prepared remarks. Audience questions, which should be encouraged by the group leader, will serve not only as a device for keeping audience attention but also as a method of prodding certain problems previously unanswered by the group.

DEBATE-FORUM

Although the debate-forum is not a "pure" form of discussion, it does have some of its characteristics and is often used as a type of public discussion. It is a more formal arrangement of the public forum. First, two speakers give their opposing opinions in prepared statements. Second, each speaker is allowed a fixed amount of time to rebut the other. Finally, a group of qualified listeners ask pointed questions of each speaker. This last phase with an open exchange of ideas gives the debate-forum the flavor of discussion.

The arrangement of speakers before the audience should permit both participants and listeners to be included in the proceedings. The arrangement is similar to the one used for the panel discussion.

The types of discussion are not fixed and the ones presented here can be used as a basis for other special arrangements. No matter what the format is, it should serve the needs of the participants and the special problems of the topic. A technical topic will probably require, for example, detailed reports while controversial topics will require a more flexible system of discussion allowing for an easy flow of opinion. The main point to remember, however, is that as the form becomes more formal so will the procedure of the discussion.

246

ARRANGEMENT FOR DEBATE-FORUM

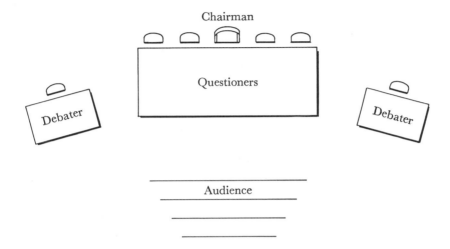

The discussion leader

The leader of a discussion is like the hub of a wheel. He keeps the parts together as an efficient unified whole. It is his responsibility to maintain the effectiveness of the discussion by acting as a guide for communication. He should control direction and, if necessary, act as an arbitrator to resolve matters of controversy.

The qualities for discussion leadership are like those for any position of responsibility. The leader must command the respect and cooperation of the discussants. To achieve this, the discussion leader must:

1. Have a thorough understanding of the discussion process.
2. Have knowledge of the subject under consideration.
3. Have an understanding of human nature.
4. Have a lively interest in the discussion of the topic.
5. Be attentive throughout the entire discussion.
6. Be fair in keeping the discussion equally balanced among the participants.

247

7. Be impartial in all decisions.
8. Be exact in guiding the discussion toward its general purpose.

DUTIES OF THE DISCUSSION LEADER

The duties of the discussion leader begin well in advance of the actual event. After the discussants have selected the topic, the leader verifies the exact phrasing and presents copies to all those involved well before the actual meeting. At this time it is also advisable for the chairman to become acquainted with each participant in order to gain some insight into their future performances in the discussion.

Next, the leader studies the topic himself in order to foresee the possible direction of the discussion and to make plans to manage it smoothly. Some chairmen actually outline their idea of the main points to be covered. However, the final decision of matters to be covered almost always comes from the discussants.

Finally, at the time of the discussion meeting, the chairman checks the physical setting and the seating arrangement. Name cards are used to assist the participants when they are not acquainted and for the convenience of the audience. The leader makes the introductions and reviews the procedure of the discussion. The discussion is then ready to begin.

During the discussion, the leader cannot relax, as his role is varied and demands an alert mind. He is narrator, questioner, interpreter, and director. The chairman has various responsibilities.

BEGINNING THE DISCUSSION

1. Introduce the discussion subject with a statement concerning the topic and the purpose of the group meeting.
2. Give an illustration emphasizing the significance or meaning of the question.
3. If they are appearing before an audience or if the discussants are unacquainted, introduce each discussant.
4. Ask each participant to make an introductory comment on the basic issue of the question and the need for its consideration.
5. Be alert to an early indication of a common attitude among the group.
6. Suggest issues to be covered by the discussion.

7. Request suggestions from the discussants on the main points to be covered and the order of discussion.

8. Settle on one issue to begin the discussion.

DURING THE DISCUSSION

1. Keep the discussion moving from point to point and avoid prolonged speaking on one matter unless it is very constructive.

2. Summarize the essence of comments made on a point before moving on to another.

3. Mediate any deadlocks.

4. Encourage contributions from each member.

5. Call on the more reticent participants to speak.

6. Tactfully interrupt those members who tend to monopolize the discussion, by summarizing and then requesting another to speak.

7. Request suggestions from the discussants on the main points to be covered and the order of discussion.

8. Remind the discussants of the value for the rational exchange of ideas during moments of tension.

CONCLUDING THE DISCUSSION

1. Review the discussion with a general summary.

2. Summarize each main point for important results.

3. Have each participant make a final comment.

4. Draw a final conclusion as to the implications or findings of the group.

The discussion participant

Just as the chairman has certain responsibilities, the participant has obligations to himself and other members of the group. Effective discussion requires the cooperative assistance of informed individuals. Before the time of the discussion, the participant should become informed on the details of the question.

When the moment of discussion arrives, each discussant should enter into the situation with a cooperative spirit, an objective mind, and an awareness of the value of group thinking.

During the discussion there are a number of guiding points which can be followed to gain more effective participation:

1. Contribute freely but have something constructive to say.
2. Follow the trend of thought and contribute accordingly.
3. Use explanation for any comments that may not be immediately and completely comprehended.
4. Include evidence when expressing an opinion.
5. Succinctly reveal the reasoning which led you to an expressed conclusion.
6. Be understanding, tactful, and reasonable when in disagreement.
7. Let the thinking of the majority determine issues, purposes, and direction.
8. Recognize the chairman as the impartial leader and respond to his direction.
9. Contribute without being asked.
10. Never monopolize the discussion or talk too long.
11. Listen carefully to what the others say and do not be in a hurry to speak.
12. Always participate in a spirit of friendly cooperation.

Discussion is designed to allow a number of individuals to work harmoniously for a common goal. If conducted properly, discussion is most beneficial to everyone concerned but when poorly performed, it is chaos. The success or failure of group discussion depends on the cooperation, preparation, and performance of all participants.

Decision-making conferences

A DECISION-MAKING CONFERENCE occurs when a group of individuals meet to make a decision. While ordinary discussion is not bound to any goal, the participants in this type of conference are expected to reach a definite conclusion.

A conference may consist of an employer and an employee making a decision on salary or the President and his advisors conferring on an international policy. This method of group communication has certain distinct characteristics that are different from those of a discussion. To help you become familiar with them, the following are *supplementary* to those given for discussion.

Organization of the decision-making conference

The chairman of a conference is completely responsible for calling, organizing, and conducting the meeting. Therefore, the greater part of this form of group communication centers upon the leader. While the participant needs only to be concerned with his particular knowledge of his specific topic, the conference leader has responsibilities, in addition to those noted under discussion, as follows:

1. Usually the chairman is permitted to select the participants.
2. The size of the conference group should be limited to the number necessary to reach a decision.
3. The selection of a place of meeting, while depending on the size of the group, should also be conducive to constructive results.
4. Each conferee should be notified in advance of the following:
    a. Time and place of meeting.
    b. Names of other participants.
    c. Specific topic of consideration.
    d. Items within the topic of concern.
    e. Approximate time of adjournment.
    f. Any specific instructions.
5. During the conference, the chairman conducts the meeting like that of a discussion leader.

Decision-making conference procedure

More than discussion, this conference adheres to a procedural outline rather closely in order to reach a final decision on its question.

251

Although in practice the two forms of communication are similar, it will be noted that the conference procedure includes steps for making this specific decision:

1. Statement of the subject and the main topic to be considered.
2. Explanation of the conference purpose and the general decision that must be reached.
3. Examinations of the subject and topics during the open discussion.
4. Collecting possible answers to the question.
5. Testing each answer against the question.
6. Making a specific choice of answer.
7. Considering the matter of implementing the decision.

Except for their organization and purpose, the conference and the discussion are similar. The participants should be equally well-informed and cooperative while the leader must skillfully deal with participants and direct the conference toward a final decision.

Parliamentary procedure

THERE ARE OCCASIONS when group communication is guided by the regulations of parliamentary procedures. With such rules, everything taking place is governed by established rules. These principles are found in *Robert's Rules of Order* and are democratic in action:

1. Every participant has the right to be heard.
2. The rights of the majority and the minority are protected.
3. Both sides to every argument should be permitted to speak.
4. Voting is the right of all participants.
5. Rule is by majority.

It is not necessary to be an expert to participate actively under the rules of parliamentary procedure. While it is desirable if one member of a group qualifies as an expert or parliamentarian, the average individual need only be familiar with the fundamentals in order to participate effectively. Therefore, the following points are condensed to give the prospective participant the necessary basic information.

Duties of the parliamentary chairman

The chairman of a meeting conducted under parliamentary procedures has responsibilities similar to the more informal discussion and conference leaders:

1. Plan the time and place of the meeting.
2. Organize the agenda of business or topics.
3. Call the meeting to order.
4. Present each point on the agenda for discussion or action.
5. Maintain proper parliamentary order.
6. Protect the rights of the minority during discussions.
7. Supervise all voting.
8. Bring the meeting to a formal conclusion.

The principal duty of the chairman is to safeguard the parliamentary rights of the participants. To do this effectively, he must have a working knowledge of the formal rules of parliamentary order and must be alert to the actual proceedings before him. He should have a copy of parliamentary rules available to resolve any questions regarding procedure.

Duties of participants

Constructive contribution and cooperative conduct are the primary duties of a participant in discussion and conference. They are the same when parliamentary procedure prevails. In this instance, however, the communicant needs to be aware of other factors affecting his relationship to the group:

1. Speak only when formally recognized and permitted by the chairman.
2. Speak only on the specific point before the group.
3. All proposals must be put to the chairman.
4. Proposals are to be stated accurately and in the formal language of parliamentary expression.
5. There is no discussion unless approved by the chairman under the rules of parliamentary procedure.

Because the parliamentary group has a more formal atmosphere than either an informal discussion or a conference group, there is a greater need for accurate framing of thoughts before expression.

Order of business

Most groups under parliamentary rule follow a similar order of proceedings. Variations can be made to adapt to the special needs of a particular group. The general order for an average group is as follows:

1. Call to order by the chairman.
2. Reading of the minutes of the previous meeting, correction, and approval by those in attendance.
3. Reading, correcting, and approving of the treasurer's report.
4. Reports of other officers.
5. Reports of standing committees.
6. Reports of special committees.
7. Consideration of unfinished or old business.
8. Consideration of new business.
9. Adjourning the meeting.

Methods of voting

Whenever a proposal, more accurately called a motion, is put before the group for a decision, some form of voting usually occurs. Different methods of voting which can be used are:

Voice Vote:	The members respond to the request of the chairman with "aye" or "no."
Show of Hands:	Hands are raised at the request of the chairman and a count can be taken if necessary.
Ballot Vote:	Voting is done secretly and privately on some type of ballot, then collected, and counted before a witness.
Roll Call Vote:	The names of the participants are read by the secretary, and each person responds with an

oral "aye" or "no" which is then recorded next to the respondent's name.

General Consent: At the discretion of the chairman, approval to a motion may be automatically given as by "general consent," unless there is an objection which then necessitates a more specific vote.

The participant in a parliamentary group should know the different methods of voting to ensure the best form of making a majority decision. This knowledge can protect the rights of both the minority and the majority against inaccurate or unfair verdicts.

The motion procedure

There is a general procedure for proposing a main motion for group consideration. There can be no deviation from the process unless permitted under parliamentary rules:

1. Recognition is first obtained from the chair.
2. The motion is stated in exact language.
3. In order to indicate other interest in the motion, a second is needed to proceed further.
4. The motion is stated by the chair.
5. Time is allowed for discussion or modification of the motion.
6. After discussion or amendment, the final wording of the motion is read.
7. A vote is taken and the results announced.

The exceptions to this procedure are specifically included in parliamentary rules and vary with the purpose of the motion. In the review of principal motions, exceptions to the standard procedure are noted.

Principal motions

In addition to the "main motion" covering all general matters and following the above procedure, there are motions having specific purposes. Those motions of principal concern to the average participant are:

To Amend:	A motion proposing a change to the main motion; it is therefore voted upon before the original motion. Debatable: majority vote.
To Commit:	A motion proposing the main motion be submitted to a committee for further consideration before a final decision. Debatable: majority vote.
To Lay on the Table:	A motion proposing to postpone consideration of another motion until some other time when the original motion can be recalled easily. Undebatable: majority vote.
To Postpone:	A motion specifically proposing to put off further consideration of a motion until a certain time or indefinitely. Debatable: majority vote.
To Adjourn:	A motion having privilege over other motions unless it interrupts a speaker, voting, or vital business. Undebatable unless a qualified motion: majority vote.
The Previous Question:	A motion proposing that discussion on a pending motion end and the vote be taken. Undebatable: two-thirds vote.
Point of Order:	A motion used to present an objection to a ruling by the chair or to some parliamentary procedure; it can be made at any time, with the chair making an immediate decision. Undebatable unless the decision of the chair is appealed; then there is a majority vote.
Question of Privilege:	A motion made at any time except while deciding adjournment or recess, affecting the rights, privileges, and comfort of those present. Undebatable: decision by the chair.

There are other motions which involve the parliamentarian. Although it is not necessary for every participant in the parliamentary situation to know all the rules, it would be best if they were able to use the preceding information. For additional details, references can be made to the following chart of motions.

Tables of Motions in Order of Precedence

Motions	May Interrupt Speaker?	Second Required?	Amendable?	Debatable?	What Type of Vote?
Privileged Motions					
1. Fix time of Next Meeting	no	yes	yes	yes[1]	maj
2. Adjourn	no	yes	no	no	maj
3. Recess	no	yes	yes[2]	yes[3]	maj
4. Question of Privilege	yes	no	no	no	ch or maj[4]
5. Orders of the Day	yes	no	no	no	chair[5]
Incidental Motions (There is no rank among these motions— they result from other motions)					
6. Point of Order	yes	no	no	no	ch or maj[4]
Appeal Ruling of Chair	yes	no	no	no	maj
Parliamentary Inquiry	yes	no	no	no	chair
Withdraw Motion[6]	no	no	no	no	ch or maj
Suspend Rules	no	yes	no	no	2/3
Object to Consideration	yes	no	no	no	2/3
Subsidiary Motion					
7. Lay on the Table[7]	no	yes	no	no	maj
8. Close Debate	no	yes	no	no	2/3
9. Limit Debate	no	yes	yes	no	2/3
10. Postpone to Fixed Time	no	yes	yes	yes	maj
11. Refer to Committee[8]	no	yes	yes	yes	maj
12. Committee of the Whole	no	yes	yes	yes	maj
13. Amend	no	yes	yes	yes[9]	maj
14. Postpone Indefinitely	no	yes	no	yes	maj
Main Motion					
15. Reconsider[10]	yes	yes	no	yes[9]	maj
16. Take off the Table	no	yes	no	no	maj
17. Rescind	no	yes	yes	yes	2/3
18. Main Question	no	yes	yes	yes	maj

[1] Not debatable if another motion pending.
[2] Amend only length of recess.
[3] Only the amendment is debatable.
[4] Decision by chair, unless on appeal then by majority.
[5] Chair must obey unless rules suspended.
[6] Only by maker of original motion.
[7] Applicable only to 4, 13, 15, 18, and appeal ruling of chair.
[8] Applicable only to Main Question and its amendments.
[9] Debatable only if original motion debatable.
[10] Applicable only for person who voted prevailing side of original motion.

G roup communication has become a vital part of our society. You should be familiar with its forms and be able to take an active role in either discussion or conference. Whether the operation of the group is informal or under parliamentary rules, the individual speaker should still be competent in both explanation and opinion.

Part VI | Exercises ∽ Assignments

1. Prepare a series of discussion questions of:
   a. fact   b. policy   c. value

2. Select a question for discussion and prepare yourself as a discussion leader.

3. Divide members of the class into discussion groups. Have each group select a topic for research and present a discussion for the class.

4. Evaluate the chairmanship of a television or radio discussion program.

5. Select appropriate discussion questions of:
   a. local problems   c. national problems
   b. state problems   d. international problems

6. Attend a lecture forum or a symposium. Write a review of both the program and the leadership.

7. Write a history of one of the current discussion programs on radio, television, or live. Suggestions are: Northwestern Reviewing Stand, Meet the Press, Ford Hall Forum.

8. Organize the class into a parliamentary club for purposes of taking a stand on current problems.

9. Phrase main motions for the above group.

10. Report on the use of parliamentary law in an organization to which you belong.

Conclusion

AFTER you have completed this course, the question is, "What next?" There are several paths open for those who need and desire further work.

First, let us consider the more formal paths to additional training. If you wish to consider another speech course, by all means consult the instructor of this course. He knows your assets and liabilities. He also is familiar with the other offerings available in your locality. In addition, most areas or communities have an educational clearing house providing an up-to-date listing of all courses offered in evening or extension programs. Check with your local educational association or your local Chamber of Commerce for information.

Some of these courses might be a continuation under the heading of "Advanced Public Speaking" or "Business and Professional Speech." On the other hand, you may feel a need for more specialized work in one of the areas covered in this book. You may be interested in a course devoted to voice improvement or oral interpretation. Perhaps special vocational or avocational speech needs may direct you to a course in "Persuasion" or "Conference Leadership."

Secondly, if you decide to follow the non-academic route to further improvement you can take several paths. You can investigate the situations providing additional speech experiences. All communities provide a wide variety of situations where interested and active people share ideas. These may range from the Toastmasters, an organization devoted to the improvement of speech proficiencies, to local volunteer groups. Today, many churches and clubs have discussion groups. An active participation in any group will eventually provide you with opportunities to do some form of oral presentation or reporting.

Finally, you may decide on your own personal program of self-improvement. In that case, the following suggestions should be helpful to you.

1. Set aside a short period of time (10-15 minutes) for daily practice.
2. Select a phase of speech training for concentration (organization, animation, etc.).
3. Use a tape recorder at regular intervals to compare performances and to measure progress.
4. Continue to observe and evaluate.
5. Practice oral summarization of the articles you read.
6. Read and study the speeches of the great communicators both past and present.

Most important, remember the three rules for improving your skills: PRACTICE! PRACTICE! PRACTICE!

Appendix A

Speech topics

IN MY OPINION:

YOU SHOULD TAKE UP GOLF
YOU SHOULD DONATE BLOOD TO A BLOOD BANK
THE SALES TAX IS UNFAIR (OR FAIR)
COMIC BOOKS SERVE A USEFUL PURPOSE
FINAL EXAMINATIONS SHOULD BE ABOLISHED
STUDENTS SHOULD GRADE INSTRUCTORS
PARENTS ARE TOO LENIENT
CENSORSHIP IS DANGEROUS
MARRIAGE IS HERE TO STAY
CENSORSHIP IS NECESSARY
OBJECTIVE TESTS ARE UNFAIR
THERE IS NO EXCUSE FOR SLOPPINESS
THE AGE OF CHIVALRY IS DEAD
MERCY KILLING IS NEVER JUSTIFIABLE
PRIZEFIGHTING SHOULD BE ABOLISHED
MOVIES ARE BETTER THAN EVER
THE AVERAGE TEACHER KILLS CREATIVITY
A GOOD PERSONALITY ISN'T EVERYTHING
POETRY IS OVERRATED
ART AND SCIENCE DON'T MIX
HISTORY IS THE STORY OF MAN'S CRIMES AGAINST MAN

YOU SHOULD VISIT:

THE ROCKEFELLER CENTER
THE GRAND CANYON
SALT LAKE CITY

CANADA
SOUTH AMERICA
THE UNITED NATIONS
WASHINGTON, D.C.
MEXICO
THE STATUE OF LIBERTY
DISNEYLAND
A COAL MINE
YELLOWSTONE NATIONAL PARK
MOUNT RUSHMORE
CONCORD, MASS.
GETTYSBURG
HAWAII
THE TAJ MAHAL
HONG KONG
A MUSEUM
A FIRE STATION
AN OLD FOLKS HOME
YANKEE STADIUM
STONEHENGE
YOUR GRANDPARENTS

WHAT HAPPENED:

TO FREE ENTERPRISE?
AT PEARL HARBOR?
TO INITIATIVE?
TO STUDENT HONESTY?
AT GETTYSBURG?
TO PERSONAL LIBERTY?
TO COURTESY?
TO THE BIG BANDS?
TO OLD-FASHIONED MATHEMATICS?
AT VALLEY FORGE?
AT THE ALAMO?
TO "GOOD OLD" PHYSICAL FITNESS?
TO RESPECT FOR AUTHORITY?
TO AMELIA EARHART?
TO THE EDSEL?
TO MOUSTACHES?
TO THE "IN" CROWD?
IN 1929?
ON THE DAY YOU WERE BORN?

In Defense of:

Laziness
Women in Politics
Our Space Program
Dropouts
Fluoridation
Unlimited Cuts
Advertising
Youth Today
Long Hair
The Large University
The Small College
Fraternities
Regular Exercise
The Honor System
Prizefighting
Free Speech
The Old-fashioned Girl
Protest Marches
Courage
Doing It Right the First Time
Teenage Marriages
Television

How It Works:

Automobile Carburetor
Printing Press
Movie Projector
Vacuum Tube
Profit Sharing
Atomic Energy
Stock Market
Teaching Machine
Anti-Missile Missile
Television Transmission
Jet Propulsion
Nielsen Ratings
Farm Cooperative
Computer-Arranged Dates
Electric Guitar
Centripetal Force
Electoral College

263

How to:

Identify Counterfeit Money
Start a Car on a Cold Morning
Enjoy Life
Manage Your Money
Develop Your Own Film
Stay Healthy
Enjoy a Vacation
Start a Fire without Matches
Rescue a Drowning Person
Fly-Cast
Wash a Car
Cut Down a Tree
Lose Weight
Put on Contact Lenses
Train a Dog
Study
Use a Slide Rule
Quit Smoking
Prevent Fires
Relax
Change a Habit
Flunk Out of College
Win Friends

A Close Look at:

The League of Women Voters
The American Legion
The United Nations
The Parent-Teacher Association
The John Birch Society
The Republican Party
The Democratic Party
The Warren Report
The Communist Party
Civil Liberties Union
Viet Nam
Rising Crime Rates
The YMCA
The Community Chest
The Red Cross
Labor Organizations

AMERICAN MEDICAL ASSOCIATION
NATIONAL ASSOCIATION OF MANUFACTURERS
THE GRANGE
THE SUPREME COURT
THE WORLD BANK
4-H CLUBS
NAACP

A HISTORY OF:

THE LEAGUE OF NATIONS
BASEBALL
BASKETBALL
FOREIGN AID
EUROPEAN COMMON MARKET
CIVIL RIGHTS
RADIATION THERAPY
JAZZ
DEPRESSIONS
FLYING
PEACE CORPS
PRINTING
CENSORSHIP
ANTIBIOTICS
THE RIGHT WING
LABOR UNIONS
THE MORMONS
PENNSYLVANIA

IN APPRECIATION OF:

EDISON
NEHRU
GANDHI
"TEDDY" ROOSEVELT
WOODROW WILSON
HARRY TRUMAN
HERBERT HOOVER
RICHARD NIXON
BARRY GOLDWATER
GERTRUDE STEIN

Appendix A

Edward Albee
Norman Thomas
Wendell Willkie
Babe Ruth
Ben Hogan
Albert Schweitzer
Jane Addams
Adlai Stevenson
Mrs. Eleanor Roosevelt

What is

Nylon?
Modern Art?
The Cyclotron?
Sleep Walking?
A Lie Detector Test?
LSD?
A Closed Shop?
Wire Tapping?
A Virus?
Air Pollution?
Zen Buddhism?
An I.Q.?
A Fossil?
Automation?
A Computer?
An X-ray?
Libel?
A Poem?
A Light Wave?
Energy?
Your Philosophy of Life?

Appendix B

Articulation and pronunciation exercises

Note the tendency to combine and distort sounds in rapid connected speech. Read both sides with rapid smooth pattern.

Jeet?	Did you Eat?
Kumere!	Come Here!
Seeyahroun	I'll See You Around
Shouldnchew?	Shouldn't You?
Ha Yadune?	How Are You Doing?
Lemesee	Let Me See
Sote Nuff?	Is It Hot Enough?
Wheyuh goin?	Where Are You Going?

∽ ∽ ∽ ∽ ∽

The following words are frequently mispronounced. Try your pronunciation and then check it against the suggested dictionary pronunciation:

chasm	*gesture*
forehead	*prestige*
squalor	*bird*
data	*Bert*
arctic	*Italian*
hostile	*picture*
verbatim	*incognito*
err	*deaf*
decade	*police*

∽ ∽ ∽ ∽ ∽

The following words usually have regional differences in pronunciation. See if you can identify these differences:

tomato	been
idea	bin
father	master
aunt	water
saw	wash
half	greasy
because	power

～ ～ ～ ～ ～

Check your pronunciation of the following to see if you omit sounds!

definite	regular
poem	usual
similar	belong
asked	Saturday
student	recognize
accessory	temperature
gentlemen	chocolate
violent	diamond
family	library
sophomore	Catholic
submarine	government
finally	liable
separation	history

～ ～ ～ ～ ～

Check your pronunciation for the following words. Be careful of additional or extra sounds:

almond	singer
across	umbrella
idea	calm
film	corps
entrance	drown

twice	*column*
athlete	*salmon*
wash	*Illinois*
subtle	*mischievous*

∽ ∽ ∽ ∽ ∽

Find the correct stress for the following words:

admirable	*theater*
cement	*exquisite*
debate	*hospitable*
interesting	*inquiry*
infamous	*precedent*
adult	*decade*
alias	*comparable*
detail	*integral*
device	*preferable*
aspirant	*pianist*
event	*cigar*
ally	*deprecate*

∽ ∽ ∽ ∽ ∽

Appendix C

Selections for analysis and practice

John F. Kennedy

INAUGURAL ADDRESS
(January 20, 1961)

MY FELLOW CITIZENS:

WE observe today not a victory of party but a celebration of freedom—symbolizing an end as well as a beginning—signifying renewal as well as change. For I have sworn before you and Almighty God the same solemn oath our forebears prescribed nearly a century and three-quarters ago.

The world is very different now. For man holds in his mortal hands the power to abolish all form of human poverty and all form of human life. And yet the same revolutionary beliefs for which our forebears fought are still at issue around the globe—the belief that the rights of man come not from the generosity of the state but from the hand of God.

We dare not forget today that we are the heirs of that first revolution. Let the word go forth from this time and place, to friend and foe alike, that the torch has been passed to a new generation of Americans—born in this century, tempered by war, disciplined by a hard and bitter peace, proud of our ancient heritage—and unwilling to witness or permit the slow undoing of those human rights to which this nation has always been committed, and to which we are committed today—at home and around the world.

Let every nation know, whether it wishes us well or ill, that we shall pay any price, bear any burden, meet any hardship, support any friend, oppose any foe to assure the survival and success of liberty.

This much we pledge—and more.

To those old allies whose cultural and spiritual origins we share, we pledge the loyalty of faithful friends. United, there is little we cannot do in a host of new co-operative ventures. Divided, there is little we can do—for we dare not meet a powerful challenge at odds and split asunder.

To those new states whom we welcome to the ranks of the free, we pledge our word that one form of colonial control shall not have passed away merely to be replaced by a far more iron tyranny. We shall not always expect to find them supporting our view. But we shall always hope to find them strongly supporting their own freedom—and to remember that, in the past, those who foolishly sought power by riding the back of the tiger ended up inside.

To those peoples in the huts and villages of half the globe struggling to break the bonds of mass misery, we pledge our best efforts to help them help themselves, for whatever period is required—not because the Communists may be doing it, not because we seek their votes, but because it is right. If a free society cannot help the many who are poor, it cannot save the few who are rich.

To our sister republics south of our border, we offer a special pledge—to convert our good words into good deeds—in a new alliance for progress—to assist free men and free governments in casting off the chains of poverty. But this peaceful revolution of hope cannot become the prey of hostile powers. Let all our neighbors know that we shall join with them to oppose aggression or subversion anywhere in the Americas. And let every other power know that this hemisphere intends to remain the master of its own house.

To that world assembly of sovereign states, the United Nations, our last best hope in an age where the instruments of war have far outpaced the instruments of peace, we renew our pledge of support—to prevent it from becoming merely a forum of invective—to strengthen its shield of the new and the weak—and to enlarge the area in which its writ may run.

Finally, to those nations who would make themselves our adversary, we offer not a pledge but a request: that both sides begin anew the quest for peace, before the dark powers of destruction unleashed by science engulf all humanity in planned or accidental self-destruction.

We dare not tempt them with weakness. For only when our arms are sufficient beyond doubt can we be certain beyond doubt that they will never be employed.

But neither can two great and powerful groups of nations take comfort from our present course—both sides overburdened by the cost of modern weapons, both rightly alarmed by the steady spread of the deadly atom, yet both racing to alter that uncertain balance of terror that stays the hand of mankind's final war.

So let us begin anew—remembering on both sides that civility is not a sign of weakness, and sincerity is always subject to proof. Let us never negotiate out of fear. But let us never fear to negotiate.

Let both sides explore what problems unite us instead of belaboring those problems which divide us.

Let both sides, for the first time, formulate serious and precise proposals for the inspection and control of arms—and bring the absolute power to destroy other nations under the absolute control of all nations.

Let both sides seek to invoke the wonders of science instead of its terrors. Together let us explore the stars, conquer the deserts, eradicate disease, tap the ocean depths and encourage the arts and commerce.

Let both sides unite to heed in all corners of the earth the command of Isaiah—to "undo the heavy burdens . . . [and] let the oppressed go free."

And if a beachhead of a co-operation may push back the jungles of suspicion, let both sides join in the next task: creating, not a new balance of power, but a new world of law, where the strong are just and the weak secure and the peace preserved.

All this will not be finished in the first one hundred days. Nor will it be finished in the first one thousand days, nor in the life of this

Administration, nor even perhaps in our lifetime on this planet. But let us begin.

In your hands, my fellow citizens, more than mine, will rest the final success or failure of our course. Since this country was founded, each generation of Americans has been summoned to give testimony to its national loyalty. The graves of young Americans who answered the call to service surround the globe.

Now the trumpet summons us again—not as a call to bear arms, though arms we need—not as a call to battle, though embattled we are—but a call to bear the burden of a long twilight struggle, year in and year out, "rejoicing in hope, patient in tribulation"—a struggle against the common enemies of man: tyranny, poverty, disease, and war itself.

Can we forge against these enemies a grand and global alliance, north and south, east and west, that can assure a more fruitful life for all mankind? Will you join in that historic effort?

In the long history of the world, only a few generations have been granted the role of defending freedom in its hour of maximum danger. I do not shrink from this responsibility—I welcome it. I do not believe that any of us would exchange places with any other people or any other generation. The energy, the faith, the devotion which we bring to this endeavor will light our country and all who serve it—and the glow from that fire can truly light the world.

And so, my fellow Americans: Ask not what your country can do for you—ask what you can do for your country.

My fellow citizens of the world: Ask not what America will do for you, but what together we can do for the freedom of man.

Finally, whether you are citizens of America or citizens of the world, ask of us here the same high standards of strength and sacrifice which we ask of you. With a good conscience our only sure reward, with history the final judge of our deeds, let us go forth to lead the land we love, asking His blessing and His help, but knowing that here on earth God's work must truly be our own.

Franklin Delano Roosevelt

DECLARATION OF WAR
(December 8, 1941)

TO THE CONGRESS OF THE UNITED STATES:

Yesterday, December 7, 1941—a date which will live in infamy—the United States of America was suddenly and deliberately attacked by naval and air forces of the Empire of Japan.

The United States was at peace with that nation and, at the solicitation of Japan, was still in conversation with its government and its emperor looking toward the maintenance of peace in the Pacific.

Indeed, one hour after Japanese air squadrons had commenced bombing in Oahu, the Japanese ambassador to the United States and his colleague delivered to the Secretary of State a formal reply to a recent American message.

While this reply stated that it seemed useless to continue the existing diplomatic negotiations, it contained no threat or hint of war or armed attack.

It will be recorded that the distance of Hawaii from Japan makes it obvious that the attack was deliberately planned many days or even weeks ago.

During the intervening time, the Japanese government has deliberately sought to deceive the United States by false statements and expressions of hope for continued peace.

The attack yesterday on the Hawaiian Islands has caused severe damage to American naval and military forces. Very many American lives have been lost.

In addition, American ships have been reported torpedoed on the high seas between San Francisco and Honolulu.

Yesterday the Japanese government also launched an attack against Malaya.

Last night Japanese forces attacked Hong Kong.

Last night Japanese forces attacked Guam.

Last night the Japanese attacked Wake Island.

This morning the Japanese attacked Midway Island.

Japan has, therefore, undertaken a surprise offensive extending throughout the Pacific area. The facts of yesterday speak for themselves. The people of the United States have already formed their opinions and well understand the implications to the very life and safety of our nation.

As commander in chief of the army and navy I have directed that all measures be taken for our defense.

Always will we remember the character of the onslaught against us.

No matter how long it may take us to overcome this premeditated invasion, the American people in their righteous might will win through to absolute victory.

I believe I interpret the will of the Congress and of the people when I assert that we will not only defend ourselves to the uttermost but will make very certain that this form of treachery shall never endanger us again.

Hostilities exist. There is no blinking at the fact that our people, our territory and our interests are in grave danger.

With confidence in our armed forces—with the unbounding determination of our people—we will gain the inevitable triumph—so help us, God.

I ask that the Congress declare that since the unprovoked and dastardly attack by Japan on Sunday, December 7, a state of war has existed between the United States and the Japanese Empire.

Abraham Lincoln

THE SECOND
INAUGURAL ADDRESS
(March 4, 1865)

At this second appearing to take the oath of the presidential office, there is less occasion for an extended address than there was at first. Then a statement, somewhat in detail, of a course to be pursued seemed very fitting and proper. Now, at the expiration of four years, during which public declarations have been constantly called forth on every point and phase of the great contest which still absorbs the attention and engrosses the energies of the nation, little that is new could be presented.

The progress of our arms, upon which all else chiefly depends, is as well known to the public as to myself, and it is, I trust, reasonably satisfactory and encouraging to all. With high hope for the future, no prediction in regard to it is ventured.

On the occasion corresponding to this four years ago, all thoughts were anxiously directed to an impending civil war. All dreaded it; all sought to avoid it. While the inaugural address was being delivered from this place, devoted altogether to saving the Union without war, insurgent agents were in the city seeking to destroy it with war—seeking to dissolve the Union and divide the effects by negotiation. Both parties deprecated war, but one of them would make war rather than let the nation survive, and the other would accept war rather than let it perish, and the war came. One-eighth of the whole population were colored slaves, not distributed generally over the Union, but localized in the Southern part of it.

These slaves constituted a peculiar and powerful interest. All knew that this interest was somehow the cause of the war. To strengthen, perpetuate, and extend this interest was the object for which the insurgents would rend the Union by war, while the government claimed no right to do more than to restrict the Territorial enlargement of it.

Neither party expected for the war the magnitude or the duration which it has already attained. Neither anticipated that the cause of the conflict might cease when, or even before the conflict itself should cease. Each looked for an easier triumph, and a result less fundamental and astounding. Both read the same Bible and pray to the same God, and each invokes His aid against the other. It may seem strange that any men should dare to ask a just God's assistance in wringing their bread from the sweat of other men's faces, but let us judge not, that we be not judged. The prayer of both could not be answered. That of neither has been answered fully. The Almighty has His own purposes. "Woe unto the world because of offenses, for it must needs be that offenses come; but woe to that man by whom the offenses cometh!"

If we shall suppose that American slavery is one of those offenses which, in the providence of God, must needs come, but which having continued through His appointed time, He now wills to remove, and that He gives to both North and South this terrible war as the woe due to those by whom the offense came, shall we discern which the believers in a living God always ascribe to Him? Fondly do we hope, fervently do we pray, that this mighty scourge of war may speedily pass away. Yet if God wills that it continue until all the wealth piled by the bondsman's two hundred and fifty years of unrequited toil shall be sunk, and until every drop of blood drawn with the lash shall be paid by another drawn with the sword, as was said three thousand years ago, so still it must be said, that the judgments of the Lord are true and righteous altogether.

With malice toward none, with charity for all, with firmness in the right as God gives us to see the right, let us finish the work we are in, to bind up the nation's wounds, to care for him who shall have borne the battle, and for his widow and his orphans, to do all which may achieve and cherish a just and a lasting peace among ourselves and with all nations.

Daniel Webster

LIBERTY AND UNION
(Jan. 26, 1830)

I profess, Sir, in my career hitherto, to have kept steadily in view the prosperity and honor of the whole country, and the preservation of our Federal Union. It is to that Union we owe our safety at home, and our consideration and dignity abroad. It is to that Union we are chiefly indebted for whatever makes us most proud of our country. That Union we reached only by the discipline of our virtues, in the severe school of adversity. It had its origin in the necessities of disordered finance, prostrate commerce, and ruined credit. Under its benign influences, these great interests immediately awoke, as from the dead, and sprang forth with newness of life. Every year of its duration has teemed with fresh proofs of its utility and its blessings; and although our territory has stretched out wider and wider, and our population spread further and further, they have not outran its protection, or its benefits. It has been to us all a copious fountain of national, social, personal happiness. I have not allowed myself, Sir, to look beyond the Union, to see what might lie hidden in the dark recess behind. I have not coolly weighed the chances of preserving liberty, when the bonds that unite us together shall be broken asunder. I have not accustomed myself to hang over the precipice of disunion, to see whether, with my short sight, I can fathom the depth of the abyss below; nor would I regard him as a safe counsellor in the affairs of this Government whose thoughts should be mainly bent on considering, not how the Union should be best preserved, but how tolerable might be the condition of the People when it shall be broken up and destroyed.

While the Union lasts, we have high, exciting, gratifying prospects spread out before us, for us and our children. Beyond that I seek not to penetrate the veil. God grant that, in my day, at least, that curtain may not rise! God grant that on my vision never may be opened what lies behind! When my eyes shall be turned to behold, for the last time, the Sun in Heaven, may I not see him shining on the broken and dishonored fragments of a once glorious Union; on States severed, discordant, belligerent; on a land rent with civil feuds, or drenched, it may be, in fraternal blood! Let their last feeble and lingering glance, rather, behold the gorgeous Ensign of the Republic, now known and honored throughout the earth, still full high advanced, its arms and trophies streaming in their original lustre, not a stripe erased or polluted, nor a single star obscured—bearing, for its motto, no such miserable interrogatory as—*What is all this worth?* nor those words of delusion and folly—*Liberty first and Union afterwards*—but everywhere, spread all over in characters of living light, blazing on all its ample folds, as they float over the sea and over the land, and in every wind under the whole Heavens, that other sentiment, dear to every true American heart—Liberty *and* Union, now and forever, one and inseparable!

Patrick Henry

GIVE ME LIBERTY
OR GIVE ME DEATH
(March 23, 1775)

MR. PRESIDENT:

No man thinks more highly than I do of the patriotism, as well as abilities, of the very worthy gentlemen who have just addressed the house. But different men often see the same subject in different lights; and therefore, I hope it will not be thought disrespectful to those gentlemen, if, entertaining as I do opinions of a character very opposite to theirs, I shall speak forth my sentiments freely and without reserve. This is no time for ceremony. The question before the house is one of awful moment to this country. For my own part, I consider it as nothing less than a question of freedom or slavery. And in proportion to the magnitude of the subject ought to be the freedom of the debate. It is only in this way that we can hope to arrive at truth and fulfil the great responsibility which we hold to God and our country. Should I keep back my opinions at such a time, through fear of giving offense, I should consider myself as guilty of treason toward my country, and of an act of disloyalty toward the Majesty of Heaven, which I revere above all earthly kings.

Mr. President, it is natural to man to indulge in the illusions of hope. We are apt to shut our eyes against a painful truth and listen to the song of that siren till she transforms us into beasts. Is this the part of wise men, engaged in a great and arduous struggle for liberty? Are we disposed to be of the number of those who having eyes see not, and having ears hear not, the things which so nearly concern their temporal salvation? For my part, whatever anguish of spirit it may cost, I am willing to know the whole truth; to know the worst and to provide for it.

I have but one lamp by which my feet are guided, and that is the lamp of experience. I know of no way of judging of the future but by the past. And judging by the past, I wish to know what there has been in the conduct of the British ministry for the last ten years to justify those hopes with which gentlemen have been pleased to solace themselves and the house? Is it that insidious smile with which our petition has been lately received? Trust it not, sir; it will prove a snare to your feet. Suffer not yourselves to be betrayed with a kiss. Ask yourselves how this gracious reception of our petition comports with those warlike preparations which cover our waters and darken our land. Are fleets and armies necessary to a work of love and reconciliation? Have we shown ourselves so unwilling to be reconciled that force must be called in to win back our love? Let us not deceive ourselves, sir. These are the implements of war and subjugation—the last arguments to which kings resort.

I ask gentlemen, sir, what means this martial array, if its purpose be not to force us to submission? Can gentlemen assign any other possible motive for it? Has Great Britain any enemy in this quarter of the world, to call for all this accumulation of navies and armies? No, sir, she has none. They are meant for us: they can be meant for no other. They are sent over to bind and rivet upon us those chains which the British ministry have been so long forging.

And what have we to oppose to them? Shall we try argument? Sir, we have been trying that for the last ten years. Have we anything new to offer upon the subject? Nothing. We have held the subject up in every light of which it is capable; but it has been all in vain. Shall we resort to entreaty and humble supplication? What terms shall we find which have not been already exhausted? Let us not, I beseech you, sir, deceive ourselves longer.

Sir, we have done everything that could be done to avert the storm which is now coming on. We have petitioned; we have remonstrated; we have supplicated; we have prostrated ourselves before the throne and have implored its interposition to arrest the tyrannical hands of the ministry and Parliament. Our petitions have been slighted; our remonstrances have produced additional violence and insult; our supplications have been disregarded; and we have been spurned with contempt from the foot of the throne! In vain, after these things, may we indulge the fond hope of peace and reconciliation. There is no longer any room for hope. If we wish to be free, if we mean to preserve inviolate those inestimable privileges for which we have been so long contending, if we mean not basely to abandon the noble struggle in which we have been so long engaged, and which we have pledged ourselves never to abandon until the glorious object of our contest shall be obtained—we must fight! I repeat it, sir, we must fight! An appeal to arms and to the God of Hosts is all that is left us!

They tell us, sir, that we are weak—unable to cope with so formidable an adversary. But when shall we be stronger? Will it be the next week, or the next year? Will it be when we are totally disarmed, and when a British guard shall be stationed in every house? Shall we gather strength by irresolution and inaction? Shall we acquire the means of effectual resistance by lying supinely on our backs and hugging the delusive phantom of hope until our enemies shall have bound us hand and foot? Sir, we are not weak, if we make a proper use of those means which the God of nature hath placed in our power. Three millions of people, armed in the holy cause of liberty, and in such a country as that which we possess, are invincible by any force which our enemy can send against us. Besides, sir, we shall not fight our battles alone. There is a just God Who presides over the destinies of nations and Who will raise up friends to fight our battles for us. The battle, sir, is not to the strong alone; it is to the vigilant, the active, the brave. Besides, sir, we have no election. If we were base enough to desire it, it is now too late to retire from the contest. There is no retreat but in submission and slavery! Our chains are forged! Their clanking may be heard on the plains of Boston! The war is inevitable—and let it come! I repeat it, sir, let it come!

It is in vain, sir, to extenuate the matter. Gentlemen may cry, Peace, Peace—but there is no peace. The war is actually begun! The next gale that sweeps from the north will bring to our ears the clash of resounding arms! Our brethren are already in the field! Why stand we here idle? What is it that gentlemen wish? What would they have? Is life so dear, or peace so sweet, as to be purchased at the price of chains and slavery? Forbid it, Almighty God! I know not what course others may take; but as for me, give me liberty or give me death!

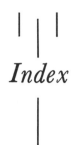

Index

Index